V·FORCE

Britain's Nuclear Bombers
and the Cold War

JONATHAN GLANCEY

Atlantic Books
London

First published in hardback in Great Britain in 2025 by Atlantic Books,
an imprint of Atlantic Books Ltd.

10 9 8 7 6 5 4 3 2 1

A CIP catalogue record for this book is available from the British Library.

Hardback ISBN: 978 1 83895 795 7
Trade Paperback ISBN: 978 1 80546 544 7
E-book ISBN: 978 1 83895 796 4

Printed in Great Britain by CPI Group (UK) Ltd, Croydon CR0 4YY

Atlantic Books
An imprint of Atlantic Books Ltd
Ormond House
26–27 Boswell Street
London
WC1N 3JZ

www.atlantic-books.co.uk

Product safety EU representative: Authorised Rep Compliance Ltd., Ground Floor,
71 Lower Baggot Street, Dublin, D02 P593, Ireland. www.arccompliance.com

MIX
Paper | Supporting
responsible forestry
FSC® C013604

Uno Animo Agimus

We act with one accord

Motto of 35 (Vulcan) Squadron RAF

Contents

V-bomber Dispersal Bases and Airfields, 1962

Prologue

In balance with this life, this death

Nuclear white knights. B.2 Vulcans at RAF Wittering, 1963

RAF Coningsby, Lincolnshire. Friday, 26 October 1962. 'I'm dashing off,' said newly commissioned Pilot Officer Peter West to his wife as he prepared to swap his married quarters for a caravan parked next to a pure white delta-wing Vulcan B.2 nuclear bomber stabled on the fringe of the airfield. The caravan was where West and his four fellow crew members were to wait for the call to 'scramble'.

'If you see us take off,' continued the young air electronics officer, 'I want you to take the children, put them in the car, put a few things in the car with them, and get the hell out of there. Drive up to Scotland. Go to your brother in Skye. You'll probably be safe there.'

Even when strapped into the cramped cockpit of the Vulcan and prepared for take-off at any moment, West thought – and hoped – the bombers would remain on the ground. For West believed in the sanity of MAD, the doctrine of Mutual Assured Destruction, by which the full-scale use of nuclear weapons by an attacker on a nuclear-armed defender with second-strike capabilities, like his Vulcan bomber, would cause the complete annihilation of both the attacker and the defender.

'In the highly improbable idea that we would take off,' West recalled in 2009, 'we knew that if we did get back, there would be nothing to get back to. Long afterwards, my wife said that she thought to herself at the time, "What a bloody fool. Where does he think I'm going to go? How far does he think I'll get? I would be passing all the airfields, all of which would be primary targets, come on!"'

If those airfields had been hit by Soviet nuclear bombs or missiles, much of Britain would have been devastated, vast swathes of its population killed, maimed or fatally weakened – very possibly for generations to come. Mrs West would have needed a brand-new 120-mph Jaguar Mk X, clear A roads, and the driving skills of Pat or Stirling Moss to have any realistic chance of speeding her family 500 miles north-west to Skye. Even then, RAF Machrihanish, on the west coast of Scotland

– one of the RAF's nuclear bomber dispersal bases – may well have been hit. And who, in any case, could be sure of which way the wind, laced with nuclear fallout, would be blowing, or even if the ferry over the sea to Skye would be sailing? Mrs West felt it would have been best to stay at home with the children. If the family was going to die, it would be with the children in their mother's arms.

These were the hours and minutes, we are taught, that the world held its breath. The Four Horsemen were mounted. The gates of Hell appeared to gape. Armageddon seemed inescapable. Apocalypse now. Was US president John F. Kennedy truly prepared to launch nuclear strikes against the Soviet Union that October weekend in 1962? Would his Soviet counterpart, Nikita Khrushchev, be forced to reply in kind? If Friday 26th, when Pilot Officer West was called away from home, was 'hot', then, if it had been possible to measure the temperature on some politico-military thermometer, Saturday 27th was scorching.

At what time should the editors of the *Bulletin of the Atomic Scientists* have set their well-known Doomsday Clock that weekend? When this graphic device first appeared on the cover of the scientific journal in its new magazine format in June 1947, it was set at seven minutes to midnight. The aim had been to alert the public at large to the imminent threat of uncontained nuclear weaponry. Founded in 1945 by the Russian-born biophysicist Eugene Rabinowitch of the University of Chicago following the dropping of atomic bombs on Hiroshima and Nagasaki, the bulletin's early contributors included Albert Einstein, Robert Oppenheimer, Bertrand Russell and Soviet physicist Nikolay Semyonov.

Newspaper editors worldwide were entranced by the Doomsday Clock. It was designed both intellectually and graphically – the memorable artwork was by the artist Martyl Langsdorf – to make alarming front-page headlines, and it did. Peter West and many of his colleagues were certainly aware of it. Following the testing of H-bombs in November 1952 in the US and August 1953 in the Soviet Union, the clock had advanced to two minutes to twelve. On Saturday, 27 October 1962, it must surely have ticked towards a minute – or even to just a few seconds – to midnight.

That afternoon, a Soviet S-75 Dvina ground-to-air missile system shot down a US Lockheed U-2 'spy' plane over Cuba – killing its pilot, Major Rudolf Anderson. Two weeks earlier, Anderson had been one of the USAF reconnaissance pilots who discovered nine Soviet nuclear missile launch sites dotted along the Cuban coastline, installed following the failed US-backed invasion to oust Castro at the Bay of Pigs the previous year. Forty R-12 and R-14 ballistic missiles with nuclear warheads, capable of striking targets across the United States, were on their way by sea from the USSR to the Caribbean island, and heading towards a US Navy blockade.

Since February, two nuclear bombers at key RAF bases had been on QRA (Quick Reaction Alert) standby. On Saturday 27th, Bomber Command ordered Alert Condition 3. This meant that as many of Britain's nuclear bombers as possible should be armed and prepared for take-off within fifteen minutes. Far from the east coast of England, a dozen Fleet Air Arm Sea Vixens on board the 23,900-ton aircraft carrier HMS *Hermes* were also on alert and ready to strike Sevastopol – a key Soviet military base – and other Crimean targets with free-fall Red Beard A-bombs. The distinctive all-weather de Havilland FAW.1 jets, featuring twin Rolls-Royce Avon engines and twin tail booms, had a maximum speed of 650 mph (a Mach 1.4 version had been considered, but dropped) and a range of 600 nautical miles. Designed by a team led by Ronald Bishop of de Havilland Mosquito fame, they could fly low over the water at high speeds. Although their primary role was to protect the fleet, they could carry air-to-ground as well as air-to-air missiles and Red Beard.

While the minutes to Armageddon ticked by, diplomacy was at work. The British prime minister, Harold Macmillan, spoke by phone to President Kennedy, who was keen to invade Cuba and destroy the nuclear missile silos. We can listen to their conversation today – the veteran British politician calming the presidential waters while Soviet diplomats negotiated with the Americans in Washington. Despite loud threats, Khrushchev had no desire for nuclear war.

What neither Kennedy, Macmillan nor even Khrushchev knew at the time was that, on Saturday 27th, one of the four Foxtrot-class submarines escorting the Soviet ships steaming to Cuba very nearly fired the opening shot of World War III. Surfacing to recharge its batteries, B-59 caught the attention of the US Navy, and Captain Valentin Savitsky ordered his crew to submerge. Because, at this moment, the sub was out of contact with anyone, including Moscow, US ships hoping to establish communication lobbed practice depth charges, aiming to encourage it to resurface. Believing he was under lethal attack, Savitsky prepared to launch a nuclear-tipped torpedo at one of his antagonists. He was stopped at the last moment by Captain Vasily Arkhipov, the submarine brigade's measured chief of staff who, very fortunately, was on board B-59. It was, although recollections vary, a very close-run thing indeed.

In the eastern and East Midland counties of England that momentous Saturday, villagers became aware of sudden preparations to launch (not that they would have known their technical specifications) 65-foot high, 11,000-mph Thor nuclear intermediate-range ballistic missiles (IRBMs). These rose from top-secret RAF Bomber Command launch pads close to the medieval parish churches and rural pubs they frequented. Sixty of these weapons – delivered to twenty sites in Cambridgeshire, the East Riding of Yorkshire, Leicestershire, Lincolnshire, Northants and Norfolk – had arrived from the US between 1958 and 1961, in the bellies of Douglas C-124 Globemaster II transport planes. Designed by US Navy rocket engineer Commander Robert Truax and program manager Adolf Thiel – who had earlier worked for Wernher von Braun on the design of the V-2 rocket in Nazi Germany – the safety record of Thor was not 100 per cent. There had been several accidents in the United States, while in December 1960 liquid oxygen spilling from one of the missiles onto its launch pad at RAF Ludford Magna, Lincolnshire, very nearly caused a fire that could have detonated its rocket fuel and very possibly its 1.44-megaton warhead.

Was anyone supping a pint in Ludford Magna's White Hart Inn that weekend aware that they were a sitting target for Soviet missiles and bombers? Or that they could have been blown to kingdom come by their own countrymen nearly two years ago by that nuclear missile, based on the design of a Nazi 'vengeance weapon', sited across the fields little more than a mile south of the pub? Did they know on that knife-edge October weekend that Mach 2 RAF Lightnings and even faster ground-to-air Bloodhound missiles were on red alert to intercept Soviet bombers entering British airspace?

This being England, something else, beknown only to a handful of cabinet ministers, senior civil servants, art gallery directors and removal firms, was afoot. The cream of the collections of the National Gallery, the Tate Gallery, the British Museum, the V&A, the Royal Collection and the Public Record Office were to be taken by road at night to the safety of the Manod Quarry in North Wales and the Westwood Quarry at Corsham, Wiltshire, as they had been during the Second World War. But this also being England, one of the gallery directors – the Surveyor of the Queen's Pictures, Anthony Blunt – was a long-standing Soviet spy. If Moscow had really wanted to 'nuke' treasured works of art, a quick call to Blunt could have revealed all.

The missile crisis ended following a meeting between Robert F. Kennedy, President Kennedy's younger brother and de facto chief of staff, and Anatoly Dobrynin, Soviet ambassador to Washington. At 10 a.m. GMT on Sunday 28th, a letter from Khrushchev was read out over Radio Moscow announcing the immediate withdrawal of missiles from Cuba. Praising Khrushchev's 'statesmanlike decision', Kennedy promised, and delivered, 'reciprocal measures to assure peace in the Caribbean area' – and, he might have added, the Western world. At what had seemed the very last minute, the Cuban Missile Crisis was solved by old-fashioned, if tightrope, diplomacy. In Britain, Bomber Command's V-Force stood down. Pilot Officer Peter West could go back home to his family.

Curiously, while for West and his RAF colleagues the world was threatened with nuclear devastation that daunting weekend, the Doomsday Clock stood unmoving at seven minutes to midnight. How so? According to the *Bulletin of the Atomic Scientists*:

The answers to this seeming anomaly are that the Doomsday Clock captures trends and takes into account the capacity of leaders and societies to respond to crises with reasoned actions to prevent nuclear holocaust. The Cuban Missile Crisis, for all its potential and ultimate destruction, only lasted a few weeks; however, the lessons were quickly apparent when the United States and the Soviet Union installed the first hotline between the two capitals to improve communications, and, of course, negotiated the 1963 test ban treaty, ending all atmospheric nuclear testing. Others have suggested that the gravity of the Cuban Missile Crisis has been defined by decades of scholarship but that, in 1962, the world population, to a large degree, was unaware of what *exactly* had just happened. Or, more precisely, what *hadn't* happened.

In Britain that Saturday, many people were simply out shopping or watching football. Arsenal beat Wolves 5–4. Hearts beat Kilmarnock 1–0. The deadly match between NATO and the Soviet Union ended in a nail-biting draw.

The nuclear deterrent remained firmly in place, with Britain's borne through the 1960s by the purpose-built bombers of V-Force. This book tells their story from the ember days of the Second World War and the white-hot development of the atom bomb to their ultimate replacement by the inverse logic of Royal Navy submarines. *V-Force* looks at these winged Cold War warriors – warts, rivets and all – through the lenses of invention and engineering, of rivalry with fellow NATO countries as well as with the Soviet Union, and of popular culture, too. It looks at how, rather surprisingly, on holidays and business trips we may well have been flying aboard civil versions of the V-bombers. And it hopes to explain why, long after their role was sensibly usurped, it proved hard to let these machines vanish from the skies they were designed to protect. A story of success, with compromise and failure along the way; of changing political and military priorities; and, not least, of derring-do by those associated with these machines, both in the air and on the ground.

B.1 Vulcan leads B.1 Victor (top) *and B.1 Valiant* (below)

Britain's V-Force was the front line of an aerial cavalry that would have charged towards targets behind the Iron Curtain if the Soviets had fired a first shot in what we think of, flinchingly, as World War III. Some hours behind these charismatic British bombers, waves of eight-engine USAF Boeing B-52 Stratofortress bombers would have been making their relentless 500-mph way east and west towards Soviet targets. V-Force was always the West's advance guard.

Vulcan, Victor, Valiant. What machines these were.

V-Force: First Impressions

I once spent a glorious summer afternoon, when young, reading in a Lincolnshire field sentried with blood-red poppies. I put my book down each time a camouflaged Vulcan bomber rose from close-by RAF Waddington. Stunning-looking, evidently powerful, and somewhat smoky, the aircraft nosed up over the field. They created, at first, elongated delta-shaped shadows, and then, as they passed over, a collective Jovian roar shot through with a demonic chorus of unearthly howls. This howling was the sound signature of the Vulcan, caused by the geometry of its air intakes at certain throttle settings. There was something strangely primeval about the noise. It was easy to imagine Vulcans howling over Lincolnshire fields into combat in some last weird battle in the East; white-clad aerial knights in their nuclear prime over Russian guns, delivering hell before thundering back across the North Sea. Back to the sky-piercing spires, potato flowers, poppy-strewn fields and rich earth of air-based Lincolnshire.

The thought of Pilot Officer West and his colleagues flying into battle in the wake of the Cuban Missile Crisis, should common sense have evaporated and diplomacy failed, calls to mind that wistful phrase 'Cavalry of the Sky' and, odd or not, the Charge of the Light Brigade. Rather like Lord Cardigan's 'six hundred' galloping into the 'valley of Death' towards Russian artillery in the Battle of Balaklava during the Crimean War (1853–56), the RAF's V-bombers in the 1960s would have faced a palisade of enemy weaponry in the guise of ground-to-air missile launch pads stretching in their hundreds from the Baltic to the Caspian Sea. A V-750VN missile from one of the S-75 Dvina air defence systems had shot down the CIA Lockheed U-2 spy plane flown at 70,500 feet by Gary Powers over the Soviet Union on 1 May 1960. Another V-750 had taken down Major Anderson's U-2 over Cuba.

How these British aircraft stirred the public imagination. At the 1955 Farnborough Air Show, Avro's chief test pilot, Wing Commander Roland 'Roly' Falk – dressed in Savile Row suit and tie – barrel-rolled the second production Vulcan, all 69 tons of it, while in his take-off climb. Recorded on film, Roly's roll astonishes still. While Alex Henshaw, Vickers' chief test pilot during the Second World War, had rolled the four-engine Avro Lancaster heavy bomber – the only pilot known to have done so – he certainly would not have been able to perform this aerobatic feat immediately after take-off.

The Avro Vulcan first flew in 1952, seven years after the end of the Second World War. It had been on the drawing board in 1947, five years after the Avro Lancaster went into service with Bomber Command. The sudden swap in the early 1950s from camouflaged 280-mph piston-engine machines bristling with machine guns pointing from Perspex turrets to pure-white, unarmed 625-mph flying-wing jets may well have dumbfounded many of those attending the Farnborough Air Show on public weekends. These two famous aircraft types belonged to eras separated by the atomic bomb. What Farnborough audiences might have found even more extraordinary is the fact that the Lancaster and the Vulcan were

Bespoke test pilot: Roly Falk about to fly a B.1 Vulcan

designed by the same engineers. Stuart Davies – who took over as head of design at Avro after Roy Chadwick, his chief, was killed in an aircraft accident in 1947 – was not only the key designer of the Vulcan. He had also turned the unsuccessful twin-engine wartime Avro Manchester bomber into the triumphant four-engine Lancaster, and before that had worked on the design of the Hawker Hart and Hawker Fury, the former a fast light bomber, the latter an aerobatic fighter, both in service with the RAF from 1930–31.

Before these superb biplanes that so thrilled crowds at the Hendon Air Shows of the 1930s, Davies had worked on the 1924 Mk X version of the Vickers Virginia biplane bomber, substituting the wood structure of earlier models for one of duralumin and steel. The Virginia was the replacement for the First World War Vickers Vimy, a modified version of which, in 1919, Captain John Alcock and Lieutenant Arthur Brown had flown when they made the first non-stop transatlantic flight. Flying in atrocious conditions, this nearly sixteen-hour flight was fuelled by petrol, soggy sandwiches, chocolate bars, and coffee laced with spirits. Virginias remained in service with the RAF until 1941, the year the Lancaster first flew.

Watching those Vulcans, by now painted in camouflage for low-level missions, howling over that Lincolnshire field was an unalloyed visceral sensation and unadulterated visual joy. However, the connection, through Stuart Davies, of the delta-wing nuclear jets to the earliest days of British bomber aircraft seemed to me improbable. They were the products of such very different technological eras.

I last saw one of these memorable machines flying – as at least 2 million other people did – at air displays between 2008 and 2015 by XH558 *The Spirit of Great Britain*, restored by the Vulcan to the Sky Trust. It was wonderful to witness this mesmerizing V-bomber put through its paces – flying, as pilots have said, like a jet fighter – and it was special to join a crowd of people falling – almost – into silence as XH558 led a brace of Lancasters close by RAF Waddington on 21 August 2014, to mark the ground-breaking of a Bomber Command memorial near Lincoln. Among those watching was 92-year-old Wing Commander George 'Johnny' Johnson, last of the famed 'Dambusters'. The generation gap between the two types of Avro bombers was reinforced by the sound of the Lancasters at full throttle, working hard to keep pace with the Vulcan, which was maintaining a nose-up attitude to keep its speed down and help counter the turbulence from the wake of its powerful exhausts.

Of the other two V-Force bombers, I never witnessed a Vickers Valiant, the first of the trio into service and the first to be withdrawn from flight. I did, though, marvel at the Handley Page Victor. It would be hard not to. Low-slung on the ground, the Victor, especially when viewed head-on, had the appearance, surreally, of some enormous and deeply strange fish. A ray of sorts. That shape. That pair of giant gills – the air intakes of its Armstrong Siddeley Sapphire turbojets – and those curious segmented crescent wings. I could imagine them flapping slowly and powerfully through the ocean depths. A very mechanical fish, though, with its Captain Nemo cockpit, that oddly spaced glazing and long probing nose. The Victor's tail, though, was not that of a fish, but of another mighty sea creature – the whale. Though whether piscine or whale-like in terms of its looks, the Victor displayed a strangely alien aesthetic.

I watched Victors fly in and out of RAF Marham in Norfolk. They were aerial fuel tankers by then, retired in 1993. Until 2021, a Victor served as a gate guardian at Marham. With neither the resources nor the time to restore the aircraft, in 2020 the RAF asked if anyone would like to take the Victor on.

The last viewings were made on 10 October 2020, during the Covid pandemic. There were no offers. No Victor has flown since.

Quieter – relatively so – than the Vulcan, the Victor sounded more like an early jet airliner than a purely military aircraft. As we will see, there were, in fact, proposals for civil airliner versions of all three production V-bombers, with that of the Valiant, the most conventional of them, coming closest to realization. This may well seem odd to anyone who has so much as peered into the claustrophobic cockpits of the V-bombers. The Vulcan's is, for everyone except perhaps those for whom this aircraft could do no wrong, almost frightening. How could five crew members – six if the crew chief, usually an NCO appointed to care for a specific aircraft and its desig-nated regular crew, was on board – cope, shoehorned for hours on end into a space just big enough for them to squeeze inside? If you think an economy seat on board a budget airline Airbus or Boeing is cramped, try the cockpit of a Vulcan for size.

Pilots of light or much smaller aircraft, or those lucky enough to have flown in a Lancaster, would have found the almost complete lack of a view ahead disconcerting. Even more discomfiting was the fact that the airframe of the Vulcan was largely invisible from the pilots' seats. Not that pilots would have seen all that much in nuclear conflict. They were even trained to fly with a patch over one eye. The light of a nuclear explosion would have been blinding.

The best view of these beguiling aircraft was either from the ground or from another aircraft – an RAF Lightning interceptor perhaps, flying in formation with V-bombers or aiming to refuel from tanker versions. The real view from inside a Vulcan was that of the instrument panels.

Three members of the Vulcan's crew – radar plotter, navigator, air electronics officer – had to sit at the bottom of a ladder, facing backwards in a dark cubby hole with no view whatsoever. No ejection seats either, unlike the captain and co-pilot above them. As for any member of the crew who might feel a call of nature during a sortie, the Vulcan was equipped with a small bin with a tube attached, at the bottom of the ladder. There was no privacy, and how on earth – or in the air – a crew member could move around this space-capsule-like area kitted out in bulky high-altitude flight gear is anyone's guess. During the 1982 Falklands War, Flight Lieutenant Martin Withers and his crew – six in all, including an air-to-air refuelling instructor – flew a 15-hour, 45-minute bombing mission from Ascension Island to Port Stanley and back, a world record. How did they avoid cramp?

Glimpses of these aircraft in early childhood aside, I knew them not in white, but in camouflage. But in my mind's eye – as well as, of course, through the medium of photography, film and video – I see them, now that none are flying, clothed as if in white samite and, as if we might yet awake King Arthur and his knights from their sleep in Avalon and its dispersal sites – Chepstow, Caerleon, Alderley Edge, Richmond, Sewingshields – ready to defend us again. A V-Force of the imagination.

Perhaps I am being too romantic. Rarely, though, has a team of aircraft rooted themselves so quickly and so deeply

in the national consciousness. Their active life in the disturbing role for which they were designed proved to be fleetingly
brief. Only one of them, the Valiant, unleashed a nuclear
bomb – and this, thankfully, on a test site, although this was
dangerous enough for anyone's good.

Bucked by turbulent politics, V-Force was an Atomic Age
weapon to be admired and feared. An aerial Excalibur, it seems
somehow appropriate that at the end of the 1960s its weaponry and defining purpose, now that there was no guarantee
that the bombers would ever reach their targets, were to be
drawn underwater into the near-silent depths of submarine
warfare. For those few years, though, how V-Force – Britain's
frontline nuclear deterrent – shone.

This book is one attempt to illustrate the history of V-Force,
to place Britain's V-bombers in their social and political,
design and engineering, and, of course, military context,
including that of their rivals. It is not a nuts, bolts and rivets
reference book. I list a number of these for further reading at
the end. Instead, it tries to capture something of this remarkable and even quixotic aerial adventure, so very short-lived
in its original form as the forces of politics and ever-more
advanced weaponry lowered it ever-closer to the ground.

The sorry part of the story is Britain's failure to either
capitalize on or to develop its own military and commercial
aviation technology when it might have done. If not always,
politics and economics – short-term, knee-jerk and international – have a habit of winning over home-grown invention
and technology. Britain's defence, and specifically its nuclear

deterrent, became increasingly reliant on US politics and technology. There are those who will argue that this was an inevitable process, yet this is not wholly true. In part it was due not just to the wiles of domestic and international politics, but to an almost wilful deindustrialization – the turning of what were factories and research institutes into poorly designed housing estates and shopping centres. In 2025, Britain finds it hard to make locomotives, trains or cars on its own.

There are, of course, outstanding examples of international collaboration in the aviation industry – Concorde, for example, or the Eurofighter Typhoon – and yet, just across the Channel, France retains an independent nuclear deterrent, and manufactures its own multi-role fighter, the Dassault Rafale – which, unlike the otherwise highly capable Typhoon, can operate from land and sea and be equipped with nuclear missiles. The British economy is said to rank sixth in the world, the French seventh. Britain's increasing lack of independence and competitiveness is not to do with a lack of money, but rather a lack of will, or interest perhaps. This is not an argument in favour of spending on guns rather than butter, nor of encouraging war over peace, but of considered self-defence, of Britain being a dynamic NATO partner, and of the desire and ability to invent, design, make and, in the case of aircraft, fly high.

The V-Force bombers, at their most deadly sixty years ago, were compelling machines fighting a strange, unfought war that we are still rightfully fearful of. Theirs – as the necessary opening chapters tracking the story of devastatingly powerful weapons, destruction on an increasingly horrifying scale, nuclear deterrence, and the role bombers were expected to play in it show – was truly a terrible beauty.

ONE

Weapons of Mass Destruction I

The bomber will always get through

10 November 1932. Thirty years before the Cuban Missile Crisis. Stanley Baldwin, the de facto prime minister of the 1931–35 national government – Ramsay MacDonald's health was deteriorating, his speeches confused – addressed parliament on the issue of rearmament. 'I think it is well... for the man in the street to realise that there is no power on earth that can protect him from being bombed. Whatever people may tell him, the bomber will always get through. The only defence is in offence, which means that you have to kill more women and children more quickly than the enemy if you want to save yourselves...'

A few weeks after the end of the Second World War, Clement Attlee, the new Labour prime minister who had been deputy leader of the Labour Party at the time of Baldwin's speech, noted that 'the modern conception of war to which in my lifetime we have become accustomed is now completely out of date. We recognised or some of us did before this war that bombing could only be answered by counter bombing. We were right. Berlin and Magdeburg were the only answer to London and Coventry. Both derive from Guernica.'

Other Spanish towns and cities, including Córdoba, Durango, Jaén and Madrid, had been bombed from the air by Hitler's Condor Legion and Mussolini's Aviazione Legionaria before Guernica was targeted on the afternoon of Monday, 26 April 1937. Lieutenant Colonel Wolfram von Richthofen, younger brother of the 'Red Baron' and head of the Condor Legion, had his tactical reasons for attacking the town, yet the only way he could see of trapping Basque forces at a particular road junction was to carpet-bomb the area. Given the existing level of technology, the pinpoint bombing of the roads and bridges he claimed to have been after was out of the question.

Guernica, *Pablo Picasso (1937)*

Made in five waves, the raid was executed by three new German bombers – a pair of Heinkel He 111s and a Dornier Do 17, proving themselves in combat – and by eighteen Junkers Ju 52s (trimotor general utility aircraft) and three Italian Savoia-Marchetti SM.79 trimotor light bombers. Accompanied by Messerschmitt Bf 109, Heinkel He 51 and Fiat CR.32 fighters, the fifth wave was the most destructive. German and Italian air crews dropped 22 tons of bombs on Guernica. As to how many civilians were killed, no one really seems to know. Numbers vary from 300 to 1,700. Of buildings destroyed, it was at least 14 per cent or perhaps as many as 74 per cent. Whatever the figures, the raid was horrific.

What made this episode so well known outside Spain is the fact that George Steer, a reporter from the London *Times* covering the Spanish Civil War, had been quick to arrive at the scene. His story, published on 28 April, was syndicated to the *New York Times* and picked up by international press agencies. Guernica was the first such raid to be reported first-hand. Steer's story was embellished as it did the rounds, leading British MPs to believe that Guernica was an 'open city' – neither occupied nor defended by military forces, and not allowed to be bombed under international law – which was untrue, while the Congressional Record shows that US senators and representatives were misled to believe that poison gas had been used. The death toll grew with rising international outrage.

Told of what had happened, Pablo Picasso, then living in Paris, read Steer's account and set to work on an ambitious and nightmarish interpretation in black, white and grey oils of the bombing of the Basque town. The giant canvas, *Guernica*, would be displayed in the Spanish Pavilion at the 1937 World's Fair in Paris. Albert Speer's towering German Pavilion topped with a Nazi eagle stood close by.

Guernica has loomed large in the collective imagination ever since. Who, from that Monday market day in April 1937, could have escaped the bombers? In 2007, the then president of the Basque parliament, Juan José Ibarretxe, met political deputies from Dresden, Hiroshima, Oświęcim (Auschwitz), Pforzheim, Volgograd (Stalingrad) and Warsaw to remember the significance of the raid on Guernica. Tadatoshi Akiba, mayor of Hiroshima, said:

> Human beings have often sought to give concrete form to our powerful collective longing for peace. After World War I, that longing led to the League of Nations and numerous rules and taboos designed to govern warfare itself. Of these, the most important was the proscription against attacking and killing civilian non-combatants even in times of war. However, the second half of the twentieth century has seen most of those taboos broken. Guernica was the point of departure, and Hiroshima is the ultimate symbol. We must find ways to communicate to future generations the history of horror that began with Guernica.

Back in England in the early 1930s, there were those who disagreed with Stanley Baldwin's assertion that the bomber would always get through – among them Air Marshal Hugh Dowding, appointed head of Fighter Command in 1936, who pushed for the development of radar, the Royal Observer Corps and the advanced eight-gun Rolls-Royce Merlin–powered Hurricane and Spitfire fighters. Even so, measured voices like that of the future Conservative prime minister Harold Macmillan, who had fought and been badly wounded in brutal front-line battles in France during the First World War, believed the opening weeks of a new war with Germany would witness the deaths of hundreds of thousands of British civilians. Writing in 1956, Macmillan said that he, among many others, had 'thought of air warfare in 1938 rather as people think of nuclear war today'.

Dowding's great victory was the Battle of Britain, his air defence system holding back an outright German invasion of England while doing its best to protect British towns and cities from aerial attacks. In the hours of darkness, German bombers did get through Dowding's defences, wreaking havoc on, among other hard-hit towns and cities, Birmingham, Bristol, Coventry, Glasgow, Kingston upon Hull, Liverpool, Manchester, Plymouth, Portsmouth and Southampton. Between September 1940 and May 1941, London was bombed on fifty-seven consecutive nights.

The RAF's attempt to hit back at Germany proved disturbingly ineffective. In August 1941, the official Butt Report – an analysis of 633 target photographs made by the War Cabinet Secretariat economist David Bensusan-Butt – revealed that by the time the British bombers, flying by night, reached the industrial complexes of the Ruhr, just one in ten flew within five miles of its target; half of all bombs dropped fell into open countryside; and only 1 per cent were within the vicinity of the target, a case of the sound and fury of bomber aircraft signifying precious little.

One immediate upshot of the Butt Report was the formation of what proved to be the highly successful Pathfinder Force – RAF Bomber Command squadrons charged with locating and marking targets. Another was the advancement of the case for the area or 'carpet' bombing of German cities by large formations of heavy bombers. To this the Lindemann Report of March 1942 added a disturbing rider. Written by Winston Churchill's close friend and chief scientific advisor, Frederick Lindemann, 1st Viscount Cherwell, it called for Bomber Command to direct its raids at working-class districts, thus destroying the German workforce.

Britain's heavy four-engine bombers – the Handley Page Halifax, Short Stirling and the brand-new Avro Lancaster – began coming into service, and in large numbers. In February 1942, Air Marshal Arthur Harris was appointed Air Officer Commanding Bomber Command. At the same time the United States Army Air Force (USAAF)'s VIII Bomber Command (called the Eighth Air Force from 1944) arrived in England – at first at RAF Daws Hill, close by Harris's headquarters at RAF High Wycombe. The Americans began ferrying fleets of heavy four-engine Boeing B-17 and Consolidated B-24 Liberator bombers across the Atlantic.

Harris made his intentions clear: 'The Nazis entered this war under the rather childish delusion that they were going to bomb everyone else, and nobody was going to bomb them. At Rotterdam, London, Warsaw and half a hundred other places, they put that rather naive theory into operation.' Borrowing from the Old Testament (Hosea 8:7), he announced, 'They sowed the wind, and now they are going to reap the whirlwind.' In a BBC radio broadcast on 28 July 1942, he added fuel to his fire: 'We are going to scourge the Third Reich from end to end. We are bombing Germany city by city and ever more terribly in order to make it impossible for them to go on with the war. That is our object; we shall pursue it relentlessly.'

A First World War fighter ace, in 1923 Harris had taken command of 45 Squadron stationed in a politically unstable Iraq. The RAF had been employed to 'police' the country following an uprising in summer 1920, in which more than 100,000 armed tribesmen rebelled against the British occupation. Flying missions totalling 4,008 hours, the RAF dropped 97 tons of bombs and fired 183,861 rounds for the loss of nine men killed, seven wounded and eleven aircraft destroyed. Nearly 9,000 Iraqis died. The uprising was quashed. With the RAF replacing ground troops, British military expenditure in Iraq fell from £23 million in 1921 to less than £4 million five years later.

Squadron Leader Harris added bomb-racks to his Vickers Vernon – a biplane introduced in 1921 and the RAF's first dedicated troop carrier – and, in doing so, almost invented the first British heavy bomber. 'The Arab and Kurd now know what real bombing means,' reported Harris after several punitive raids against Iraqi rebels. 'Within 45 minutes a full-sized village can be practically wiped out and a third of its inhabitants killed or injured, by four or five machines which offer them no real target, no opportunity for glory as warriors, no effective means of escape.'

From spring 1942, the tables were about to be turned on Germany. The major Allied air raids were to prove devastating. The first American heavy bomber raid on German-occupied Europe was made on 17 August 1942, by twelve B-17s of the 97th Bomb Group (motto: *Venit Hora*, 'The Hour Has Come') from RAF Grafton Underwood, Northamptonshire, on railway marshalling yards at Sotteville-lès-Rouen. The pilot of the lead aircraft in the first flight of six B-17s, *Butcher Shop*, was Captain Paul W. Tibbets. On 6 August 1945, Tibbets would fly the B-29 Superfortress *Enola Gay* from Tinian, an island under US control in the western Pacific, to Hiroshima.

With the Americans flying by day and the RAF at night, German cities reaped Harris's whirlwind. The most concentrated assault was Operation Gomorrah (the Old Testament again – 'Then the LORD rained upon Sodom and upon Gomorrah brimstone and fire from the LORD out of heaven', Genesis 19:24), a raid on Hamburg protracted over eight days and seven nights, which at the time was the heaviest in the history of air warfare. It hit Hamburg's shipyards, U-boat pens and oil refineries, yet Allied bombers were after bigger game – the city itself. Careful calculations relating to the flammability of the city's building stock, as well as wind direction and humidity, were made before the bombers set off. On the night of the most intense raid (27/28 July 1943), an aerial armada

Reaping the whirlwind: aftermath of Allied bombing in the
Eilbek district of Hamburg

of 787 RAF bombers – 74 Wellingtons, 116 Stirlings, 244 Halifaxes and 353 Lancasters – headed to the tinder-dry city guided by RAF's Pathfinder Force, with 739 aircraft attacking.

The bombing caused an unpredicted and unprecedented vortex of superheated air that turned into a 150-mph tornado of fire rising 1,500 feet and howling demonically through the working-class districts of Borgfelde, Hamm, Hammerbrook and Rothenburgsort. People were swept off their feet from pavements into the burning air. The temperature rose to 815°C, causing the asphalt streets to burst into flames. Fuel spills ignited fires in the harbour and along the canals. Air-raid shelters were of no use; the air was sucked from inside them. Over three infernal hours, the firestorm destroyed thousands of apartment buildings, adding significantly to the total number of people killed in Hamburg – perhaps as many as 42,000 over those eight days. Hundreds of thousands more fled the city.

The raid that night had been meticulously planned. There were diversionary sorties by twin-engine Wellingtons and Mosquitos on targets including Bremen, Duisberg, Kiel and Lübeck. In the process, the mighty Krupp steelworks at Essen was badly damaged, with Dr Gustav Krupp suffering a severe stroke the morning following the raid. New techniques including Window (or chaff) – aluminized paper strips dropped from bombers to baffle enemy radar on the ground and in the air – helped the Allied crews immeasurably. Searchlights and night-fighters were unable to locate the hundreds of British bombers as a result. A follow-up raid by 777 RAF bombers was hugely damaging, although there was no second firestorm.

On the night of 27/28 July, Hamburg had witnessed the jaws of a medieval hell gaping wide. In the wake of Gomorrah, Air Marshal Harris wrote to Marshal of the Royal Air Force, Sir Charles Portal, assuring the Chief of the Air Staff that Bomber Command was now able 'to produce in Germany by April 1st 1944, a state of devastation in which surrender is inevitable'. Harris also called on the government to be honest with the British public concerning the nature and purpose of the area bombing campaign:

The aim of the Combined Bomber Offensive... should be unambiguously stated [as] the destruction of German cities, the killing of German workers, and the disruption of civilised life throughout Germany... the destruction of houses, public utilities, transport and lives, the creation of a refugee problem on an unprecedented scale, and the breakdown of morale both at home and at the battle fronts by fear of extended and intensified bombing, are accepted and intended aims of our bombing policy. They are not by-products of attempts to hit factories.

Following criticism of the devastating Allied bombing of Dresden over four raids made between 13 and 15 February 1945, when some 25,000 people were killed and the old city destroyed, the by now Air Chief Marshal Harris noted, 'The feeling, such as there is, over Dresden, could be easily explained by any psychiatrist. It is connected with German bands and Dresden shepherdesses. Actually, Dresden was a mass of munitions works, an intact government centre, and a key transportation point to the East. It is now none of these things.'

Harris's bombers had certainly got through, but at a terrible cost both for German civilians and for his aircrew. And if Allied confidence had been mounting with good reason, there were still nights when it went wrong. On a raid made on Nuremberg under a full moon – 30/31 March 1944 – Bomber Command lost 106 aircraft out of the 795 taking part, and 545 men. Of every hundred airmen who joined Bomber Command, forty-five were killed, six were seriously injured and eight were held as prisoners of war.

There was, though, another school of thought to Harris's. The English inventor and Vickers-Armstrongs engineer Barnes Wallis, for one, believed from the outset that the war might be won through the destruction of German infrastructure, major manufacturing plants and military installations. To this effect, early in the war he proposed a six-engine Vickers Victory bomber with a pressurized hull, designed to cruise at 320 mph at 45,000 feet (beyond the reach of German fighters) carrying a single 22,400-lb (10-ton) bomb. The idea seemed fanciful to many in the Air Ministry at a time when the Lancaster four-engine bomber was under development.

Although Wallis was able to conduct wind-tunnel tests on a model of his six-engine bomber, in 1941 the project was shelved. Though not before it had helped to further a key question over the efficacy of RAF bombing. What if a Vickers Victory should make it to the heart of the Ruhr only to miss its target – very possibly by some distance? What a waste that would be of invention, construction, testing, training, preparation, fuel, adrenaline and sweat. In the event, Wallis found a mechanical ally in the guise of what proved to be the highly capable Avro Lancaster. On the night of 16/17 May 1943, nineteen specially modified Lancasters of 617 Squadron flew from RAF Scampton in Lincolnshire at 'zero feet' (actually 100 feet) to avoid radar, and headed to the Möhne, Eder and Sorpe dams – key strategic targets that between them supplied water and hydroelectricity to the industrial, arms-manufacturing Ruhr district.

Each aircraft carried a single weapon, a cylindrical 9,000-lb 'Upkeep' mine designed by Barnes Wallis. Hanging from the bellies of the Lancasters, the mines were to be spun backwards at 500 rpm before being released precisely 425 yards from the walls of the dams, with the aircraft flying at a prescribed 232 mph and 60 feet above the water – and this in bright moonlight and into heavy flak. Several attempts were made on the dams that night with Wallis's 'bouncing bombs', which lived up to their name, clearing defensive torpedo nets as they skipped towards the dam walls before spinning down them and exploding underwater at a depth of 30 feet.

Two dams, the Möhne and Eder, were breached. Local towns were flooded, trains were washed off their tracks and six electricity stations were put out of action. Thirteen hundred civilians were killed, including nearly 500 slave labourers, mostly women, from Ukraine. According to Field Marshal Erwin Rommel, 20,000 labourers were diverted from building the defensive Atlantic Wall along the Normandy and Brittany coasts to reconstruct the vital dams. Joseph Goebbels, Hitler's propaganda minister, described the attack as 'an act of war against the state, but one to be admired, for the English had navigated and planned so thoroughly'. The story made the front page of the *New York Times* and won American admiration. The raid was a huge morale booster.

Air Vice Marshal Ralph Cochrane, commander of 5 Group, which included 617 Squadron, sent a message to Wing

Commander Guy Gibson, the 24-year-old commander of Operation Chastise – and, to date, veteran of more than 170 bombing and night-fighter missions. 'The disaster which you have inflicted on the German war machine was a result of hard work, discipline and courage. The determination not to be beaten in the task and getting the bombs exactly on the aiming point in spite of opposition have set an example others will be proud to follow.'

Flying skill, pinpoint accuracy and sheer bravery. It was a heady mix. The King and Queen visited Scampton and the Lancaster crews soon after the raid. In June 1943, Gibson was presented with the Victoria Cross at Buckingham Palace. There were thirty-three other decorations for his fellow Dambusters. That evening, the 'boys' were wined and dined by A. V. Roe, founder of Avro, at the Hungaria restaurant on London's Lower Regent Street – ration books thrown to the wind – and entertained, impromptu, by fellow diners, the comedian Arthur Askey, band leader and impresario Jack Hylton, and Elsie Carlisle, the singer best known for her renditions of 'A Nightingale Sang in Leicester Square' and Cole Porter's 'What Is This Thing Called Love?'. Other guests included Tommy Sopwith, of Sopwith Camel and Hawker Aircraft fame, and Barnes Wallis.

Oddly, Roe was a keen supporter of Oswald Mosley, and had been a member of the British Union of Fascists in the 1930s. Two of his sons, 26-year-old Squadron Leader Eric Alliot Verdon-Roe and 22-year-old Squadron Leader Lighton Verdon-Roe DFC, were killed serving with the RAF. Eric had been flying a twin-engine Armstrong Whitworth Mk V on a 102 Squadron bombing mission to Hanover; Lighton, an Avro Lancaster III with 156 Squadron to north Germany.

Gibson and his wife Eve, a chorus girl, lunched with Winston Churchill at Chequers before the wing commander was packed off on a PR tour of Canada and the United States, where he had a private meeting with President Roosevelt. Back in England, he was Roy Plomley's guest on *Desert Island Discs* on 19 February 1944. Along with Bing Crosby's sentimental 'If I Had My Way', Gibson's choice of eight gramophone records included Wagner's 'Ride of the Valkyries' from *Die Walküre* and the same composer's overture from *The Flying Dutchman,* the latter played by the Berlin State Opera Orchestra. These must have seemed odd choices at the time.

Serialized in the *Daily Express* over the winter of 1944–45, the first print run of Gibson's memoir, *Enemy Coast Ahead,* sold 50,000 copies on publication in 1946. The pugnacious wing commander was long dead by then, killed in September 1944 when his Mosquito crashed at Steenbergen in the Netherlands, returning from a mission marking targets for 5 Group over Mönchengladbach in North Rhine-Westphalia. He was twenty-six.

On the night of 16/17 May 1943, eight of 617 Squadron's nineteen Lancasters had been lost, with fifty-three crew killed. For Barnes Wallis, the success of Operation Chastise 'was almost completely blotted out by the sense of loss of those wonderful young lives'. The British bombers had got through, but at great cost.

While Arthur Harris thought the raid a waste of resources, others clearly disagreed. Wallis was able to push on with his designs for 'earthquake' bombs – huge weapons with which to destroy heavily fortified German installations and infrastructure impregnable to conventional bombing.

The first was Tallboy, a 12,000-lb (5-ton) bomb employed for the first time within forty-eight hours of the D-Day landings. On 8 June 1944, eighteen Lancasters of 617 Squadron, led by Wing Commander Leonard Cheshire, dropped the streamlined, ground-penetrating weapons accurately on the 1,000-yard Saumur Tunnel. Exploding 60 feet below ground, the railway tunnel was destroyed, stopping the 17th SS Panzer Division *Götz von Berlichingen* and the 2nd SS Panzer Division *Das Reich* in their tracks, impeding their armoured advance north to Normandy. This time, there were no RAF losses.

Among other celebrated Tallboy successes was the capsizing of the formidable 42,000-ton German battleship *Tirpitz* – 'a floating fortress' – near Tromsø, Norway. Operation Catechism was conducted by 9 and 617 Squadrons; the Lancasters dropped twenty-nine Tallboys and there were two direct hits, the second causing the demise of *Tirpitz*. Tallboys also put paid to the V-2 rocket launch complex at Calais and the V-3 supergun installation at Mimoyecques in the Pas-de-Calais. Buried in a 4½-mile tunnel dug by hand into a limestone hill by slave labour and lined with 482,000 tons of concrete, the gun emplacement had seemed an impossible target.

The V-3 itself, with its multiple rocket-boosted 130-metre barrels, was to have fired six hundred 140-kilogram (310-lb) shells an hour at London. Before it was ready to do so, it was destroyed on 6 July 1944 by Tallboys dropped by fourteen Lancasters of 617 Squadron led by Cheshire on his hundredth and last bombing mission. The site, which can be visited today, is close to the French entrance to the Channel Tunnel.

Although out of action, the V-3 gun site attracted the attention of the USAAF, who used it as a target the following month under the banner Operation Aphrodite, to test a very different type of weapon: pilotless bombers packed with explosives directed by remote control from another aircraft. In theory, this alternative to Wallis's earthquake bombs seemed a promising idea. In practice, the test flight made on 12 August 1944 – killing Lieutenant Joe Kennedy, elder brother of the future US president John F. Kennedy, and his flight engineer Lieutenant Wilford J. Willy – proved otherwise.

Their four-engine Consolidated PB4Y-2 Privateer took off from RAF Fersfield, Norfolk. The plan was for the two-man crew to set the bomber on the right trajectory at 2,000 feet before bailing out. The Privateer would then be under the control of one of a pair of twin-engine Lockheed Ventura medium bombers flying with it. The Privateer blew up over Blythburgh on the Suffolk coast. Operation Aphrodite was called off after fourteen fruitless missions.

RAF Bomber Command followed up with the deployment of the second of Wallis's new bombs. This was Grand Slam, which was as long as a 1940s London double decker bus and, at 22,400 lb (10 tons), much heavier. It was, in fact, the largest and most powerful conventional bomb used by both sides in the Second World War. Employed in the final weeks of the war in Europe, just forty-two Grand Slams were dropped from the bomb bays of modified 617 Squadron Lancasters. The effectiveness of the bombs was not in question, but because Lancasters armed with Grand Slams were barely able to manoeuvre once airborne, they required extensive fighter escorts for missions to Germany. At this time, although the Luftwaffe was a largely spent force, it could still field the Me 262 jet fighter, a dangerous foe.

The first successful Grand Slam raid, on 14 March 1945, was on the Bielefeld Viaduct. Its destruction would, it was thought, stop railway traffic between Hanover and the Ruhr. What with the sheer number of aircraft involved – fifteen Lancasters, seventy-four Mustang escort fighters, eight Pathfinder Mosquitoes to mark the target and a ninth Mosquito to capture the raid on film – the mission was something of a sledgehammer to crack a nut, and yet mission after bombing mission to date had failed to demolish the strategic viaduct. While a success in terms of its immediate objective, the raid did not stop a diversionary route that kept rail traffic on the move.

Grand Slams and Tallboys were also used successfully against the vast concrete Valentin submarine pen at the port of Farge close to Bremen – which, under construction since 1943, was expected to be complete and to begin producing all-electric Type XXI U-boats from August 1945. The structure was 426 metres long, 97 metres wide and up to 27 metres high. Its walls were 4.5 metres thick, and the roof as much as

7 metres deep. Designed by the distinguished civil engineer Erich Lackner, then working for Organisation Todt – the Nazi state civil and military engineering concern founded in 1933 by Fritz Todt – the pen was built by some 10,000 concentration camp inmates and prisoners of war. The air raid by 617 Squadron on 27 March 1945 – twenty Lancasters carrying thirteen Grand Slams and seven Tallboys, and accompanied by ninety Mustangs – caused sufficient damage to bring the Valentin project to a close.

There was, though, a ghastly postscript. Five thousand prisoners held at the Neuengamme concentration camp and its satellite camps who had worked on the submarine pen were among those evacuated on board two former ocean liners, the SS *Cap Arcona* and SS *Deutschland*, and the freighter SS *Thielbek*, and held below decks without food or water. The SS was probably intending to sink the ships as British forces closed in. The British, thinking the ships were about to sail SS soldiers and high-ranking officials to Norway, chose to attack them. Five squadrons of puissant RAF Hawker Typhoons armed with bombs, rockets and cannons sank the ships. Starving, skeletal survivors struggling in the cold sea were strafed and killed. Those few nearing the shore were machine-gunned by Nazi officials. The date was 3 May 1945, the day before the German surrender to Field Marshal Bernard Montgomery at Lunenburg Heath.

Five days later, VE (Victory in Europe) Day was celebrated in London, Paris, New York (9 May in Moscow), and other towns and cities across Europe and around the world. The war in the

East, however, raged on. Until November 1944, while it was effectively out of range, Japan had been spared US bombing raids. That month, the US regained control of the Mariana Islands, a crescent-shaped archipelago of volcanic and coral formations in the western Pacific, some 1,500 miles east of the Philippines and a similar distance from Tokyo to the north. This put the imperial capital in range of the USAAF's new four-engine Boeing B-29 Superfortress bomber. But, although this massive machine was able to fly beyond the reach of most Japanese fighters, the tempestuous Pacific climate was far from ideal for raids made at high altitudes. Accurate bombing in high winds proved to be almost impossible.

In February 1945, General Curtis 'Bombs Away' LeMay took over command of XXI Bomber Command. Stripped of guns and packed with napalm-filled M-69 incendiaries, B-29s were now to attack Japanese cities at low altitude by night. Tests to find the ideal bomb were conducted at Eglin Air Force Base, Florida, and the Dugway Proving Ground in Utah. At Dugway, a model village of Japanese houses, designed and decorated down to the last detail – including choice of paints and children's toys – was bombed, rebuilt and bombed again.

LeMay was pretty sure of what his bombers would achieve. Operation Meetinghouse, executed on the night of 9/10 March 1945, ought to have sealed Japan's fate. A fleet of 325 B-29s, each with a take-off weight twice that of a B-17 or an RAF Lancaster, headed from the Marianas to Tokyo. Those that made it there dropped 1,665 tons of bombs, causing a fire that destroyed 16 square miles of buildings and killing around

84,000 people. Except for Kyoto – as even LeMay recognized its cultural importance – major Japanese cities were set on fire, one after another, while B-29s also mined Japanese ports and shipping routes to devastating effect in Operation Starvation. By August 1945, LeMay's B-29s had set sixty-three Japanese cities ablaze – in the process killing half a million people and leaving 8 million homeless. The bomber had got through with apocalyptical effectiveness. And still, the Japanese fought on.

TWO

Weapons of
Mass Destruction II

All changed, changed utterly

G roup Captain Leonard Cheshire VC, DSO & Two Bars, DFC, did not turn to the Roman Catholic Church in 1948 and devote the rest of his life to charitable work because of his experience of witnessing the atomic bomb explode over Nagasaki. He said it was the experience of the war as a whole. After his retirement from the RAF in January 1946 – he was twenty-eight – and treatment for psychoneurosis at St Luke's Woodside Hospital for Functional Nervous Disorders, Muswell Hill, the distinguished bomber commander worked briefly as a journalist for the *Sunday Graphic* before setting up the charitable homes that bear his name to support disabled people to live, learn and work as independently as they choose.

Cheshire, however, could not but be affected by his direct experience of the effects of the explosion of the uranium fission bomb over Nagasaki on 9 August 1945. Flying in the

B-29 *Big Stink*, assigned to monitor and film the attack, he witnessed a very singular expression of the way humankind could choose to destroy itself, in a manner it had been unable to do before the first successful atomic test – conducted less than a month before, at Alamogordo, New Mexico.

> By the time I saw it, the flash had turned into a vast fire-ball which slowly became dense smoke, 2,000 feet above the ground, half a mile in diameter and rocketing upwards at the rate of something like 20,000 feet a minute. I was overcome, not by its size, nor by its speed of ascent but by what appeared to me its perfect and faultless symmetry... 'Against me,' it seemed to declare, 'you cannot fight.' My whole being felt overwhelmed, first by a tidal wave of relief and hope – it's [the war] all over! – then by a revolt against using such a weapon.

'With such utter devastation before our eyes,' he wrote in *The Face of Victory* (1961), 'how imperative [it was] to do something to see that it should never happen again.'

Since 1945, not even the most aggressive despot has chosen to drop a nuclear bomb on an enemy. Two were dropped, of course: the one on Nagasaki witnessed by Cheshire; the other – 'Little Boy' – from the B-29 *Enola Gay* three days earlier, over Hiroshima. It seems strange that the only nuclear bombers to attack a foreign nation were piston-engine machines, the last of a line of aircraft about to be made redundant in the Jet Age.

It had taken more than 700 Lancasters dropping several thousand tons of bombs to destroy the heart of Hamburg. It took one B-29 to annihilate 90 per cent of the fabric of Hiroshima in an instant and to kill 140,000 people, as well as causing many more deaths, further suffering, long-term medical complications and future deformities. It took one more B-29 to destroy half of Nagasaki and 70,000 people. Returning to the Tinian airbase, Captain Robert A. Lewis, co-pilot of *Enola Gay*, opened his logbook and wrote, 'My God, what have we done?'

An article published on 11 March 1946 in *Life* magazine describing the effect of the bomb dropped on Hiroshima read: 'In the following waves [after the initial blast] people's bodies were terribly squeezed, then their internal organs ruptured. Then the blast blew the broken bodies at 500 to 1,000 miles per hour through the flaming, rubble-filled air. Practically everybody within a radius of 6,500 feet was killed or seriously injured and all buildings crushed or disemboweled.'

When in December 1968 the crew of Apollo 8 came out from behind the Moon on their fourth pass, they witnessed something no human had seen until then: Earthrise. That exquisite orb, so far from their Gemini space capsule, was home. Seen from space, it appeared whole and beautiful. Who would ever have guessed that this was a world long divided into squabbling states and bickering religions, beset by savage wars and fouled by pollution created by its own inhabitants? From the perspective of deep space, it must have seemed absurd that any human would want to harm this planet, yet the American astronauts – ex-USAF and US Navy test and fighter pilots – who experienced this epoch-changing vision, knew full well that humans were now capable of the wilful destruction of their own species, the flora and fauna they shared the planet with, entire natural environments, and even, perhaps, the Earth itself. *Boom!* Nuclear war might see to that.

'As we got further and further away,' recalled James Irwin, the Apollo 15 astronaut who walked on the Moon in July 1971, 'it diminished in size. Finally, it shrank to the size of a marble, the most beautiful marble you can imagine. That beautiful, warm, living object looked so fragile, so delicate, that if you touched it with a finger, it would crumble and fall apart. Seeing this has to change a man, has to make a man appreciate the creation of God and the love of God.'

Taylor Wang, a Chinese-American Space Shuttle crew member in 1985, thought of a Chinese tale of 'some men sent to harm a young girl who, upon seeing her beauty, become her protectors rather than her violators. That's how I felt seeing the Earth for the first time. I could not help but love and cherish her.' Alexei Leonov, the Soviet cosmonaut who in March 1965 became the first person to walk in space, during the Voskhod 2 mission, saw that 'the Earth was small, light blue and so touchingly alone... our home that must be defended like a holy relic'. For Edgar Mitchell, a member of the Apollo 14 crew and the sixth man to walk on the Moon, 'My view of our planet was a glimpse of divinity.'

On the night before Christmas 1968, as they emerged from the dark side of the Moon for the ninth time, the crew of Apollo 8 made a live television broadcast. Showing viewers shots of outer space which Commander Frank Borman described as 'a vast, lonely, forbidding type of existence or expanse of nothing', the crew took turns to read from the Book of Genesis. 'In the beginning,' began William Anders, 'God created the heaven and the earth. And the earth was without form, and void; and darkness was upon the face of the deep. And the spirit of God moved upon the face of the waters. And God said, Let there be light: and there was light. And God saw the light, that it was good: and God divided the light from the darkness.'

Apollo 8's mission was taking place at the end of a year of upheaval and division around the world. Soviet tanks had rolled, unwelcome, into Prague. Martin Luther King, Jr and Robert F. Kennedy had been assassinated. The Vietnam War had escalated with the Tet Offensive. University campuses across the United States had witnessed rioting. The events of May 1968 had brought France close to revolution. In October, troops had opened fire on students in Mexico City, killing hundreds. High above the fray, Apollo 8 brought home a message. There was only one Earth. It belonged to us all and it needed our loving care.

The searing light Leonard Cheshire witnessed over Japan on 9 August 1945 was an inverted Genesis seen through dark glasses. This was light as destroyer. Lucifer's moment. As calm as ever in flight, Cheshire had wanted to fly closer to the towering, mushroom cloud, but his pilot kept his distance, insisting he was looking after the safety of his passengers rather than, as Cheshire thought, feeling 'overwrought as well he might be by the scene in front of him'.

Back in London, Cheshire made his report to the prime minister. Winston Churchill had sent him to join the B-29s in the Pacific, but Clement Attlee was in 10 Downing Street now. Attlee was somewhat baffled when Cheshire said that he thought atomic energy should be used to further space exploration rather than weapons. But, as historian Max Hastings says, Cheshire was a remarkable man with 'a mystical air about him, as if he somehow inhabited another planet from those around him, yet without affectation or pretension'. If he had not found God, then God was about to find him. In recent years, this extraordinary and very brave airman has been considered for sainthood.

Cheshire's fellow observer on board *Big Stink* was the equally quietly spoken William Penney, a gifted English mathematician and physicist with a seraphic smile who had played key roles in the development of the A-bomb, both in Britain before the war and in the US during the conflict. At the Manhattan Project's Los Alamos Laboratory, New Mexico, he had been on the committee that chose targets for atomic bombs, Hiroshima and Nagasaki included.

A cumulative train of thought and experiments conducted by British, Italian and German scientists from the early 1930s had led to the discovery of nuclear fission by Otto Hahn, Lise Meitner and Fritz Strassmann – for which Hahn alone was awarded the 1944 Nobel Prize in Chemistry. Hahn had pursued postdoctoral studies in London and was a postgraduate pupil of New Zealand–born Ernest Rutherford, the 'father of nuclear physics', during his tenure at McGill University in Montreal. In 1932, under the direction of Rutherford at the Cavendish Laboratory, Cambridge, John Cockcroft and Ernest Walton split the atom. In Rutherford's words, they had 'touched the ghost of matter'.

The scientific community at this time was just that – an international connection of brilliant men and women who, until war broke out in 1939, were often eager to share knowledge to further progress in their fields of research. Quite who knew what exactly, whether in Britain, Canada, the United States, Nazi Germany or the Soviet Union, was never clear. With scientists like Otto Hahn, Germany was in a strong position in terms of developing a nuclear bomb before the Allies. Yet the scientists themselves did not always see their discoveries through a nationalist lens. Hahn, for example, had no liking for the Nazis and detested their treatment of the Jews. He was sorry to lose Lise Meitner, a Jew whose conversion to the Christian faith in 1908 would not, she knew, save her from the concentration camps. She was helped to escape to Sweden. When invited by the British to join the Manhattan Project, Meitner refused, saying, 'I will have nothing to do with a bomb.'

Britain was ahead with nuclear research when the government concluded it would be best to merge its secret Tube Alloys project (a deliberately humdrum name aimed at diverting attention from its secret purpose) with the Manhattan Project. The deal was signed by Winston Churchill and

Franklin Roosevelt at the Quadrant Conference held in Quebec City in August 1943. Joseph Stalin had been invited but was unable to attend for 'military reasons' – the big and critical Soviet Donbas offensive was in full swing. Moscow, however, had been receiving information on Tube Alloys for several months and would continue to be supplied with information from the Manhattan Project. The source was Klaus Fuchs, a German physicist who had joined the Communist Party and fled Germany in the aftermath of the Reichstag fire of February 1933. Whoever actually set fire to the German parliament building, Hitler chose to blame the Communists – and used this act of arson to trigger the Enabling Act, allowing the government to bypass parliament and establish totalitarian rule.

Safe in England, Fuchs worked for Tube Alloys, and later for the Manhattan Project in Los Alamos under Robert Oppenheimer. After the war, he was with the new Atomic Energy Research Establishment, working on the development of Britain's go-it-alone H-bomb. Finally uncovered as a spy in 1949, Fuchs was arrested, tried and sentenced to fourteen years in prison. In his defence, he said – truthfully – that there had been no money involved. He had been assisting a British and American ally in the fight against Nazi Germany. After serving nine years, Fuchs left Britain for the German Democratic Republic, where he became deputy director of the Central Institute for Nuclear Physics in a rebuilt Dresden. It is difficult to say what real contribution Fuchs made to the realization of Soviet nuclear weapons. The USSR had its own brilliant scientists, who tended, as did its technical engineers, to question ideas from the West and to do things, whatever information they received, their own way.

Fear of espionage was to play a key role in the drama that unfolded in August 1946, when the signing into law of the US Atomic Energy Act on the first of that month by President Harry Truman ended technical nuclear cooperation with Britain with immediate effect. British scientists who had yet to return home were refused access to papers they had written only days before the Act. This was a blow to Clement Attlee's recently elected Labour government. A certain Alan Nunn May had not helped matters. May, a Soviet spy, was a Birmingham-born physicist and member of the Communist Party who had been at Trinity Hall, Cambridge, with Donald Maclean, one of the infamous Cambridge Five – Maclean, Kim Philby, Guy Burgess, Anthony Blunt and John Cairncross – who between them and over many years had served Moscow with thousands of top-secret documents. May, who had worked in Canada for the Manhattan Project and shared secrets with the Soviets, was arrested in March 1946 and sentenced to ten years' hard labour.

Truman's signing of the Atomic Energy Act came less than five months after the 'Sinews of Peace' speech given by Winston Churchill at Westminster College in Fulton, Missouri, on 5 March. The US president had encouraged Churchill to travel to Missouri, promising he would be there. He was. This was a very important speech indeed.

'From Stettin in the Baltic to Trieste in the Adriatic, an iron curtain has descended across the continent,' orated Churchill, introducing a phrase that was taken up immediately and which stuck in the political mind and the popular imagination until the fall of the Berlin Wall in November 1989.

'Behind that line,' he continued, 'lie all the capitals of the ancient states of Central and Eastern Europe. Warsaw, Berlin, Prague, Vienna, Budapest, Belgrade, Bucharest and Sofia, all these famous cities and the populations around them lie in what I must call the Soviet sphere, and all are subject in one form or another, not only to Soviet influence but to a very high and, in many cases, increasing measure of control from Moscow.'

Given the daunting reality of the atomic bomb, Churchill spoke of the necessity of strengthening Anglo-American ties:

No one in any country has slept less well in their beds because this knowledge and the method and the raw materials to apply it, are at present largely retained in American hands. I do not believe we should all have slept so soundly had the positions been reversed and if some Communist or neo-Fascist State monopolised for the time being these dread agencies. The fear of them alone might easily have been used to enforce totalitarian systems upon the free democratic world, with conse-quences appalling to human imagination. God has willed that this shall not be, and we have at least a breathing space to set our house in order before this peril has to be encountered: and even then, if no effort is spared, we should still possess so formidable a superiority as to impose effective deterrents upon its employment, or threat of employment, by others.

Churchill was well received in Missouri and his speech was heard through one medium or another around the world. Still, though, Truman withdrew US cooperation. All of a sudden, the 'special relationship' between Britain and the United States spoken of by Churchill – himself half-American and, from 1963, an honorary US citizen – seemed not so very special after all.

Britain, though, had already determined that, if necessary, it would strike out by itself. On 9 August 1946, the Chief of the Air Staff, Lord Tedder, signed an official request on behalf of the military for an atomic bomb. At much the same time, Lord Portal – Tedder's wartime precursor, staunch supporter of Air Chief Marshal Arthur Harris's area bombing, and now Controller of Production (Atomic Energy) in the Ministry of Supply – asked William Penney to plan an atomic weapons section within the Armaments Research Department to design, develop and construct atomic bombs.

The situation was clearly a complex one. The US was shifting into one of its isolationist phases. The British economy was impoverished. The fear in government and military circles that the Soviet Union might develop its own nuclear bomb sooner or later, while it was itching to expand its European empire, was all but tangible. The thought of the budget needed to create an independent nuclear arsenal was, to say the least, challenging. But could Britain afford to sit back and take a secondary role in world affairs? Ernest Bevin, Attlee's formidable Foreign Secretary, thought not.

'His Majesty's Government do not accept the view,' Bevin told the House of Commons in May 1947, 'that we have ceased to be a great Power, or the contention that we have ceased to play that role. We regard ourselves as one of the Powers most vital to the peace of the world, and we still have our historic part to play. The very fact that we have fought so hard for liberty, and paid such a price, warrants our retaining this position; and, indeed, it places a duty upon us to continue to retain it. I am not aware of any suggestion, seriously advanced, that by a sudden stroke of fate, as it were, we have overnight ceased to be a great power.'

As for a nuclear plant in Britain, Bevin was equally forward. 'We've got to have this thing over here, whatever it costs. We've got to have the bloody Union Jack on top of it.' Attlee and Bevin led the charge against US policy under Truman and against their own MPs, a substantial number of whom were pro-Soviet – Stalin's willing fools – as well as those who simply felt there was no money to spend on hugely expensive weapons that would, in any case, not be in service with the RAF for several years to come.

With the decision taken by a small group of cabinet ministers huddled around the prime minister to go ahead with an independent British bomb, the House of Commons was informed in May 1948, although there were no details given of its design or construction and certainly nothing about where it was to be built and stored. Just like Tube Alloys, the secret organization in charge of developing Britain's atomic bomb was given an unrevealing name: High Explosive Research. Penney was appointed to direct research and development at Fort Halstead, a Ministry of Defence site on the Kentish North Downs near Sevenoaks.

In 1950, the team moved to the new Atomic Weapons Establishment at Aldermaston, Berkshire, where from Easter 1959, 'Ban the Bomb' marches organized by the Campaign for Nuclear Disarmament (CND) set off for Trafalgar Square, 50 miles away. The very first march had been in the opposite direction the year before. The marchers sang as they walked. In 1959 Topic Records released an LP, *Songs Against the Bomb*. Tracks included 'Hey Little Man', 'Doomsday Blues', 'The H-Bomb's Thunder' and 'The Bomb Has Got to Go'.

On 29 August 1949, before High Explosive's move to Aldermaston, the Soviets unsettled London and Washington by testing their first atomic bomb, codenamed 'First Lightning', at Semipalatinsk in the Kazakh SSR (Soviet Socialist Republic). The general understanding in the West had been that this was unlikely to happen before 1954. The brain behind the Soviet bomb was Igor Kurchatov's. Kurchatov had been researching radioactivity and then nuclear science at the Soviet Academy of Sciences, Leningrad, for twenty years when in 1943 Stalin authorized a Soviet nuclear programme and appointed the talented physicist to direct it.

The brawn was provided by the nightmarish Lavrentiy Beria, chief of the Soviet secret police, the NKVD. Beria's personal interests lay more in kidnapping, rape, brutal torture

in which he gleefully took part, and the destruction of intelligent and decent people's lives and careers than in science,
yet he was appointed political head of the nuclear programme
the day after the explosion of Little Boy over Hiroshima.
Beria's fierce energy, and information from his extensive spy
network, pushed the project on quickly while making the lives
of those working on it deeply uncomfortable. The principal
target of his paranoia was Kurchatov, who was kept under
constant surveillance.

Yuli Khariton, a key member of Kurchatov's team, said of
Beria: 'This man personified evil in the country's modern
history [and] possessed at the same time tremendous vigour
and efficiency. It was impossible not to admit his intellect,
willpower, and purposefulness. He was a first-class manager
able to bring every job to its conclusion.' Khariton's father,
a political journalist, had been arrested by Beria's NKVD in
1940, and sentenced at the age of sixty-four to seven years'
forced labour. He died before completing his wholly unjust
sentence.

The one consolation for Kurchatov's staff, scientific success
aside, was Beria's immediate fall following Stalin's death.
Tried and convicted of treason, Beria was executed in Moscow
on 23 December 1953. Unsettled by the destructive power of
the atomic and hydrogen bombs he created, Kurchatov began
calling for the peaceful development and use of nuclear technology. He was fortunate that Stalin was dead when he did.

The Soviet nuclear physicist's ashes were buried in the
Kremlin Wall Necropolis on Red Square, through which

nuclear missiles are paraded every year on Victory Day. In recent years, President Vladimir Putin has watched gigantic RS-24 Yars intercontinental ballistic missiles (ICBMs) – each of which contains up to ten nuclear warheads – rumble past the Kremlin on sixteen-wheel trailers.

Kurchatov's life was cut short by his exposure to radioactive gases at Chelyabinsk-40, the closed city in the south-west Urals where the Soviet Union's first weapons-grade plutonium plant was built as part of the nuclear programme established there from 1946. While workers were looked after comparatively well in Chelyabinsk-40 (Ozersk today), the environment was of little or no importance to those in charge. Nuclear waste was dumped in the local river flowing out to the Arctic Ocean. Contaminated water from the reactors was discharged into Lake Kyzyltash and Lake Karachay. On 29 September 1957, a failure in a cooling system caused one of fourteen steel tanks containing some 80 tons of radioactive waste to explode, releasing more radioactive contamination than the 1986 meltdown at the Chernobyl Nuclear Power Plant. It settled over an area of more than 7,700 square miles, home to 270,000 people. While news of Chernobyl was squeezed from a reluctant Moscow and relayed to the outside world within forty-eight hours, the full extent of what happened at Chelyabinsk would remain unknown both within and without the Soviet Union until 1980.

Still, by 1960, the CIA had pieced together a pretty clear idea of the true story. Washington, however, was keen to downplay it. Why? Because Chelyabinsk-40 was the Soviet

counterpart to the Hanford Engineer Works, which incorporated the world's first plutonium production reactor in the
purpose-built new town of Richmond, on the Columbia River,
Washington. Day by day, Hanford polluted the local environment. The complex's safety could not be guaranteed. It seemed
best to keep the American public in the dark.

There was, though, even more to fear, not least the question of how powerful the nuclear-fusion H-bomb promised
in the wake of the A-bomb would be. The short answer was
about one thousand times more powerful. *One thousand times*.
The A-bomb is a fission device in which the atomic nucleus
of uranium or plutonium is split, releasing huge amounts of
energy. The H-bomb employs atomic fission to trigger the
fusion of hydrogen atoms or isotopes that, working in the way
the sun does, produces colossal energy.

The first US test took place at Enewetak Atoll in the
Marshall Islands on 1 November 1952, a month after the first
British A-bomb was detonated in the hull of the Royal Navy
frigate HMS *Plym* in the Montebello Islands off the coast of
Western Australia. In the way more of Ealing comedies than
the Cold War, when Britain's first operational nuclear fission
bomb, the Blue Danube, was delivered to RAF Wittering the
following November, there was no aircraft there, or anywhere
else in the country, designed to carry this very particular
payload.

Churchill had been back in Downing Street since October
1951, and it was he who decided that Britain should press
ahead with an H-bomb of its own. The first detonation was

made over Christmas Island in the Indian Ocean south of Java and Sumatra on 8 November 1957, followed the same day by the dropping of a bomb from a Vickers Valiant V-bomber on the edge of Malden Island in the central Pacific. This achievement impressed Washington, which at the time was in a state of crisis over the successful launch of Sputnik 1 a month earlier. What worried the Americans was not so much the fact that the USSR had sent the first artificial satellite into orbit around the Earth – much as this rankled – but that the launch had been made by an ICBM that, with a 1,000,000-lb thrust, demonstrated in no uncertain terms that Soviet missiles could now reach the US. Washington felt the need for buddies. The US–UK Mutual Defence Agreement was signed the following July, committing the two countries to work together again on a nuclear weapons programme, although the word should probably be spelled 'program', as Britain's nuclear arsenal was to be essentially American.

Now that these terrifying bombs and warheads had been proven to work, the big question on both sides of the Atlantic – and in Moscow too – was how they would be delivered to enemy targets. By the time of Sputnik, missiles appeared to be the way forward. But while this had been foreseen early on, in 1946 missiles were in their infancy and the one existing possible way was by long-range bomber aircraft. In the event, as we will see, the two methods of delivery were to work, uneasily, together.

Despite an initial lack of enthusiasm on Hitler's part, Germany had raced ahead with rocket research during the

Second World War. Ultimately, it was impossible not to realize the importance of the work of the team of scientists and engineers at the Army Research Centre at Peenemünde on the German Baltic Coast. Wernher von Braun, then just in his thirties, was the establishment's technical director. On 20 June 1944, one of his V-2 long-range guided ballistic missiles – MW 18014 – crossed the Kármán line, drawn at 100 kilometres above sea level, and thus by the terms of the international agreement made in the 1960s entered outer space. Its maximum altitude was a remarkable 176 kilometres. Von Braun's interest in rockets had always been in terms of space exploration rather than weaponry and, famously, he was eventually able to return to his preoccupation with NASA, where his 363-foot Saturn V rocket with a thrust something like 135 times that of his V-2 vengeance weapon lifted Neil Armstrong, Buzz Aldrin and Michael Collins from Cape Canaveral, Florida, on the way to the Moon in July 1969.

Before then, though, and after four Allied bombing raids on Peenemünde – the first by a fleet of 596 Halifaxes, Stirlings and Lancasters on the night of 17/18 August 1943 – V-2 production had been moved to Mittelwerk, a construction plant dug into Kohnstein, a hill near Nordhausen, Thuringia. This grim place was built by slave labour drawn from the nearby concentration camp. Infamously, more people died making V-2s than were killed by V-2s on the near 3,000 launches made against Antwerp, London and Liège in 1944 and 1945. What everyone learned was that, just as there was no way of knowing where a V-2 would meet the ground, there was also no way of intercepting this 3,600-mph projectile. The missile, it seemed, would always get through.

With examples of the V-2 captured by both the Americans and the Soviets, von Braun's rocket went on to inform the design of armed missiles and space rockets in both countries – notably his Redstone, which was used in the first US live nuclear ballistic missile tests and, in May 1961, for the launch of the first American into space, Alan Shepard. From 1958 until 1964, production models of the Redstone, built by Chrysler, were stationed in West Germany.

Von Braun was brought to the US from Germany after the war under the auspices of the secret intelligence programme Operation Paperclip, along with some 1,600 other German scientists, engineers and technicians. Adolf Busemann, pioneer of swept-wing aircraft design, was among them. His influence in the US was to be immediate.

In May 1945, a team of US aerodynamicists and aero-engineers had gone to Germany to glean information from their counterparts there. After discussions with Busemann, George Schairer, Boeing's inventive chief aerodynamicist, wired his office, 'Stop the bomber design.' He was referring to Boeing's large long-range nuclear jet bomber, which would emerge as the six-engine B-47 Stratojet, first flown in December 1947. Its straight wings were now to be swept back by 35 degrees.

During the American fact-finding trip to Germany, Busemann reminded Schairer that he had presented a paper – 'High Velocities in Aviation' – on swept wings at the Fifth Volta Conference, held in Rome in 1935, and that five of the conference dinner guests were there at the meeting in Germany a decade later. While Busemann had been ahead of the game in the late 1930s, swept wings – which delay the onset of wave drag and are thus helpful in high-speed flight – were not important for bombers like the B-17, B-29 or Lancaster, with top speeds of 280–350 mph. They were, though, critically important now the need had arisen, after Little Boy and Fat Man, for bombers that, flying ever closer to the speed of sound, would get through to targets as quickly as technically possible.

THREE

Weapons of Mass Destruction III

Inception

The Air Ministry specification – B.35/46 – that led, officially, to the Valiant, Vulcan and Victor bombers was issued on 7 January 1947, the day Clement Attlee's Labour government committed Britain to the development of an atomic bomb. Six companies – Armstrong Whitworth, Avro, Bristol, English Electric, Handley Page and Short Brothers – were invited to tender designs for consideration that July, by a committee of expert aeronautical engineers chaired by Morien Morgan, chief aerodynamicist at the Royal Aircraft Establishment, Farnborough, and the future 'Father of Concorde'. From the ember days of the war, these independent companies had been considering the form and general arrangement of future military aircraft. The leaps and bounds made in aircraft technology and design by the Germans did much to set the pace and tone of post-war research and development.

From early 1946, for example, Handley Page's chief designer, Reginald Stafford, and the company's head of research, Godfrey Lee, who had been in Germany immediately after VE Day on behalf of the swept wings committee of the Aeronautical Research Council, were busy at work on a design of a long-range jet bomber. Originally, Lee had been thinking of a jet airliner, but he was asked by Sir Frederick Handley Page to look at a replacement for the Avro Lincoln – the slow, if competent, piston-engine successor to the Lancaster. The Lincoln was the aircraft that might carry Britain's first nuclear bomb should progress with jet bombers be delayed. An artist's impression of Lee's Handley Page HP.80 jet bomber proposal of 1947 reveals a sleek, futuristic aircraft with inboard engines and wings swept back at 45 degrees, their tips curved upwards like those of twenty-first-century airliners – although not for the same reason. It was a stunning design, evoking some wholly new, if as yet technically unresolved, future.

What seems remarkable from today's perspective is that Stafford, Lee and others on the Handley Page team had begun working on this design, which would morph one way or another into the Victor V-bomber, when Avro's Lancaster was still in production and the first Avro Lincolns were being delivered to RAF Bomber Command. Designed for missions in the Pacific theatre during the Second World War, the Lincoln – the RAF's last heavy piston-engine bomber – was superseded by events. The war was over before it could be called on to attack Japanese targets. It was, in any case, inferior in terms of performance and payload to the Boeing

B-29 Superfortress, which, after having bombed mainland Japan extensively, dropped the atomic bombs on Hiroshima and Nagasaki. In 1950, the RAF leased eighty-seven B-29s – redesignated Washington B.1s – as stop-gap long-range bombers to supplement the Lincolns before the arrival of, first, the twin-engine jet English Electric Canberra and, then, the four-engine jet V-bombers. These Washingtons returned home to the US in 1954.

Compared to the Lancaster, Lincoln and Handley Page's own Halifax heavy bomber – in service with the Pakistan Air Force until 1961 – Lee's HP.80 proposal belonged to a very

Bomber Command's Rolls-Royce Merlin-powered Avro Lincoln

different era, as if several generations rather than a mere few years separated these aircraft types. Gone were the Merlin piston engines, bulbous turrets bristling with Browning machine guns, and tail-dragging fuselages of the 1940s bombers. Fine machines in their own right and realm, these earlier aircraft seemed almost Gothic in design next to Lee and his colleagues' resolutely modern HP.80.

In late 1947, both the reconfigured crescent-wing HP.80 put forward by Handley Page and Avro's striking delta-wing 698 bomber were approved by Morien Morgan's committee. These marked new territory in terms of design and engineering. They were unlike any other aircraft at the time, outward signs of original thinking – although, as yet, untried and tested. As both designs might have failed to meet expectations, a less ambitious 'back-up' nuclear bomber was ordered from Shorts of Belfast. This was the SA.4 Sperrin, named after Northern Ireland's beautiful, boggy Sperrin Mountains, and in the end just two were built.

In the 1930s, Shorts had established its name with distin-guished flying boats. The company's reputation was enhanced in the Second World War with the impressive S.25 Sunderland long-range double-deck flying boat patrol bomber. Complete with a galley for hot meals and cups of tea, comfortable bunks, a flushing porcelain lavatory, and an arsenal of bombs, depth charges and machine guns, the Sunderland – a fiery porcupine of an aircraft – sank U-boats, rescued sea and aircrews, and drove off attacks from, in one famous episode from 1940, as many as six formidable twin-engine Junkers

Ju 88C fighters at once. Shorts also designed the RAF's first four-engine heavy bomber, the S.29 Stirling – bigger, slower and with a shorter range than the later Handley Page Halifax and Avro Lancaster.

Events conspired against the stop-gap Sperrin. Both London and Washington were rattled when in February 1948, and with Soviet backing, the Communist Party of Czechoslovakia staged a *coup d'état*, toppling the government in Prague. In June, in a move made to isolate Berlin and bring the city lock, stock and barrel into Stalin's empire, the Soviets blockaded all road, rail and water routes to the German city from the west, leading to the 1948–49 Berlin Airlift. Thereafter, the threat of war with the USSR increased and there was a boost to Britain's military spending, with the US contributing following the outbreak of the Korean War in June 1950. The Air Staff ordered a fourth four-engine jet bomber, the Vickers 660. A halfway house between the staid, straight-wing Sperrin and the avant-garde Avro and Handley Page swept-wing designs, it promised to be in the air sooner than its competitors.

The Sperrin was cancelled. It was, at heart, a Second World War aircraft reconfigured for the Jet Age rather than a Jet Age bomber entering the nuclear era. Its one unorthodox feature was the mounting of its four Rolls-Royce Avon jets in stacked pairs in vertical nacelles above and below the middle of each wing. Contrary to appearance, these did not impede air flow. One clear advantage of this arrangement was that the engines were readily accessible for servicing and replacement. When the first of the

Bulbous Short Sperrin with stacked mid-wing Avon engines

two Sperrins built made its public debut at the 1951 Farnborough Air Show in a civilian-like red, grey and black colour scheme, it was put into the shade by the svelte, natural metal Vickers 660 – newly dubbed the Valiant, a name selected through a poll among the Vickers staff. The Sperrin looked slightly awkward and old-fashioned in comparison with the Valiant. It was certainly inferior in terms of outright performance.

We might stop here to ask why the Ministry of Supply, the Ministry of Air and the RAF were toying with four competing designs of jet bombers, at a time when rapid innovation in ground-to-air missile technology threatened to destroy them all. Between September 1944 and March 1945, London alone had been struck by several hundred rocket-powered German V-2 ballistic missiles. Launched from sites around The Hague, V-2s reached their targets in five minutes. Climbing to around 250,000 feet and accelerating to 3,400 mph, in flight the V-2 was immune from attack. At this stage of its development, however, it was a blunt weapon of war. Without an accurate guidance system, it struck targets randomly. The most lethal V-2 hit on London was on a branch of Woolworths on New Cross Road. The final blow was on a block of working-class flats in Stepney. V-2s were a sign of things to come – but, as yet, not quite the 'wonder weapon' Hitler had dreamed of.

While in October 1945 the British tested V-2s assembled from scattered components at Cuxhaven on the north German coast, their interest then and for some years yet was focused on long-range strategic bombers, leaving the Soviets and Americans to push ahead with surface-to-air and long-range ballistic missile technologies in tandem with new bomber types. Space rockets, too. From 1941, the Germans had been working on a radio-controlled surface-to-air missile, the Wasserfall ('Waterfall'). Derived from the V-2, this smaller device could be stored safely for up to a month before being launched. While wartime success eluded the Wasserfall, it was another valuable lead for Allied and Soviet scientists and engineers to follow after the war.

Missile technology in general, however, was not expected to be up to speed for several years. The RAF wanted the new-generation bombers. As the Chief of the Air Staff, Marshal of the Royal Air Force Sir John Slessor, put it in 1952, considering the possibility of a Soviet invasion of Western Europe: 'I do not believe the Red Army could be stopped by the Divisions and Tactical Air Forces which NATO can in fact build up without busting Europe and the UK economically – which may well be the Russian game. I believe the only really sound course would be to build up a completely overwhelming British/American bomber force with the A-bomb, capable of pulverizing Russia itself and eliminating the Red Air Force at its bases.'

Slessor's 1957 book, *The Great Deterrent*, brought his ideas on the subject together in crystal-clear prose and no uncertain manner. In Slessor, the British nuclear bomber had a highly intelligent and dynamic champion. Coining – or certainly spearheading – the term 'V-Force' for what became the Valiant, Vulcan and Victor bomber squadrons, Slessor represented British determination against the odds at its best.

Born in Ranikhet, an Indian hill station in Uttarakhand – warm summers, winter snows, set against a backdrop of the Himalayas – Slessor had contracted polio as a boy. Lame in both legs, he walked for the rest of his life with the aid of a stick. Rejected by the British Army on medical grounds, he was helped into the Royal Flying Corps through family connections. Overcoming his physical limitations, he proved to be a fine fighter pilot, serving with distinction in the Middle East and over the Western Front during the First World War.

During the Second World War, Slessor was the highly effective Air Officer Commanding Coastal Command, keeping vital transatlantic convoys on the move – notably with the help of those long-distance Short Sunderlands – before his appointment as the equally energetic Commander-in-Chief RAF Mediterranean and Middle East. What he and his colleagues saw in the V-bomber designs was a transition from heavily armed, slow and low-flying propeller-driven machines to unarmed, high-flying jets able to outpace enemy fighters. The appeal must have been enormous for those who, like Slessor, had begun their active careers flying 90-mph biplanes, hopping over enemy gun emplacements at the risk of being shot down by small-arms fire – and for those, too, who had battled through flak and been pursued by fast and often expertly flown fighters over Germany and German-occupied Europe between 1939 and 1945.

So, while in 1947 four bomber designs might have seemed three too many, the wisest decision was, it seemed then, to invest in several designs and see how they performed. Much the same reasoning had been at play in the Second World War, when the RAF fronted three heavy, four engine-bombers: the Short Stirling, the Handley Page Halifax and the Avro Lancaster.

Shorts, meanwhile, had in fact put forward a more daring proposal than the Sperrin. This was a tailless, five-engine design – four Avons above and below swept-back wings, with a fifth installed in the rear of the fuselage – featuring pivoting wingtips to control pitch and roll. Although this innovative wing was tested with some success on a small demonstrator aircraft – the SB.4 Sherpa, first flown in 1953 – the Air Ministry saw no especial advantage in aerodynamicist and chief Shorts designer David Keith-Lucas's effort.

VALIANT

Brand new Valiant B(K)1 flown to RAF Marham, November 1956

Vickers' chief designer, George Edwards, had courted the Air Ministry assiduously, claiming that he could have the 660 flying by the end of 1951 and in service with the RAF by early 1955. He met both these self-imposed deadlines. His team had been thinking about a jet bomber since the late stages of the Second World War. Now was the opportunity to get one built and into service. Such was the Valiant's progress, it flew before the Sperrin, taking off from Wisley Airfield, Surrey, on 18 May 1951, with Joseph 'Mutt' Summers at the controls. In 1936,

Summers, who was the chief test pilot for Vickers, had been first to fly both the Supermarine Spitfire and the Vickers Wellington, a twin-engine long-range bomber of which more than 11,500 were built. The Wellington served throughout the Second World War.

The Valiant received a thumbs-up from Summers, just as it did from his colleague Brian Trubshaw, a wartime Stirling and Lancaster pilot and later chief British test pilot for Concorde. The first Valiants were flown to RAF squadrons in January 1955. Small wonder the persuasive and highly effective Edwards went on to lead the British Concorde team. He and Vickers could certainly deliver.

Getting the Valiant into the air within just twenty-seven months of the signing of the contract for the nuclear bomber was an impressive achievement. The speed of progress, however, meant that it was a more conventional machine – in George Edwards's words, an 'unfunny' aircraft – than either the Avro Vulcan or the Handley Page Victor that followed in its wake. Development was straightforward. Six engines gave way to four as the power of the Rolls-Royce Avon increased. These were installed, like on the Comet airliner, in the roots of each shoulder-mounted wing. While this made maintenance awkward, the arrangement gave the aircraft a clean, aerodynamic form.

First run in 1947, the Avon engine proved to be a bestseller for Rolls-Royce. As well as the Valiant, it was to power military and civil aircraft as diverse as the Canberra (retired by the RAF in 2006 after half a century's service), the English

Electric Lightning, the Hawker Hunter, and the de Havilland Comet 4 and Sud Aviation Caravelle airliners. It remains in production in the mid-2020s as an industrial gas generator manufactured by Siemens, a German company.

The wings of the Valiant were swept back in two stages – at 37 per cent from close to the wing root to delay high-speed shock waves, and 21 per cent for the main section – blended with a curved leading edge. Several of the main structural components of the aircraft were made of an aluminium, copper, magnesium and zinc alloy (DTD683) that, while safe in the relatively calm air of high flight, was to be subject to critical stress when the aircraft was flown at 500 feet and below for prolonged spells. As early as 1956, concerns were expressed, notably in the *Journal of the Institute of Metals*, over the unstable behaviour of DTD683 when airframes were stressed close to their design limits. In the event, DTD683, as we shall see, proved to be the Valiant's Achilles heel.

Other materials employed in the Valiant might well raise eyebrows today. I was surprised to find this paragraph in Tim Laming's *V-Bombers*:

Shortages of steel girder sections, largely due to the needs of the Korean War, led to the employment of *pre-stressed concrete* [my italics] in the construction of the Valiant's main assembly jig pillars. Glass-fibre plastic bonding was introduced for the production of the various dielectrical components, such as the huge nose radome and a number of suppressed aerial panels, and synthetic bonding was

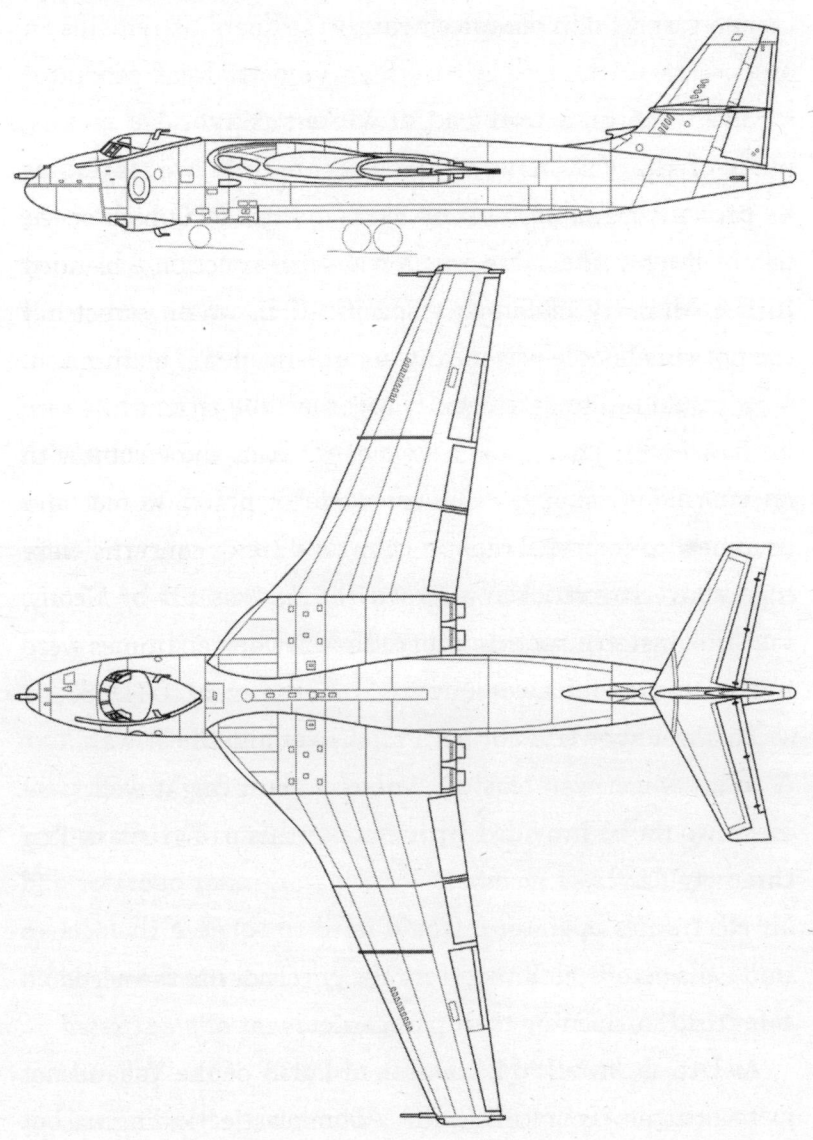

B.1 Vickers Valiant

used for the production of control surface doubling plates and various skin reinforcements.

Given the high workload at Vickers' Weybridge factory, parts of the Valiant were manufactured off site, including its pressurized cabin built by Saunders-Roe at Cowes on the Isle of Wight. The cabin was a source of concern. According to the Ministry of Supply's specification, in an emergency the entire caboodle was meant to be jettisoned. The five-man crew would fall to earth gently together, the cabin supported by parachutes. This would have meant fitting the Valiant with an enormous canopy, while considerable power would have been needed to propel canopy, cabin and crewmen sufficiently high above the stricken aircraft. Discussions led by George Edwards concerning this demanding design requirement led to its being quietly abandoned.

This would be true for both the Victor and the Vulcan, too. A compromise was reached whereby the pilot and co-pilot alone would be provided with ejection seats. The remaining three regular crew members – navigator, radar operator and air electronics operator – would need to squeeze themselves into balls before tumbling from the entrance hatch and, when safe to do so, opening their parachutes.

As late as June 1964, a House of Lords debate tussled not just with the technicalities of V-bomber ejection seats, but also with the moral questions that the lack of them for the three – occasionally four – rear crew members raised. 'Roughly speaking three-quarters of people using an ejector seat come down safely,' Lord Amulree, a physician whose father had been Secretary of State for Air under Ramsay MacDonald, reminded the House, 'but of those having to bale out the fraction is about one-quarter.' Were, perhaps, some crew members more expendable than others?

The government's response was that cost alone had never been a factor in the design of V-bomber cabins. It was time that had been of the essence, and this was still the case in 1964, when the V-bombers were needed in service. It would take too long to redesign them, although improvements had been made since their introduction, with swivel seats fitted with pneumatic cushions allowing the rear crew to exit their aircraft within thirty seconds. According to Lord St Oswald, a junior minister in Sir Alec Douglas-Home's government, 'even if a fault suddenly developed at 250 feet, it is considered that their chance of escape is good, and we must also take into account that the pilot should be able to gain height and give them a still better chance'. Not quite so encouragingly, members of the House of Lords learned that such escape procedures were practised regularly on the ground.

As fate would have it, the prototype Valiant WB210 caught fire on 12 January 1952, during internal noise measurement trials for a potential civil version of the bomber conducted over the Hampshire coast, which required the shutting-down and refiring of the aircraft's Avon engines several times. This is when a fire broke out in one of the jet pipes. The crew abandoned ship shortly before the aircraft exploded, and four men escaped unharmed. The fifth, co-pilot Squadron Leader

Brian Foster, struck the tail fin after ejecting. His injuries were fatal. Nevertheless, the Valiant would prove to be a safe aircraft – few crashes, few fatalities – in its short service life.

While the Victor and Vulcan were more advanced aircraft, it was the Valiant that carried out the entire gamut of tasks asked of V-Force, short of dropping a live nuclear bomb on an enemy target. It conducted conventional bombing raids, in Aden in 1956; dropped Britain's first A-bomb over Maralinga, South Australia, that same year and Britain's first H-bomb over Malden Island in the Pacific Ocean in 1957; served as a key part of Britain's nuclear deterrent; flew reconnaissance and air-to-air refuelling missions; and offered PR rides to VIPs, among them the Duke of Edinburgh and Anthony Eden, prime minister when the aircraft entered squadron service in 1955. And, of course, it was the public's introduction to V-Force.

Although not as impressive to look at as the near-other-worldly Victor and the Space Age Vulcan, the Valiant was up-to-the-minute in terms of electric control systems and, at the time, speed and altitude. And it was certainly big. It had to be, to carry the hefty first-generation Cold War nuclear bombs while also containing fuel sufficient to power it over and beyond the Ministry of Supply specifications of 3,300 nautical miles, 50,000 feet and 500 knots (575 mph). Imagine a Valiant parked alongside a Lancaster. At 108 feet, the Valiant was much longer than Britain's best Second World War bomber (the Lancaster measured 70 feet). Its 114-foot wingspan was just under 12 feet greater than the Lancaster's. More significantly, at 140,000 lb, a fully loaded Valiant weighed twice as much as a mission-ready Lanc. Despite being 18 inches taller than the Lancaster, the 32-foot-high Valiant sat low on the ground. There it looked more than a little hunched and even awkward – a pelican among military eagles, especially with its bulbous nose. But like the pelican, another accomplished long-distance flyer, the Valiant was elegant in flight.

By the time production ended in August 1957, 107 Valiant B.1s, including prototypes, had been built. Within eight years, however, the entire fleet was grounded, with all but one aircraft scrapped soon afterwards. The end came quickly. Switched in 1962 from high- to low-level nuclear bombing missions now that the lethal effectiveness of Soviet surface-to-air missiles was impossible to ignore, the newly camouflaged Valiant was out of its comfort zone. Buffeted by turbulence, airframes designed for high flight showed signs of critical stress. A key part of the cause was that DTD683 alloy. In 1964, fatigue and crystalline corrosion were found in wing-spar attachments. Vickers had detected the problem, but the danger was not fully exposed until early that August, when, on a training mission, the starboard rear wing-spar of Valiant WP217 fractured. The aircraft was flying at 30,000 feet. It was, the crew reported, as if it had been struck by a rocket. Skilfully, Flight Lieutenant 'Taffy' Foreman brought the stricken V-bomber down to a safe if flapless landing – the flaps were inoperable – at RAF Gaydon. Here, the wing was seen to sag.

An immediate check made on the Valiant fleet revealed stress fractures that could have, at any time, caused the wings to fail in flight. While Vickers was confident it could repair the fleet, the Valiant was out for the count. Repairs would be expensive, and, in any case, it was due to be withdrawn 'within the next four years', according to Denis Healey, Secretary of State for Defence, speaking to the House of Commons in February 1965. When 49 Squadron disbanded in May 1965, the pioneer V-bomber was history. As fate would have it, V-Force had been at its zenith the previous year, with fifty Valiants in service alongside seventy Vulcans and thirty-nine Victors.

While very few changes were made to the Valiant B.1 – with the notable exception of uprated Avon engines – a B.2 version, of which just a single example was built, could have seen the first of the V-bomber types in the air well beyond the mid-1960s. First flown in September 1953, the B.2 featured a stronger airframe than the B.1. It was designed for low flight, not as a bomber but as a Pathfinder that would serve as a guide for V-Force, just as de Havilland Mosquitoes had led Lancaster bombers to targets during the Second World War. In contrast with its pure-white, high-flying siblings, the jet-black B.2 would skim the surface, avoid enemy radar and pinpoint targets with stealthy élan.

A capable machine, cleared for 580 mph at sea level compared to 414 mph for the B.1, the B.2 was to remain a solitary aircraft. The Pathfinder concept was considered out-of-date by the time it flew. New radar technology meant that V-bombers would be able to locate and home in on their targets without help. Few then saw the need for a low-level nuclear bomber.

While the B.2 might have been the remedy for the B.1's low-level ills, it was a fine, though ultimately redundant, design. Rather sadly, this impressive machine, powered by Rolls-Royce Conway turbofan engines (the first of their kind), was packed off to Foulness on the Essex coast after withdrawal from service, where it was shot up in tests designed to determine the ability – or otherwise – of contemporary airframes to withstand various weaponry.

A B.3 proposal dating from 1953 outlined a Valiant with a greater sweep to its wing and the promise of improved performance, but this was little more than a gleam in the eyes of the Vickers design team – as was, even more so, an outline for a Mach 4 Valiant powered by four afterburning Conway engines. At this time Barnes Wallis, Vickers' head of research and development, was working on the design of his 'Swallow', a rapier-like swing-wing Mach 2 interceptor that this inventive designer imagined being developed into a future V-bomber. Such ideas are reminders of how British design engineers and aviation drawing offices crackled with fecund life and creativity in an era when companies were far less 'corporate' than they would become in the late twentieth century and beyond.

A single, gleaming white Valiant survives today, B.1 XD818, on display in company with a Victor and a Vulcan as part of the National Cold War Exhibition at the RAF Museum Midlands in Cosford, Shropshire. This is the aircraft that dropped Britain's first H-bomb, a reminder of how important a role the Valiant played in the Cold War. A reminder, too, that although the Valiant led a short life, it was a notably active one. The plane's sorry demise should bely neither its successes nor its versatile service.

The museum's Valiant, delivered new to 49 Squadron, RAF Wittering, in November 1956, was one of four bombers, suitably modified, flown to Christmas Island (Kiritimati) in the mid-Pacific Ocean in March 1957. There it took part in Operation Grapple, the testing of Britain's 'Short Granite' nuclear fusion H-bomb. Valiants had been pressed into service seven months earlier to test drop Britain's first nuclear fission A-bomb. The brief gap between these two epochal events underscored the pressure British scientists were under to catch up with the Americans.

Britain's first nuclear weapon had been tested in October 1952, when an early version of the Blue Danube device was exploded in the hull of HMS *Plym*, a Second World War River-class cruiser off the coast of Trimouille Island in Western Australia. From 1954, when the Americans successfully exploded an H-bomb, the British nuclear weapons programme became a full-throttle priority. The A-bomb and H-bomb programmes ran closely in tandem. Because the H-bomb worked in two stages, with nuclear fission triggering nuclear fusion and thus a vastly powerful and theoretically limitless explosion, an effective and reliable atom bomb was critical to the development of the hydrogen bomb.

Such was the haste involved in the nuclear weapons programme, the first of Britain's atom bombs, the 10,000-lb Blue Danube, was delivered to RAF Wittering in November

1953, ahead of the arrival of the Valiant. In other words, the RAF had a nuclear bomb before it had an aircraft capable of carrying it. The Blue Danube, though, was more of a scientific experiment than a practical military weapon. A much smaller and lighter (1,750-lb) free-fall fission bomb, Red Beard, was now in development. This was designed to be carried into war not just by V-Force bombers when these became available, but also by RAF and Royal Navy twin-engine tactical bombers – the English Electric Canberra, de Havilland Sea Vixen, Supermarine Scimitar and Blackburn Buccaneer – all of which were either in or soon to be in operational service.

The big question, meanwhile, for William Penney and his High Explosive Research team had been where A-bombs could be tested and, ideally, dropped from aircraft. The ideal choice was the Nevada Test Site, but this was off limits because of the decision made by the US in 1946 to cut Britain from its nuclear testing programme. The answer lay in the vast level spaces – *terra nullius* – of the Southern Australian outback. Keen to develop nuclear power, the Australian government was happy to play host to what was quickly established as a long-term joint venture with Britain.

Speaking in 1955 on behalf of the federal government, Howard Beale, Australia's Minister for Supply, said it was 'necessary that we should expand our knowledge of the problems of radiation as fully and as quickly as possible... England has the know how; we have the open spaces, much technical skill and a great willingness to help the Motherland. Between us we should help to build the defences of the free world and make historic advances in harnessing the forces of nature.'

The test site selected for Operation Buffalo, 500 miles north-west of Melbourne, was named Maralinga, a word meaning 'thunder' from an extinct Aboriginal language. Aboriginal people themselves, of whom about a thousand lived in the Central Australian reserve on the fringes of the 20,000-square-mile test range (measuring a twentieth of the area of South Australia, or three times that of East Anglia), had to be encouraged to move away for the duration of the tests. These were to last for seven years, during which time the Maralinga base grew to the size of a small town, providing accommodation for up to 1,600 personnel and equipped, alongside laboratories, workshops and its own power station, with restaurants, a church, cinema, shops, a swimming pool and sports grounds.

The worlds of Aboriginal peoples and the Maralinga site represented the alpha and omega of human existence. The nomadic indigenous peoples lived in tune with the rhythms of the natural world, as they had done for tens of thousands of years. Those working at Maralinga were exploring the very latest science and, in terms of the weapons they were testing, held the very future of humankind, and perhaps the Earth itself, in their hands. While it seems impossible – a biblical lifetime on from Operation Buffalo – to think of the Australian outback as *terra nullius* or its peoples of little concern, this was not the case when the first test bomb, a 3-kiloton Red Beard suspended from a pair of makeshift towers at Maralinga, was detonated at 5 p.m. local time on 27 September 1956.

Walter MacDougall, a Presbyterian missionary and native patrol officer working with the Ministry of Supply, had been assigned the task of persuading the Pitjantjatjara and Yankunytjatjara people to move from harm's way. According to his biographer, W. H. Edwards, MacDougall's empathy with the Aboriginal people led to one senior Maralinga scientist writing that, while sincere in his work, his lack of balance placed 'the affairs of a handful of natives above those of the British Commonwealth of Nations'. Fifteen years later, and not long after the banning of supersonic flights over the US and noise restrictions at US airports put Concorde's future as a transatlantic airliner in jeopardy, BAC (British Aircraft Corporation) executives talked up the possibility of Mach 2 services from London or Paris to Sydney. This would have meant flying supersonic over land. The BAC executives' case was not helped when Charles Gardner, the company's chief press officer, suggested the airliner's supersonic path over the Australian outback would 'only affect a bunch of old Abos'.

Crucially, the third A-bomb test at Maralinga was conducted from the air in the mid-afternoon of 11 October 1956. Group Captain Cecil 'Ginger' Weir, a wartime Lancaster pilot, was Operation Buffalo's task group commander. He called in 49 Squadron's Valiant WZ366, descending from 38,000 feet to 30,000 feet over the site, piloted by Squadron Leader Edwin 'Ted' Flavell, veteran of numerous secret wartime missions flown over and in and out of German-occupied Europe and Scandinavia. Bomb aimer Flight Lieutenant Eric Stacey pressed the button. Down went Britain's first air-released atomic bomb, a 10,000-lb Blue Danube, eleven years after Hiroshima, exploding at 490 feet above the ground, just short of its target, with a force of 3 kilotons. The Valiant was now a nuclear bomber in fact as well as name.

The chosen target for the British H-bomb tests seven months later was Malden Island, a flat and uninhabited atoll 400 miles from the operation's Christmas Island base in the central Pacific. The mission, Operation Grapple, involved 4,000 servicemen, scientists and support staff. It was a major investment, deeply important to Britain – especially in terms of the UK's relationship with the United States.

The Operation Grapple Valiants' long route out from England, each plane hosting a tightly packed crew of six, was via refuelling and leg-stretching stops at Aldergrove (Northern Ireland), Goose Bay (Newfoundland), Namao (Alberta), Travis Air Force Base (California) and Honolulu. The Valiant's transatlantic capability had been demonstrated the previous November, with one of the bombers flying non-stop from Lowing Air Force Base, Maine, to RAF Marham, Norfolk, in 6 hours and 25 minutes.

On 15 May 1957, Wing Commander Kenneth Hubbard DFC flew XD818 to the target, releasing its terrifying cargo, code-named Grapple 1, at 45,000 feet. The bomb missed its mid-air target by 418 yards – not bad – exploding at 7,200 feet and producing a yield, or force, of 300 kilotons of TNT. While this was a cosmic punch – Little Boy had exploded over Hiroshima with

86

a force of 15 kilotons – it was disappointing to scientists, if not for the crew of the Valiant. 'It really was a sight of such majesty and grotesque beauty,' Hubbard was to recall, 'that it defies adequate description.' The explosion the observers wanted to see and record – Grapple Y – finally came on 28 April 1958, when the 'Dickens' H-bomb released over Christmas Island from the belly of a Valiant flown by Squadron Leader Bob Bates produced a yield of 3 megatons of TNT (a megaton bomb has a thousand times more explosive power than a kiloton bomb) – the largest ever from a British thermonuclear device.

As the future Rear-Admiral Paul Bass, then a Royal Navy engineering officer on board the frigate HMS *Ulysses*, employed in Operation Grapple, would later recall:

When the test was imminent, we had to sit on the upper deck, on the side remote from the target area, with our heads between our knees and eyes tightly shut. About twenty seconds after the burst, we were allowed to open our eyes and go to the other side of the ship, where we saw an enormous orange ball of fire in the sky, which slowly developed into the now familiar mushroom cloud. Twenty minutes later there was a loud crack, like the sound of an aircraft breaking the sound barrier, and a short breeze – which was the blast and sound of the explosion reaching us. We were told that this test had been very clean as it had taken place at a height which did not suck up sea or earth which could become radio-active and subsequently contaminate the area.

Now Britain had joined the H-bomb club. The Americans were duly impressed. On 3 July, the US–UK Mutual Defence Agreement was signed. Britain would be the junior partner and in hock from now on to the US nuclear armaments programme, yet for the prime minister Harold Macmillan – who, like Winston Churchill, was half-American – it was 'the Great Prize'. The Valiant had played its part in the winning of it, although for V-Force the Great Prize would prove to be a double-edged sword.

The Valiant pilots had certainly done their bit. The bombs were 10,000-pounders. The aircraft had to be flown at a steady Mach 0.76 at 45,000 feet towards the target. So far, so easy. But once the bomb was released, a full-throttle 60-degree turn to the left while maintaining Mach 0.76 was the order of the day. Then, making a second, 135-degree turn, the Valiant would need to line up its tail-mounted cameras with the explosion point in forty seconds, ten seconds ahead of the bomb. All going to plan, it would be ready to snap away from 9 nautical miles – close enough for accurate photography, far enough for the crew to escape the effects of nuclear fallout. Not all did. Certainly not the crews of Canberras flying through the mushroom clouds to take readings of the radiation.

Bob Bates would die from leukaemia, but this was many years later, after his retirement from the RAF. Kenneth Hubbard, who had flown Vickers Wellingtons in extensive action with 70 Squadron from Foggia against heavily defended targets in northern Italy and the Balkans in 1944–45, went on to command RAF Scampton and its three Vulcan squadrons. He lived a long life.

Various claims for compensation were to be made over the decades by servicemen and islanders alike. Most have led nowhere, partly because as years go by it becomes increasingly hard to tell whether a particular individual involved one way or another in Operation Grapple might have fallen ill anyway. The matter remains uncomfortably unsettled. Malden Island is now a wildlife sanctuary, a haven for frigatebirds.

As a Bomber Command navigator in his early twenties with 49 Squadron, Flight Lieutenant Kenneth Edmonds flew on board supporting Valiants during both Operation Buffalo and Operation Grapple. He witnessed, close-up, the dropping of the A-bomb over Maralinga on 11 October 1956 and the Grapple X H-bomb over the southern tip of Christmas Island on 8 November 1957.

In July 2024, I met Ken Edmonds at home in Norfolk, 12 miles east of RAF Marham, the last Victor base. Marham's F-35 multi-role stealth fighters thundered somewhere unseen across the big, burning blue East Anglian sky.

'I was very young then,' said Edmonds, 'as were most of us, so it was all a big adventure and for much of the time great fun. I'd been flying with PR [Photo Reconnaissance] Canberras on ops over the Mediterranean and as far as Baghdad, which was pretty exciting, and jumped at the opportunity of flying all the way to Australia. I had no real idea of what I'd volunteered for until we arrived at Maralinga. Once there, we quickly understood the enormity of the operation – politically, scientifically and militarily – but the camaraderie was such that it was a real pleasure to be involved. The set-up was happily

Grapple 1 thermonuclear mushroom cloud, Christmas Island,
May 1957

informal. We all mucked in together on a level – aircrews and ground crews including recruits on National Service, and the scientists from Aldermaston led by Sir William Penney himself, a delightful man. There were no heroics involved on our part in either operation. We were doing a job.'

Edmonds handed me the logbook of his late friend and colleague Flight Lieutenant John Ledger, Ted Flavell's co-pilot. It opened with Ledger training on Tiger Moths before moving in crisp, one-line entries to a 1-hour, 35-minute flight on 11 October 1956: 'Valiant WZ366. Live atomic bomb released over Maralinga desert. First UK air drop.'

Such a sensational moment; the logbook entry so cut and dry. The reality had been a pair of pure white bomber jets flying at 30,000 feet over that great Australian plain, the lead aircraft releasing a 10,000-lb, 3-kiloton bomb. And before being caught in the blast and its aftershock, the Valiants pulling up, around and away, back to base. The crews had practised for three months over the RAF bombing range at Wainfleet on The Wash, south of Skegness, and at Orford Ness, a shingle spit on the Suffolk coast. They did their bit, according to Edmonds, without undue drama, although the shock waves from the H-bomb explosions provoked severe turbulence.

The H-bomb clouds were, said Edmonds – referring to Operation Grapple – 'strangely beautiful, rising up to 60,000 feet and even higher in shimmering orange, yellow and gold. Of course, theirs was a terrible beauty.' While he believes that Valiant crews escaped the effects of radiation, this was not true for those of the Canberra B.6s flown through the towering clouds to gather atmospheric samples. Flight Lieutenant Eric Denson, one of the Canberra pilots, reported horrendous turbulence. He recalled muttering over and again Tennyson's 'Into the jaws of Death / Into the mouth of hell / Rode the six hundred' as the twin-engine jet see-sawed through Grapple Y's shape-shifting pillar of death.

On landing, Denson's Canberra was so hot that the crew had to wait fifteen minutes before being allowed to clamber out from the cockpit. Denson vomited frequently during the following forty-eight hours. Back home in England, he developed gastric problems and dermatitis on his chest. His wife, Shirley, said he suffered 'dreadfully deep depressions and mood swings', while before the mission he was described as 'full of life, confident, kind, thoughtful with a keen sense of humour, and unflappable'. After three attempts, in 1976 Eric Denson committed suicide.

Commenting on a report sent to him in 1955 by Sir Harold Himsworth, the distinguished medical scientist and secretary of the Medical Research Council, on the damage exposure to radiation from H-bombs could have on the DNA of armed services personnel involved in their testing, the prime minister Anthony Eden noted: 'A pity, but we cannot help it.' The Grapple Y Dickens bomb was over a hundred times more powerful than the Fat Man A-bomb dropped on Nagasaki.

Had the experience of fighting and surviving the Second World War hardened the hearts of even the most civilized English men and women? So many on the home front as well as the front line had experienced danger and death as never before. In 1944, Ken Edmonds' family home in Croydon had been targeted by a German V-1 'doodlebug'. The flying bomb exploded at the end of the garden, the house stripped to a shell. The staircase remained intact, with young Ken tucked up fast asleep beneath it, and the family survived. They found a large piece of shrapnel buried in what was Ken's regular bed.

Between Operations Buffalo and Grapple, the Valiant was called to action for the first time during the Suez Crisis, for a sequence of conventional, Second World War–style bombing raids on Egyptian airbases made under the banner Operation Musketeer between 31 October and 5 November 1956. Twenty-four Valiants from 138, 148, 207 and 214 Squadrons were dispatched to RAF Luqa, Malta, their crews surprised by the targets assigned to them.

The 'crisis', precipitated by President Gamal Abdel Nasser's nationalization of the Suez Canal, would prove to be a fiasco. Eden had joined the French, following Israeli attacks on Egypt, in trying to topple Nasser, wrestle back control of the canal – a vital passage for trade and the supply of oil – and to restrict Soviet influence in the Middle East. The British prime minister and his government were seen to fail on all accounts, and as public support dwindled, Washington expressed the strongest disapproval and Moscow growled threateningly. Eden resigned soon after British troops withdrew from Egypt.

The role the Valiant played was theoretically major, yet minor in practice. Bomber Command was instructed to take

Egyptian military airfields out of action. The forty-nine sorties flown by Valiants at night, targeting the airbases at Abu Sueir, Almaza, Cairo West, Fayid, Kabrit, Kasfareet and Luxor, caused significant damage to just three of the seven. Relying on Second World War target sights – the Valiants had yet to be fitted with the latest navigation and bombing kit – crews dropped 1,000-lb high explosive bombs inaccurately. This was Bomber Command 1956, but it might have been 1939.

Curiously, despite being well equipped with fighter jets, the Egyptian air force put up little or no resistance to the British bombers. One crew spotted a lone Egyptian Gloster Meteor but was able to evade it with ease.

Back home, the Valiant proved to be a competent reconnaissance plane and successful air-to-air refuelling tanker. It took part in the development of the Blue Steel stand-off nuclear missile, launched some considerable distance from its intended target, and in that of the Bristol-Siddeley Pegasus engine, with its rotating exhausts, intended for the Hawker P.1127 jump jet, precursor of the Harrier. Valiants made their final operational flights on 9 December 1964, when 214 Squadron's tanker XD812 was ordered to return to RAF Marham while refuelling a Lightning interceptor, and XD818, piloted by Flight Lieutenant Pettit, returned from a 2-hour, 15-minute cross-country exercise. It was the very last to fly.

VULCAN

Prototype 'tin triangle' Avro Vulcan, first flown August 1952

'If one can imagine an aircraft the size of an Airbus A320 being thrown around the sky as if it was a Spitfire,' wrote former Avro chief test pilot Tony Blackman, 'then it is possible to have some idea of what flying and displaying a Vulcan was like.'

The Vulcan was a revelation. Before it entered squadron service in September 1956, prototypes and early production models of the striking delta-wing bomber had thrilled the public at the Farnborough Air Show. Movietone footage allows us to watch test pilot Roly Falk blasting off from Farnborough at the controls of Vulcan XA890 during the 1955 show, barrel-rolling the 69-ton machine at the crest of its display climb as top brass, international VIPs and a raincoated public – it was a wet and slightly chilly July day – gawped from the ground. Any doubts as to the efficacy of the delta wing, a largely untried and tested proposition in 1947, were well and truly dispersed. That same day – also caught by Movietone – the Fairey Delta 2, a supersonic delta-wing test aircraft, put on a spectacular, fast-rolling aerobatic display.

Among the guests at Farnborough was the prime minister, Anthony Eden. He had a flight in XA890 and was allowed to handle the controls. Clearly thrilled by the experience, the PM, who had been a distinguished young First World War infantry officer, was also flown away from Farnborough in the Vulcan. Eden was riding high at the time. Unemployment was at a historic low – less than 1 per cent – and the Suez fiasco more than a year in the future.

Eden's hugely experienced pilot, Roly Falk, was busy playing yet another theatrical role in the promotion of the Vulcan. Falk was a brilliant test pilot and natural PR man with a good understanding of the media. Having attended the de Havilland Aeronautical Technical School in the mid- and late 1930s, he had flown newsreel journalists to cover the wars in Abyssinia and Spain. A test pilot with the Royal Aircraft Establishment, Farnborough, during the Second World War, he had piloted a wide variety of aircraft including captured German machines. A crash in a modified Wellington bomber with a new type of propeller in 1946 left him, according to fellow test pilot Tony Blackman, with 'two broken legs, a broken arm, a fracture of the spine and metallic fragments in his head'. Within a year of the crash, the irrepressible Falk was flying again, impeccably dressed as always when he did so in bespoke pinstripe suit, tie, cufflinks, pocket handkerchief and sunglasses. A consummate professional, he enjoyed making flying a V-bomber seem no more difficult than – and as stylish as – turning up at Claridge's for a cocktail.

Falk played a significant role in the early development of the Vulcan. The first prototypes, flown from 30 August 1952, were exciting but not perfect. Adjustments to the leading edge of the wing, for example, proved necessary to alleviate buffeting. These led to the distinctive kinked profile of the production Vulcan's delta wing. Another Falk contribution was the fitting of fighter-style control sticks instead of the spectacle-like control wheels familiar to bomber and airliner pilots. This was possible because power-assistance meant there would be no heaving on the Vulcan's controls even in the most demanding manoeuvres. Falk also preferred this arrangement because control wheels had to be removed before pilots could eject from the cramped cockpit. Failure to do so would spell the loss of their kneecaps.

By July 1956, the production Vulcan B.1, powered by the mighty Bristol Olympus – first run in 1950 and later developed for use in the BAC TSR-2 and Concorde – was an impressive and much publicized aircraft. A decade earlier, Morien Morgan's design committee had needed more information on the way the aircraft would handle than Avro could provide. Scaled-down versions of the proposed Avro 698 were

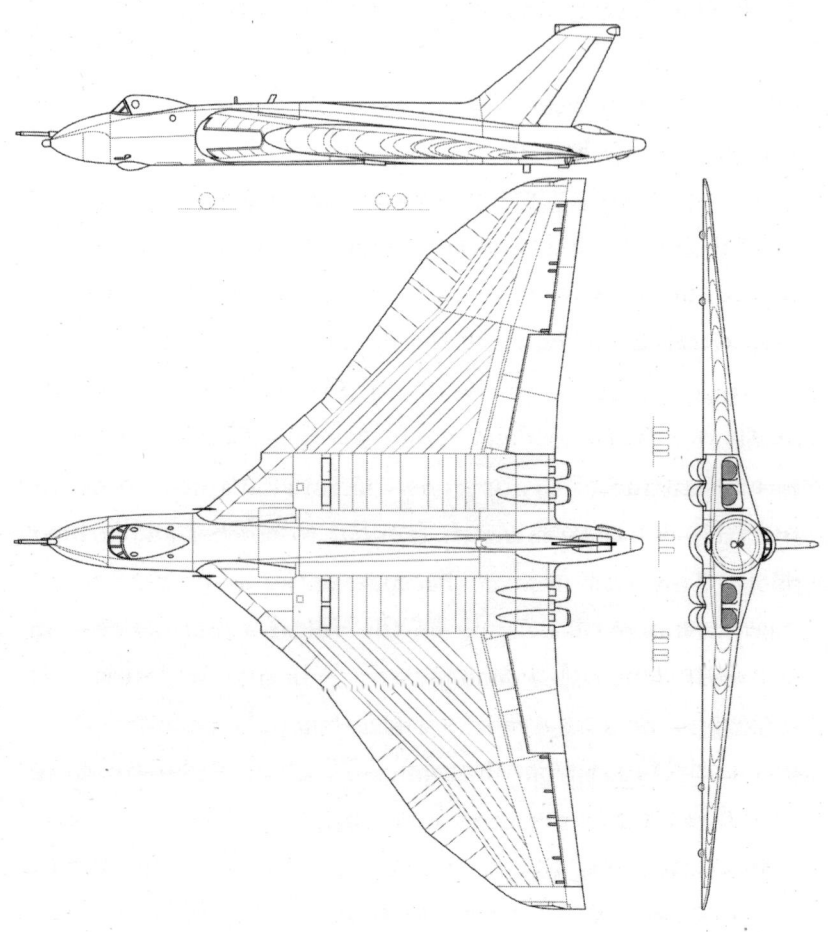

B.2 Avro Vulcan

recommended and ordered by the Ministry of Supply. These were the 'proof of concept' Avro 707s – five of them altogether, including a side-by-side two-seater, delightful-looking red, bright blue, orange and unpainted metal single-engine jet, a third of the size of the 698. The first – VX784, Britain's pioneer delta-wing jet – was flown by Avro test pilot Squadron Leader Samuel 'Red' Esler DFC from RAF Boscombe Down (close to Stonehenge, an ancient engineering marvel) on 4 September 1949. On 30 September, a control circuit failure caused the 707's air brakes to lock open in flight. The aircraft stalled irrecoverably, dived into the ground near Blackbushe, Hampshire, and burst into flames, killing Esler. While his death was tragic, when the findings of the accident report were confirmed, Avro engineers breathed a certain sigh of relief. They had been concerned that perhaps the delta wing itself was at fault. If this had been so, the 698 project would have been in peril.

Fortunately, the four 707s built between 1950 and 1953 proved to be competent aircraft. One of the type's most influential fans was Air Marshal John Boothman. Praising its handling after flying a 707B in September 1951, Boothman said 'twenty-five pilots must fly it at once'. Avro was happy. Not only was Boothman a hugely experienced and highly regarded commanding officer, he was also, at the time, Controller of Supply (Air) at the Ministry of Supply. Pilots, aircraft engineers, politicians and the public at large knew him as the modest thirty-year-old flight lieutenant who had won the coveted Schneider Trophy for Britain in 1931 at the controls of Reginald Mitchell's devilishly fast and beautiful Supermarine S6.B seaplane.

The 707s were testbeds for high- and low-speed delta-wing flight, and helped establish the kinked delta-wing design adopted for all production Vulcans. They also tested powered, fly-by-wire and sidestick controls, all of which helped to make the Vulcan a pleasure to fly. Popular at Farnborough in 1953, with Falk leading they were flown to that year's air show in memorable formation, with the first prototype Vulcans looking for all the world like a flock of birds – the young ones keeping close to their parents. These captivating delta-wing aircraft were designed by teams led by Avro's Stuart Davies. J. G. Willis was the project designer, and Eric Priestley chief aerodynamicist.

Initial concepts for the 698 had been sketched out by Avro's chief designer Roy Chadwick, a former engineering apprentice with the Lancashire and Yorkshire Railway at Horwich locomotive works. He had been with the company, founded the year before he joined by Alliott Verdon Roe, from 1911. From his work on the 35-hp, 49-mph D-Type biplane flown that April, Chadwick, appointed chief designer at the age of twenty-six, went on to outline the Manchester, Lancaster, Lincoln and Vulcan bombers. He was killed in August 1947 when his Avro Tudor II – a sixty-seat version of Britain's first pressurized airliner, the Tudor I, based on the Lincoln bomber – crashed. Installed the wrong way round, the aileron control circuit had caused the aircraft to dive when commanded to climb. One of the survivors of that crash was

Chadwick's deputy, Stuart Davies. While the Vulcan was very much Davies' aircraft in terms of practical design through to production, it is remarkable that this futuristic machine was conceived and outlined by Chadwick – whose boss at Avro had first flown a powered aircraft in 1908, just five years after the Wright Brothers, and the following year had built and flown the first all-British aircraft.

Born in London in 1906, Stuart Davies worked for Vauxhall Motors from the age of sixteen before joining Vickers in 1925. At Brooklands he was involved in the production of the Vickers Virginia Mk X, a duralumin and steel version of the long-lived biplane bomber. The last Virginias were retired in December 1941, two months before the introduction of the Lancaster. After moving to Hawker, Davies was on Sydney Camm's design team for the supremely agile Hart light bomber and Fury fighter biplane, and from late 1934 the eight-gun Rolls-Royce Merlin–powered Hurricane. In January 1938, Davies was appointed assistant chief designer at Avro, since 1935 owned by Hawker Siddeley, moving to Manchester and working in Chadwick's vast drawing office at the company's handsome new aircraft works at Chadderton, a few miles north of the city.

The first shot at a fully resolved design in response to the 1947 Ministry of Supply specification was of a fuselage-free, tailless and finless delta-wing, with a cabin projecting forward from between two large air intakes for two pairs of stacked engines tucked as closely as possible to the centre line of the aircraft. Wingtip fins were not – as they are on modern airliners – to reduce wingtip-induced drag, but rather, in lieu of a conventional tail rudder, to give directional control. No one really knew how they would perform at the high altitudes and high speeds the 698 was required to operate at. The maximum speed aimed at was Mach 0.95, just below the sound barrier.

Two bomb bays on either side of the engines were set in the depth of the wing. Essentially a flying wing – Chadwick had been excited by this concept, developed by Alexander Lippisch in Germany and Jack Northrop in the US – the 698 was a daring and dashing design. Intriguingly, its internal layout suggests it would have been a more comfortable machine to fly long distances in than any of the three production V-bombers. Like an airliner, crew accommodation was on a level and, wonder of wonders, a proper 'toilet' cabin was marked on the drawings. With tightly packed and strictly functional cabins, in practice V-Force crews were presented with rubber tubes, a covered bucket and no privacy.

From an initial design team of six formed at Chadderton in 1947, the number of those involved in draughting the design of the 698 grew to 190, while thousands of Avro and subcontractor engineers were drawn into the project as approved drawings were passed along to workshops and assembly lines. By the time a prototype, VX770, emerged in August 1952, it had been named 'Vulcan'. In his book *V-Bombers*, Tim Laming tells the rather funny story of Gilbert Whitehead, project engineer on the 698, who in later years said, 'I never liked the name. After it was announced, I went to look it up in a mythology book and the definition of Vulcan was "misshapen god of war thrown out of heaven".' Most Avro staff did like it, however, and the name sounded exactly right in company with 'Valiant' and 'Victor'.

While a tailplane had been considered for Avro's god of war, the prototype Vulcan appeared with a tall wingless tail fin. A more compact design than the Valiant, it promised to be faster and nimbler than the first of the V-bombers. It made its maiden flight, with Roly Falk at the controls, on 30 August 1952. The production B.1 version followed suit on 4 February 1955. The earliest of these were soon refitted with those kinked leading edges to their wings.

The first of six Vulcan B.1 squadrons, 49, was formed at RAF Waddington in May 1957. The squadron shifted base to RAF Scampton three years later, by this time equipped with the more powerful and more thoroughly equipped B.2. Design work on the B.2, under the direction of Roy Ewans – who succeeded Stuart Davies in 1955 – had begun in 1958, and the first production B.2 – XH533, the forty-sixth Vulcan – took to the air in August of that year. Predicting the effects of future and increasingly powerful versions of the Olympus engine, the B.2's much larger and thinner wing featured a kinked trailing edge, adopting lessons learned concerning the efficiency and stability of crescent wings at high cruising speeds close to the sound barrier. From certain angles, this new wing gave the Vulcan an almost organic appearance, as if this was indeed some aerial creature rather than a machine. The large air intakes gave the Vulcan B.2 its signature, otherworldly howl, adding to its living, breathing character. The B.2 was fitted with an autopilot, a flight refuelling probe, a new electrical system and an ECM (electronic counter measure) 'suite' in its tail. These features were also retrofitted to B.1s.

The power of the Vulcan's engines more than doubled between VX770's maiden flight in 1952 and the delivery of the last B.2 to the RAF in 1965– with a 21,000-lb thrust available from each of its four Bristol-Siddeley Olympus turbojets. The most powerful engine fitted to a Vulcan was the Rolls-Royce/Snecma Olympus 593. This had been developed for Concorde. Vulcan B.1 XA903, which had been used for Blue Steel stand-off missile testing, was dispatched to BAC's Filton works in January 1964 and flew with the 35,080-lb thrust engine for five years from September 1966. The single 593, mounted centrally beneath its airframe, was almost as powerful as all four of the Vulcan's Olympus turbojets together. While the Vulcan could, theoretically, fly with the 593 alone, the other engines were needed to generate power for the aircraft's electrical systems, and everyone involved was keen to have the reassurance of those four jets – especially during tests when the Olympus 593 was flamed on and off.

The flying testbed B.1 was further used in the development of the Turbo-Union RB.199, the multinational after-burning turbofan designed for the supersonic, swing-wing, multi-role, nuclear-capable, twin-engine Panavia Tornado that was to serve with the RAF from 1979 to 2019. With reheat, the compact engine generated a thrust of 16,400 lb. One of the tests with the RB.199 involved measuring and evaluating the effect on the engines of firing the 27mm Mauser cannon to be installed internally under the Tornado's fuselage. As a result, XA903 became the one and only Vulcan equipped with a gun. H-bombs aside, the Vulcan – like the Valiant and Victor – was unarmed.

The quest for greater engine power led to the sorry and disturbing demise of the very first Vulcan at much the same time as the B.2 began to fly. On 20 September 1958, VX770 was on a round trip from RAF Hucknall in Nottinghamshire – home since 1934 of the Rolls-Royce Flight Test Establishment – when its pilot Keith Sturt, a former RAF flight lieutenant, was asked by the air traffic controller at nearby RAF Syerston if he could perform a flypast at the Battle of Britain Day air show taking place that very moment. There was a gap in the programme. Could VX770 fill it? Sturt and the Rolls-Royce and RAF test crew were happy to do so. The crowd would be treated not just to the sight of a Vulcan – never less than thrilling – but also to the distinctive sound of a potent new version of the Rolls-Royce Conway turbofan engine.

Flying over the Syerston runway at 250 feet and 350 knots, Sturt made a right turn after the control tower. Caught on camera, the Vulcan's right wing began to disintegrate, causing fuel to leak. Then both wings caught fire. The Vulcan crashed into the end of the runway, killing all four on board as well as three RAF fire and rescue personnel crew members on the ground. The Vulcan was a strong aircraft and Sturt a seasoned test pilot. He had clocked over ninety-one hours with VX770. But it seemed that the V-bomber had been pushed to critical limits during earlier tests involving rolls and even loops over a long and intensive period. It was tempting, although not necessarily wise, to treat the Vulcan like some giant fighter.

Such tragic incidents aside, V-bombers certainly gave Bomber Command a new confidence and fresh allure, after the doldrum days of the early 1950s and the reliance on hand-me-down American B-29s. Now every opportunity was taken to woo and awe the public with this new-generation, all-British bomber. On public display, however, errors or failures were captured and magnified through print, radio, cinema and television news.

On the morning of 14 October 1956, the press was out in force at London Airport (now Heathrow). Despite heavy rain, journalists and assorted VIPs were expecting the arrival soon after 11 a.m. of a special flight from Aden. This was Vulcan B.1 XA897, the first in RAF service, on the final leg of a 26,000-mile world tour that had taken the delta-wing bomber, flawlessly, out as far as Sydney and Wellington, setting speed and distance records along the way. The pilot was Squadron Leader Donald 'Podge' Howard DFC & Bar; his co-pilot was Air Marshal Sir Harry Broadhurst DFC & Bar, DSO & Bar, AFC, head of Bomber Command.

On what proved to be an arduous descent, someone blundered. Visibility was limited. Neither the Vulcan's instruments nor the control tower's instructions appear to have been a match for the weather. Even without the rain, Broadhurst's intuition had been to give London a miss and to head home to RAF Waddington. Arrival arrangements relayed to the air marshal in Aden had given him and Howard the choice. 'You have been cleared to land at London Airport... for reception at the central terminal... In the event of diversion, alternative arrangements will be made... Keep rolling and best of luck.' Howard and Broadhurst should have diverted, and given the press, the VIPs and the reception in the Queens Building a miss.

In the event, Howard touched down momentarily in a field of Brussels sprouts, a little over a thousand yards short of the runway. He was not helped by the limited view ahead through the Vulcan's shallow windscreen, nor by the poor performance of its windscreen wipers. The Vulcan's landing gear broke apart and, as it did, damaged the elevators to the extent that, although applying full throttle and beginning to climb, Howard had no proper control of the aircraft. Close to the runway, he and Broadhurst made the decision to eject. Howard landed on grass and was unhurt. Broadhurst came down on concrete, damaging his feet and back. Their four crew-member colleagues were killed as the Vulcan struck the ground and exploded.

The pilots were snuck away out of sight of the press to the RAF hospital at Uxbridge. The crash was written off by the Royal Air Force Court of Inquiry as an accident for which, although mistakes were made both in the cockpit and the control tower, 'the failure of the controller to warn the captain that he was going below the glidepath was the principal cause of the accident'.

Although a stunning-looking and exciting aircraft to fly and display, the Vulcan's primary purpose was not, of course,

PR, but nuclear deterrence, flying at high altitude garbed in anti-flash white paintwork devised to protect the aircraft from the searing effects of thermal radiation from nuclear explosions. When switched to low-level missions, Vulcans might be spotted flying as low as 50 feet across flat landscapes and through valleys, which was alarming if you happened to be walking, riding or driving towards one of these big jets.

New weapons and the perceived need for greatly increased speed led to further Vulcan design concepts shaped on Avro drawing boards. One of these was for a 'Phase 6' Vulcan equipped with, at first, four, and then, in a reworked example, six 11,000-lb Skybolt missiles. The Phase 6 would have hosted two crews, so one could rest as the other worked, with the Vulcan maintaining an around-the-clock nuclear vigil in the air in much the same way as USAAF B-52s did. The Phase 6 Vulcan would have been an enormous aircraft, powered, presumably, by reheat Olympus turbofans. The take-off weight of the four-Skybolt Phase 6 was calculated at 339,168 lb (compared to the B.2 at 204,000 lb), while the six-Skybolt version would not have been far off the British Airways Concorde. Another proposal, dating from as early as 1956, was for a supersonic Vulcan.

There were altogether headier ideas, including a VTOL (vertical take-off and landing) Vulcan and a Vulcan 'mothership' cradling three Folland Gnat fighters, each armed with a nuclear bomb. But in any field of design and engineering, drawing board fantasies abound. The Vulcan was generally an excellent aircraft that did what was asked of it during the Cold War years. Although the idea of extending its life may have been attractive to some, 'secret projects' or 'what if?' designs take something away from the inherent rightness of this special machine in its prototype, B.1 and B.2 configurations.

VICTOR

Victor B.1 landing, parachute brake deployed

The most striking feature of the Handley Page Victor was its crescent wing – a true rarity among production aircraft that, nevertheless, allowed the big bomber to fly efficiently, smoothly and safely at high speeds and high altitudes. Quite who came up with this crescent wing first – Arado's Rüdiger Kosin and Walther Lehmann or Handley Page's Gustav

Lachmann and Godfrey Lee – remains something of a mystery, or perhaps a case of muddled professional pride, eighty years on. With the wing married to an equally distinctive and efficient tailplane, the Victor could happily barrel-roll, loop-the-loop and break the sound barrier in shallow dives. Ultimately, the Vulcan proved the better low-level bomber when in 1962 V-Force adopted this new role, but the Victor was to be the last of the V-bombers in service, albeit performing other duties in its later years, and it served through the Cold, Falklands and Gulf wars.

A significantly bigger aircraft than the Vulcan, the Victor was designed to carry either a pair of 12,000-lb Tallboys, a single 22,000-lb Grand Slam earthquake bomb, up to forty-eight 1,000-lb high explosive bombs, thirty-nine 2,000-lb sea mines, or, of course, a nuclear bomb. Appropriately, perhaps, for what proved to be a successful multi-role machine, the Victor was a complex aircraft to behold. Especially in its later B.2 form, it had the look – seen head-on and on the ground – of some fantastical deep-sea creature, its air intakes like giant gills, its cockpit glazing like some form of compound eye and its refuelling probe resembling the anatomical appendage of some monstrous angler fish. The inverted wings of its high tailplane and the vast sweep of its crescent wings only added to this peculiar impression. And yet, when it was in its natural element scything through the air, from certain angles the fleet Victor had the look of a swift. That bird, the most accomplished high-speed aerobat – a creature that can spend ten months airborne, without coming down to land – also sports a crescent wing. What works for a bird weighing less than 1.5 ounces worked for a nuclear bomber weighing more than 200,000 lb.

The distinctive shape of the Victor's wings was determined by tests to find the optimum profile for all flying conditions – and, all importantly, an even critical Mach number across the entire wing, thus countering the problem of sonic shock as air goes supersonic over one but not all parts of a wing, causing instability in flight. Handley Page's deputy chief designer, Godfrey Lee, had been on an official visit on behalf of the Royal Aircraft Establishment to what survived of the German aero industry in October 1945. He learned much about swing wings from Arado Flugzeugwerke at Warnemünde on the Baltic coast, information he passed on to Handley Page. Although a crescent wing had been constructed in April 1945 for an advanced V16 version of the Ar 234, the world's first jet bomber, it was destroyed during fighting at Warnemünde that same month. Lee maintained that the Victor's wing was Handley Page's own.

Handley Page had a long history of left-field design, going back as far as its Type E single-engine monoplane of 1912, its wings featuring curved leading and swept-back trailing edges. This intriguing aircraft survived until 1940, when it was thought to be taking up too much space at the company's Radlett factory and broken up.

After joining the Royal Aeronautical Society in 1907, Frederick Handley Page had formed a friendship with the French-born landscape artist and aviation pioneer José Weiss, who was fascinated with the stable-wing flight characteristics of *Zanonia macrocarpa* (Javan cucumber) seed pods. The large, crescent-shaped papery wings of the seeds enabled them to glide remarkably long distances. Weiss had presumably read an 1897 paper on this very seed written by Ignaz 'Igo' Etrich, the Austrian aircraft inventor whose endeavours led eventually to the Etrich Taube ('Dove') of 1910, an aircraft with beautiful, curved wings – reflecting Etrich's intense interest in the flight of both *Zanonia macrocarpa* and birds. Manufactured by Edmund Rumpler, the Taube became the world's first bomber on 1 November 1911, when the Italian pilot Lieutenant Giulio Gavotti dropped 4-lb grenades by hand from 600 feet onto Ottoman positions in the Tajura oasis and onto the military camp at Ain Zara, near Tripoli, during the Italo-Turkish War of 1911–12.

In 1919, Frederick Handley Page patented his leading-edge slot for aircraft wings, aiding lift while hindering stalls at low speeds. Few modern airliners are built without them. Unbeknown to Handley Page, in Germany Gustav Lachmann had come up with the same invention a year or so earlier. Sportingly, the two men agreed to share the patent. Within a few years Lachmann had been appointed head of research at Handley Page. A German national when war broke out in 1939, he was interned as an enemy alien, first in Canada and then on the Isle of Man. While incarcerated, he continued his work for Handley Page. As the post-war director of research, he worked closely with his deputy, Godfrey Lee, and the design team that shaped the Victor's wing, which swept back in three angles – 48.5, 37.5 and 26.75 degrees – and became thinner as it stretched out. One unresolved question is why the Victor was the only production aircraft with a crescent wing, given its efficient nature. Lee's slightly offhand answer was 'perhaps we were the only firm brave enough and daft enough to do it'.

If the Victor's wing was distinctive, its massive tailplane was, too – set high to avoid the turbulent exhaust flow from the aircraft's engines and the wash of air over its wings. Common knowledge among Victor enthusiasts, the wings of the tailplane had almost the same span as those of a contemporary Hawker Hunter jet fighter. Another well-known fact was the Victor's early ability to land with its pilot's hands off the controls, as if automatically, due to the way air flowed over and under its wings and tailplane. An adjustable tail-mounted airbrake added to the Victor's manoeuvrability, as did its light controls.

A friendly and stable aircraft to fly, the Victor was the biggest of the three V-bombers. Compared to an eight-engine USAF B-52, however, the Victor seemed quite small. Size aside, the fundamental difference between the Stratofortress and all three V-bombers was highlighted in the arrangement of their engines. Where those of the B-52 hung in pods from the 185-foot span of its wing, the engines of the Valiant, Victor and Vulcan were tucked inside the wing roots. As such, the British bombers could roll and even loop. No sane or sober pilot would attempt such manoeuvres with a B-52. In any case, it was (as far as I know) impossible.

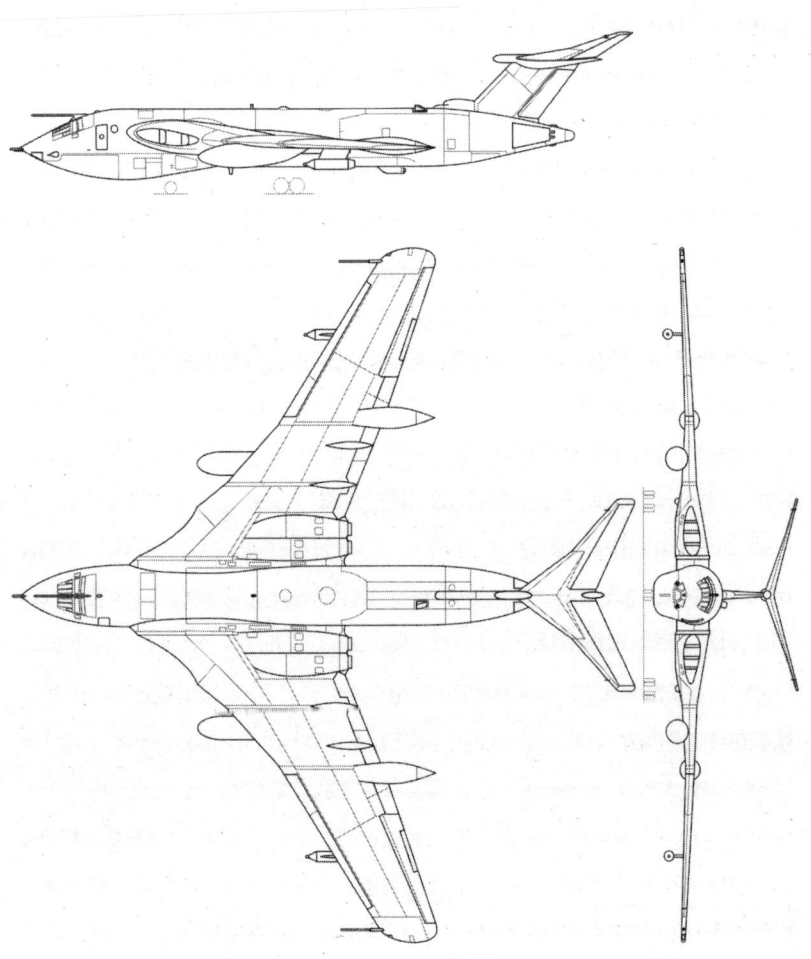

Handley Page B.2 Victor

A disconcerting video dating from June 1994 shows what would happen when a B-52 was pushed beyond its limits. During a practice flight for an air show at Fairchild Air Force Base, Washington, Lieutenant Colonel Arthur 'Bud' Holland chose to manoeuvre his B-52 into a low, steep banked turn. The aircraft stalled, dropped to the ground, broke up and burst into flames, killing all on board. Switching from this clip – used ever since in USAF training courses – to that of Roly Falk rolling the Vulcan at the top of his take-off climb at the 1955 Farnborough Air Show, the viewer can see, in dramatic fashion, the contrasting natures of the US and British heavy bombers of the time.

The Victor flew for the first time on 24 December 1952. As with the Vulcan, a one-third scale proof-of-concept aircraft had been built – farmed out to General Aircraft of Feltham, Middlesex, an outfit taken over during construction by Blackburn Aircraft of Brough, Yorkshire – based on the fuse-lage of a prototype of the new Supermarine Swift jet fighter. Rather oddly, the development of what was designated the Handley Page HP.88 lagged behind that of the V-bomber itself, and little or nothing was gained from the experiment. It came to a sorry end on 26 August 1951, when the HP.88 was being prepared for an appearance at the Farnborough Air Show. Handley Page test pilot Douglas 'Duggie' Broomfield began a straight pass at speed over the airfield at Stansted, when the HP.88 was seen to pitch violently before breaking up. Broomfield, it appears, had accidentally engaged the emergency airbrake and the sudden, brutal forces on the airframe were too much for it to bear. Unable to eject in time, he was killed.

The Victor was a far more sophisticated machine than the ill-fated HP.88. Its spot-welded alloy sandwich construction was novel, light and strong, while its wing was tested and adjusted several times before the prototype, WB771, was shipped from the Radlett factory in Hertfordshire to Boscombe Down, Wiltshire, for its maiden flight. 'Shipped' is the appropriate word, as WB771 was delivered by road – an immensely demanding operation – concealed under a tarpaulin, in the guise of a boat. No one driving past this mammoth load on London's North Circular Road would have known that this was the latest top-secret British nuclear bomber.

Handley Page's chief test pilot, Squadron Leader Hedley 'Hazel' Hazelden DFC & Bar, a wartime Lancaster veteran, flew the Victor that Christmas Eve. The V-bomber appeared in public for the first time at RAF Odiham, Hampshire, on 15 July the following year. The occasion was the new Queen's RAF Coronation Review. That same day, John Christie was hanged at Pentonville prison for the string of murders he had committed at 10 Rillington Place, Notting Hill. Christie's dingy world, his dropping from the end of a rope in a grim Victorian prison, and the general state of disrepair in Notting Hill at the time could hardly have been more different from the gleaming realm of nuclear jet bombers, of rapid and optimistic technological progress and of a glamorous, newly crowned young monarch. Britain was at once ration-book poor and grubby behind the ears and yet newly buoyed on the glittering wings of science. Christie had once served with the RAF as a 'motor driver'. Having joined shortly before Christmas 1923, he was discharged, for whatever reason, just eight months later.

Hazelden and the test crews would have enjoyed not just the smooth transit of the Victor, but the spacious cabin stretching forward to the tip of the aircraft's nose and arranged on a level throughout – unlike the Valiant and Vulcan with their cramped upstairs-downstairs configuration. But the prototype Victor was not perfect. On 14 July 1954, a set of airspeed instrument tests conducted at the College of Aeronautics, Cranfield, witnessed the loss of WB771 and its crew, skippered by Squadron Leader Ronald 'Taffy' Ecclestone DFC AFC. While Ecclestone had been with Handley Page for just three months, he was a highly experienced combat and test pilot, having flown Stirlings and Lancasters during the war with Bomber Command, and Spitfires and Hurricanes with the Bomber Defence Tactical Unit. His skill could not have saved the Victor that day, however. Streaking above the runway, full speed at 100 feet, the black, red and silver-grey V-bomber smashed into the ground, bursting into flames, after its newly fitted replacement tailplane sheared off. The tailplane of the second prototype was 15 inches lower than that of WB771. It is odd and not a little disturbing to hold your hands 15 inches apart and think that the small gap between them represents the difference between acceptable and unacceptable stress on an aircraft's tailplane – between, that is, life and death.

The first production Victor B.1, XA917, took to the air on 1 February 1956, a week in which Frank Sinatra, Lonnie

Donegan and Bill Haley & His Comets battled for the number one position in the UK charts against two versions of 'The Ballad of Davy Crockett' and one of 'Robin Hood'. With its uprated Armstrong Siddeley Sapphire Sa.7 engines, the B.1 was fast. On a flight from RAF Gaydon over Hertfordshire on 6 June 1957, test pilot Flight Lieutenant Johnny Allam tipped the nose of the Victor into a shallow dive, no more than two degrees, from 40,000 feet and – *boom!* – 'inadvertently', according to a Handley Page press release, broke the sound barrier. It was the largest aircraft yet to do so.

In service, Victors were restricted to fast subsonic flight (Mach 0.95), but quite how fast they could fly is a matter for conjecture. John Saxon, an electronics, navigation and, later, NASA engineer, tells the alarming story of his flight on board a Victor B.2 in August 1962 from RAAF Edinburgh, South Australia. Saxon was working on the navigational system of the Blue Steel stand-off missile designed to be carried by all three V-bombers. At the time, Victors, Valiants and Vulcans were based at RAAF Edinburgh for operations at the Woomera Test Range. The captain of Victor XL161 was Avro's chief test pilot down under, Johnny Baker, who during and after the war had flown many different aircraft – from Lancasters, Mosquitoes and Flying Fortresses to the latest jets – with the Aeroplane and Armament Experimental Establishment at Boscombe Down. His co-pilot was Flight Lieutenant Jimmy Catlin DFC, a wartime Lancaster pilot.

At 46,000 feet, the Victor went out of control. Baker gave the order to abandon ship, but with the aircraft spinning in a vertical dive, the crew were unable to do so. The bomber plummeted to 16,000 feet, pulling −3 and +5 Gs as it dived, and reaching a velocity well above the speed of sound. By releasing the brake parachute from the aircraft's tail, Baker was able to regain control. After jettisoning the test Blue Steel missile – filled with nothing more extreme than kerosene and peroxide – over St Vincent's Gulf, Baker made a safe emergency landing back at RAAF Edinburgh.

The crew decided to have a few drinks. That evening, Saxon recalled, Jimmy Catlin turned up at a local church social. Tottering across the dance floor, he told the vicar, 'I saw your God today,' before collapsing at his feet. It had been an unnerving day, but the Victor seemed little worse for wear, and the crew gathered soon afterwards for a celebratory dinner where they were photographed looking quite relaxed. Back in England, XL161 was converted to a K.2 tanker. Making its last flight in 1993, it was scrapped two years later.

Victors were operational with RAF 10 Squadron, Cottesmore, from April 1958. V-Force was now ready to carry 20-kiloton Blue Danube A-bombs. Yellow Sun H-bombs, designed for several different nuclear warheads, entered service the following year. Such was the pace of the V-Force programme, the prototype Victor B.2 – with its 17,250-lb-thrust Rolls-Royce Conway RCo.11 engines, 120-foot wingspan, greater range and 60,000-foot service ceiling – was already flying while B.1s were on the production line at Radlett. The B.2 incorporated developments designed to improve the performance and safety of the aircraft, among them ram-air turbo alternators in the rear fuselage. If the engines fell below minimum rpm (revs per minute), the alternators' intakes would unfold from the fuselage, enabling the Victor to generate an emergency electricity supply.

In August 1959, the very first B.2, XH668, spun out of control after high-speed turns over the Pembrokeshire coast, breaking into fragments as it struck the Irish Sea. The cause of the incident was a broken pitot tube, a small protruding instrument critical to pilots that measures airspeed.

While the B.2 proved to be a fine aircraft, it was to equip just two bomber squadrons. As, in theory, Victors would be able to carry two or even four of the American nuclear Skybolt missiles, the number of new aircraft, government thinking went, could be halved at least. This happened to suit Westminster and Whitehall, as Handley Page refused to merge with one of the two new aviation giants, BAC (British Aircraft Corporation) and Hawker Siddeley Aviation, despite official insistence that orders for new military aircraft would be given to these conglomerates alone. Handley Page did begin negotiations with Hawker Siddeley, but the Victors were cancelled anyway. The last B.2 was delivered to the RAF in May 1963.

Handley Page struggled on until 1970, when it went into voluntary liquidation. Its final offering was the HP.137 Jetstream, a small turboprop commuter aircraft designed by Charles Joy, one of the Victor team, and first flown in 1968. Later models were manufactured by Jetstream Aircraft and Scottish Aviation. The RAF stayed loyal to the Jetstream, with its T.1s employed from 1972 as multi-engine trainers and seen in company with Victors at Cottesmore. By now, the Victor's role had shifted to reconnaissance and aerial refuelling. A machine designed for John Gillespie Magee's 'high untrespassed sanctity of space', it was not exactly at home skirting the ground as a low-level bomber. It gave up that role in 1968, leaving this to the more adaptable and tougher Vulcan.

Valiant. Vulcan. Victor. These three pure-white V-bomber types were designed first and foremost to fly high and fast, carrying H-bombs to Soviet targets. That objective proved to be short-lived.

FOUR

QRA and Other
Early Service

Between the Cuban Missile Crisis and the Beatles' fourth LP, V-Force was at its peak strength. Fifty Valiants, seventy Vulcans and thirty-nine Victors stood ready to fly or assist, through reconnaissance or aerial refuelling, in the delivery of Blue Danube, Yellow Sun and US Project E atomic bombs and air-launched Blue Steel nuclear missiles against Soviet targets.

From 1962, V-Force's Quick Reaction Alert (QRA) programme required two aircraft from each squadron stood on Operational Readiness Platforms at the ends of runways around the clock, to be ready for take-off at a moment's notice on any day and at any time. Their crews were to 'scramble', as RAF fighter pilots had done in the Battle of Britain. Fired up at the press of a button that also brought the aircraft's instruments and controls alive, a V-bomber could be up in the air within two minutes.

RAF Gaydon, Quick Reaction Alert Valiant scramble

While there was talk of twin-crewed Vulcans flying on continuous aerial alert, this never happened. Vulcans would have needed to be much bigger than existing versions to accommodate a pair of crews and their sleeping arrangements. A bigger aircraft would, of course, require greater power and therefore more fuel and so on, in an escalating spiral of weight, wear-and-tear and cost.

The idea of continuous airborne alert was the brainchild of USAF General Thomas S. Power, Commander-in-Chief Strategic Air Command (SAC). Beginning in 1960, Power's Operation Chrome Dome kept approximately twelve B-52s

– the number varied – each armed with four nuclear bombs – this number did not vary – in the air at any one time. At the height of the Cuban Missile Crisis, the number of B-52s rose to sixty-five. General Power made darn sure Moscow knew SAC was on the warpath. As this keen advocate of Mutual Assured Destruction put it, 'The whole idea is to kill the bastards. At the end of the war if there are two Americans and one Russian left alive, we win.'

In 1964, cinema audiences could laugh, a little nervously, at a satirical version of MAD and Operation Chrome Dome in action. This was Stanley Kubrick's *Dr Strangelove, or: How I Learned to Stop Worrying and Love the Bomb*. Chrome Dome was called off in 1968 after a B-52 crew abandoned ship when their cockpit caught fire near Thule Air Base, Greenland, 750 miles north of the Arctic Circle. The burning bomber plunged through the ice sheet of North Star Bay. Although a nuclear explosion did not occur, radioactive material spread across Baffin Bay. The clear-up was difficult, expensive and embarrassing. What if there were to be other incidents with even more serious consequences? Chrome Dome was a deterrent too far.

Back in England, crews were ready to scramble in an instant from dispersal huts set close by their aircraft. On exercise, they might be strapped in their seats for prolonged spells, as they were in the Cuban Missile Crisis. If the word came, V-Force bombers could be up and away remarkably quickly. Within two minutes of the order to scramble, and leaving 5,000 feet of tyre-blackened runway in its wake, a howling Vulcan B.2 would be climbing hard, trailing veils of smoke and turning precipitously north-east to ride its Valkyrian flight path over the North and Baltic seas.

The public had more than an inkling of what V-Force was and, this side of the Official Secrets Act, how it operated. Aside from the dramatic sight and thunderous sound of the aircraft themselves over the skies of eastern England, as well as their appearances on TV news, in articles in the press and in children's comics, their crews were also frequent and welcome guests at the annual Farnborough Air Show. Over six of the seven days of the 1960 show, four V-bombers were up into the air in less than two minutes – the best time of 1 minute, 24 seconds recorded by the agile crew of a 617 Squadron Vulcan.

V-Force's primary role, as the nuclear 'Light Brigade', was to move as quickly as possible to destroy forward enemy missile positions and military bases ahead of the US B-52 'Heavy Brigade'. For many – perhaps most – V-Force crews, this would have been a one-way ticket. While Vulcan and Victor B.2s were to be equipped over time with the latest radar and electronic jamming equipment, none of this guaranteed safe passage through enemy airspace. If unable to fly home, survivors were instructed to head for the nearest friendly airbase. If they made it back to Britain, their own bases – along with entire cities and even counties – might well have been blown to Comintern come. This would not have come as a surprise to V-Force crews and their families. Its ten main bases were always in danger of attack. Exposed and highly visible on flat east England landscapes, for the most part in a wide arc around the Fens, and with glistening white QRA bombers sitting ducks on the exposed Operational Readiness Platforms at the ends of runways, V-Force needed all the defence it could get.

Nine out of the ten main V-Force bases were existing RAF airfields – Gaydon in Warwickshire was the exception – mixing Neo-Georgian officers' messes and matter-of-fact new brick or concrete panel housing with lengthened runways. Here standard Vanguard estate staff cars with column gear shifts (or Standard Ensigns from 1958) and peaked-cap dog handlers were to be found alongside the latest nuclear bombers. The bases were much like small towns, inhabited by truly tight-knit communities of aircrews, ground crews, air staff and families. The nuclear weapon stores of some, like RAF Finningley, resembled Bronze Age funerary barrows. In balance with this life, they seemed to say, this death. The bases might, of course, face lethal attack at any moment.

One line of defence was dispersal. If the call to action came, V-bombers would make their way in twos and fours from these major airfields to twenty-six subsidiary bases peppered along the length and breadth of the United Kingdom, from Aldergrove in Northern Ireland to Kinloss in Morayshire, from St Mawgan in Cornwall to Manston on the Isle of Thanet. One reason Harold Macmillan, in an act of what proved to be successful nuclear brinkmanship, refused to disperse V-Force at the height of the Cuban Missile Crisis was to signal to Moscow that Britain was not precipitating nuclear war. For that moment, at least.

A second line of defence was Fighter Command. From 1960, the RAF took delivery of the twin-engine, afterburning Mach 2 Lightning interceptor. Supremely aerobatic, capable of breaking the sound barrier in rocket-like vertical climbs if pressed to as high as 88,000 feet, the Lightning was a military phenomenon that had very nearly been rejected by the Macmillan government. Its Defence White Paper of 1957 had set out the case for ground-to-air missiles in preference to future RAF fighter jets. Intelligence, however, suggested that a new generation of Soviet supersonic bombers beginning with the Tupolev Tu-22 would be far more than a match for Britain's existing jet interceptors. As for the much-vaunted Bloodhound ground-to-air missile – capable, it was believed, of destroying Mach 2 enemy aircraft at high altitudes and significant distances – this was not ready quite yet. The gap needed filling. While the White Paper caused several promising new projects to be abandoned – the Avro 730 Mach 2.5 nuclear bomber among them – the Lightning flew between the gaps in its budgetary logic.

The Lightning's design was primarily the work of English Electric's Freddie Page and Ray Creasey, two brilliant grammar-school scholarship boys and a formidable team, who went on to work on the highly promising, though ill-fated, BAC TSR-2 and the swing-wing Panavia Tornado, two nuclear strike aircraft. In service until 1988, the Lightning progressed through several iterations. Like its spiritual predecessor, the Spitfire, its performance was impressive, but its range was limited. Where, though, a Spitfire needed to return to base to refuel,

Lightnings were able to top up in the air courtesy of Valiant, Victor or Vulcan tankers.

In 1962, the Ministry of Defence issued *Streaked Lightning*, a gem of a propaganda (or recruitment) film capturing the enduring allure of this enthralling aircraft. Set to a jazzy score, ranging in tone from big and brassy John Barry/Laurie Johnson–style theme tunes to cool evening cocktail jazz, it asked the questions: 'Want to fly a Lightning?', 'Want to climb two Everests in three minutes?' and 'Want to fly a Lightning and take your own thunder with you?' How could anyone remotely keen on flying not answer 'yes' to all three? While seeing off non-threatening yet invasive Soviet bombers over many years, the Lightning never fired its Firestreak or Red Top air-to-air missiles in anger, yet in its prime this scintillating aircraft was a most forbidding deterrent.

Should Mach 2 Lightnings fail to bring down Soviet bombers intent on vaporizing V-Force bases, and much of the rest of eastern England along with them, radar-guided Bloodhounds, Britain's first surface-to-air guided missiles, promised to track and strike them down. Developed from the early 1950s by Bristol Aircraft and Ferranti, much of the testing work was conducted at the Weapons Research Establishment at Woomera, where the Bloodhound was first unleashed, successfully, against a high-flying, remote-controlled Government Aircraft Factories (GAF) Jindivik jet target drone, of which more than 500 were built between 1952 and 1986. A 1958 Pathé newsreel tracked a Woomera Bloodhound taking out a remote-controlled twin-engine

Canberra, with the fleet twin-engine jet unable to out-manoeuvre the snaking missile.

With their twin Bristol Thor ramjets assisted by four Gosling booster rockets, Bloodhound Mk Is shot up from the ground to a maximum speed of Mach 2.2 and, following a radar beam, to targets at up to 70,000 feet. The Mk I carried a 200-lb warhead; its range was 28 miles. A Mk II version followed in 1964 with increased speed, range – up to 100 miles – and altitude, carrying a 395-lb warhead that could destroy its target without a direct hit. Its powers of acceleration were impressive – as, of course, they needed to be. The Bloodhound Mk II cleared its launcher at 400 mph. Within 25 feet it broke the sound barrier. Three seconds after launch, it was up to Mach 2.5, or 1,800 mph. Just a bit faster, then, than the RAF's staff car of choice at the time. With a top speed of 77.6 mph according to *The Motor*, a Standard Ensign could accelerate flat out along a V-Force base's runway to reach 60 mph in 24.4 seconds. Fired singly or in salvos, the Bloodhound would have been effective against close-quarter enemy aircraft, but not against ICBMs. Although a Mk III Bloodhound equipped with a 6-kiloton nuclear warhead was planned, the project was cancelled in 1960.

It was the threat of air-to-ground missiles that changed the way V-Force operated. The days of the white-garbed nuclear cavalry of the sky was short-lived. While V-Force bases appeared unchanged, from March 1964 the bombers – newly painted in green and grey camouflage on their upper sides and white below – were to fly at low levels to avoid enemy radar.

At the time, this was inaccurate below 3,000 feet; at 500 feet, Valiants, Vulcans and Victors would be all but invisible. Some pilots proved capable of flying V-bombers, where possible, for considerable distances as low as 50 feet. Aside from the stress such low-level flying placed on aircraft frames, it also raised the question of how V-bombers would be able to drop nuclear bombs. The answer was: with difficulty. One method was to fly low and close to the target, and then climb rapidly at the last moment to 12,000 feet before releasing their bombs. The by-now standard Yellow Sun Mk 2 H-bomb could not be dropped from low altitude.

Short of investing in some fabulous Mach 3 bomber that might fly higher than Soviet ground-to-air missiles, one relatively safe way of delivering nuclear weapons was in the form of missiles fired from V-bombers. Thus equipped, the aircraft would be able to keep well away from the target. The first of these missiles, and the one Victors and Vulcans would carry throughout their nuclear deterrent years, was Blue Steel. Work on this British stand-off guided nuclear missile had begun as early as November 1954. It had been assumed, correctly – and as the U-2 incident over the Soviet Union was to prove beyond doubt – that by 1960 it would be very difficult to attack enemy targets with free-fall weapons. The bombers would be blown out of the sky.

Avro was awarded the contract to design, develop and build Blue Steel, despite never having built a guided weapon before. There was a great deal to learn. One key question was how big the missile should be, given that its thermonuclear warhead had yet to be selected. What emerged over nine years was a 35-foot-long pilotless stainless-steel and titanium rocket plane with canards – small forewings designed to improve airflow over the main wing – and clipped delta wings. Looking at a surviving Blue Steel in the RAF Museum, Hendon, it is easy to imagine it fitted with a cockpit and flown by a pilot.

The idea is not so far-fetched. In 1944, Germany had been preparing itself for an invasion of its occupied European territory that it assumed would be led by warships. What if the V-1 vengeance weapon – a proto cruise missile – could be flown by the best volunteer pilots and smashed into Allied ships from high and deadly accurate dives? Quite by surprise, I encountered one of the very few surviving original Fieseler Fi 103R 'Reichenberg' rocket planes, preserved in company with a Von Braun V-2, at the Flying Heritage and Combat Armor Museum housed in a hangar at Seattle Paine Field International Airport in Everett, Washington.

The pilot's seat is plywood and the cramped cockpit is tucked immediately in front of the pulse rocket engine. Pilots were instructed to bail out shortly before hitting the decks of Allied ships. Their chance of survival would have been next to zero. As it was, the pilots of Leonidas Squadron – named, of course, after the Spartan king who with his 300 warriors held back, if temporarily, the Persian horde at Thermopylae in 480 BCE – signed their lives away: 'I fully understand that employment in this capacity will entail my own death.' Launched from twin-engine Heinkel He 111 bombers, Reichenbergs had no landing gear.

The project was cancelled by Hitler himself for at least three reasons. Tests proved disastrous; the Fi 103R was an expensive drain on severely strained resources; and suicide warfare was not in the German military tradition. While this might seem rich coming from Hitler, one understands what he meant. The Japanese and their infamous kamikaze squadrons were to have no such qualms.

Launched from the bellies of Victors and Vulcans, Blue Steel was powered by a two-stage liquid-fuel Armstrong Siddeley rocket engine burning a mix of hydrogen peroxide and kerosene. Its guidance system was designed by Elliott Brothers (London), a firm that had been making aircraft instruments since 1912. The Elliott system would allow the Mach 3 missile to trigger in the air within 100 metres of its target – close enough, given the 1.1-megaton force of its adapted American Red Snow warhead. The Elliott system was, in fact, more advanced than that fitted to the V-bombers themselves, and was soon also used to guide the aircraft towards targets.

In practice, Blue Steel would dive from its host bomber flying at 40,000 feet and approximately 100–150 miles from its target. With the first stage of its rocket engine ignited at 32,000 feet, it would then climb to up to 70,000–90,000 feet, the second stage of the engine boosting the missile's speed to Mach 3. The engine would then cut out, and the missile would free-fall before detonating in the atmosphere.

Test flights and missile launches were carried out as part of Operation Blue Ranger in 1960 with the Valiant – which would not carry Blue Steel operationally – Victor and Vulcan at the Woomera rocket range. Established in 1947, Woomera was the size of North Korea, and took its name from an Aboriginal spear-throwing device that projected the weapon further and more accurately than the human arm could by itself. Appropriate, then, for Blue Steel.

Within its limited range, Blue Steel promised accuracy, yet by September 1962 – when it was ready to be first fitted to the Vulcans of 617 Squadron – enhanced Soviet ground-to-air missiles were ahead of its game. There were, too, a number of concerns with the weapon itself. Fuelling, a hazardous process, took half an hour, after which the missiles were driven to the bombers on the backs of custom-designed half-cab AEC Mandator lorries with the same engines as London Transport buses.

Fitting Blue Steel to the Victor proved an awkward job. Because it had a very low ground clearance, the bomber had to be jacked up so that fitters could squeeze beneath and position Blue Steel into what was a very restricted workspace. With nuclear warheads so close to the ground, Victor take-offs were nail-biting. More concerning, though, were questions relating to Blue Steel's reliability. A 1963 RAF report estimated that only 40 per cent of launches were expected to be successful; and, of these, no more than 75 per cent would reach their target. The report was issued at the same time as newly camouflaged, low-level Victors and Vulcans were directed to release Blue Steel from 1,000 feet.

Understandably, there was talk then of a dedicated

low-flying nuclear bomber. The ideal aircraft, some argued, would be a 450-mph turboprop. The idea, however, was liked by few in the RAF, for whom a modern bomber had to be a sleek supersonic beauty and not some propeller-driven contraption, even though turboprops are, of course, jets.

In 1960, the Deputy Chief of the Air Staff had already written to the defence minister Harold Watkinson with concerns about the missile's use:

> In considering Blue Steel and any possible developments of it we must take note of some pretty unpalatable facts. We first started thinking about this weapon in 1952. The operational requirement was accepted by the Ministry of Supply in 1954 for an in-service date of 1960 and events have I think proved that had this been met the weapon would have had a useful and viable life. An in-service date of 1963 for a weapon with a range of only 100 miles is, however, a different matter.

Although more advanced Blue Steels were proposed, including a Mach 4.5 version with a range of 900 nautical miles, these were confined to Avro's drawing boards. Because of the lack of a credible alternative, Blue Steel was to remain Britain's principal nuclear deterrent alongside the much longer-lived WE.177 bomb until 31 December 1970. The last V-bombers to carry the missile were the Vulcans of 27 and 617 Squadrons, by which time the aircraft were painted in wrap-around green and grey camouflage.

In terms of their original Cold War remit, the bombers proved more than capable. In October 1961, Vulcan B.2s flew high above USAF B-52s during Operation Sky Shield II, one of three comprehensive exercises involving hundreds of aircraft conducted across the United States to test the nation's defences against Soviet bombers. Crews of the eight Vulcans, flown from Kindley Air Force Base, Bermuda, and RAF Lossiemouth, distinguished themselves by successfully 'attacking' all their assigned targets without being detected or intercepted. While V-Force was critically challenged by new missile technology, such exercises underlined a key consideration in the bombers' favour. This was General Thomas S. Power's point that, unlike missiles, bombers could be recalled (except, of course, Major 'King' Kong's B-52 in *Dr Strangelove*) or redirected.

Between 1963 and 1966, V-Force was involved in a Cold War shadow play. This was the Indonesia–Malaysia Confrontation occasioned by Indonesian president Sukarno's refusal to recognize the legitimacy of the recently created state of Malaysia. Sukarno was supported by the Soviet Union and China. Britain, the US, Australia, New Zealand and Canada sided with Malaysia, not least because they feared Indonesia turning into a Communist state. Fighting took place mostly along the east Malaysia–Indonesia border of Borneo, extending into west Malaysia during 1964, Sukarno's 'Year of Living Dangerously'. Along with ground troops and Royal Navy helicopter squadrons, V-Force played its part. B.2 Vulcans of 9, 12 and 35 Squadrons and B.1A Victors of 15 Squadron were dispatched to RAF Tengah, Singapore, and RAAF Butterworth,

Malaysia. So, too, were stocks of Red Beard nuclear warheads sent to Tengah, although these were part of Britain's long-term commitment to the Southeast Asia Treaty Organization (SEATO) and not a specific threat to Sukarno.

Britain also sent squadrons of Hawker Hunter fighters, Gloster Javelin all-weather interceptors and Lightnings east to Tengah. Armed with conventional 1,000-lb high-explosive bombs, Victors and Vulcans served as a deterrent but were not called into combat. The conflict ended in March 1966 when Sukarno was overthrown in a coup and hundreds of thousands of Indonesian Communists and suspected Communists were killed – an atrocity backed covertly by the British government and its intelligence agencies.

One unexpected and positively cheerful duty, in May 1965, was escorting Avro Lancaster G-ASXX to Calcutta on the first leg of its epic 12,000-mile flight from RAAF Butterworth to Biggin Hill in London. A camouflaged 57 Squadron Victor joined an RAAF Canberra and Sabre fighters for the occasion. Most recently, the white-painted Lancaster had been on reconnaissance, patrol and air-sea rescue duty with the French Navy's Escadrille de Servitude 9S based at Noumea, New Caledonia. Donated to what is now the Lincolnshire Aviation Heritage Centre, the veteran bomber was flown by a French crew to Sydney. At this time, G-ASXX was the only airworthy Lancaster. It should be back in the air as NX611 *Just Jane* before 2030.

Although they were involved in a variety of support roles, women did not serve with Victors, Vulcans or Valiants. A press photo of 27 June 1966 captioned 'first women to fly in a Vulcan' shows senior aircraftwomen Margaret Drabble and Rita Smith, operations clerks in the control tower at RAF Finningley, stepping away from a newly landed V-bomber. It would be another twenty-eight years before Flight Lieutenant Jo Salter, flying Tornados with 617 Squadron, became the RAF's first fast-jet combat-ready female pilot.

Always a star in the public eye, the Vulcan played a key supporting role in the 1965 James Bond spy film *Thunderball*. In this Cold War–era caper, the SPECTRE villain hijacks and sinks a Vulcan carrying two H-bombs in a bay in the Bahamas, in a bid to hold the US to ransom. A full-scale model was made on location for the film's underwater scenes. The flying sequences feature the perfectly real B.1A XH506. The art direction was by Ken Adam (also responsible for the sets of *Dr Strangelove*), who from 1943 to 1945 had been a hard-fighting Typhoon pilot with 609 Squadron. As a Jew and a German national, Adam – born Klaus Adam, son of a First World War Prussian cavalry officer – knew how to live dangerously, with dash and élan. Rewatching *Thunderball*, it is hard to imagine the USAF allowing their nuclear bombers to be involved in a film depicting a weakness, if only fictional, in their nuclear deterrent, especially in a year in which the Soviets shipped anti-aircraft missiles to Vietnam and the Cold War was still hot.

FIVE

Missiles

V-Force's nemesis. A Soviet S-75 missile system launch in Romania

I n the late stages of the Second World War, the potency of Wernher von Braun's rockets had come as something of a shock to the Allies. Though the V-2 vengeance weapon may have been too late to save Nazi Germany, it heralded a disturbing new form of warfare. Flying from an altitude of 100 kilometres at Mach 3 towards its targets, the German missile was effectively invisible and impossible to shoot down. After the war, it led to the development not only of new weaponry, but also of ever-mightier NASA rockets, culminating in Saturn V. This – von Braun's *meisterwerk* – was the tallest, heaviest and most powerful rocket yet flown. Launched for the first time from Cape Canaveral days before Christmas 1968, the 363-foot Saturn V – with the power, according to NASA, of thirty-five Hoover Dams (whatever that means!) – blasted the crew of Apollo 8 off towards its orbit around the Moon. Its 7,600,000-lb thrust was more than that of a hundred Vulcan B.2s.

While NASA turned what had been instruments of death into potent tools for the peaceful exploration of space, the military on both sides of the Cold War had their own plans. Surface-to-air missiles (SAM) have never been anything like as powerful as Saturn V, yet their debut in the US in 1954 in the guise of Bell Labs' Nike Ajax demonstrated that they could fly, if not to the Moon, then as high as the latest jet aircraft. At this time, new Soviet jets were causing concern. In 1956, Nigel Birch, the British Secretary of State for Air, and senior RAF officers witnessed the new MiG-21 Mach 2 interceptor at Moscow's Tushino Airfield. Its ceiling, they were told, was 20,000 metres (65,610 feet). Now, what if, along with this impressive high-performance fighter, the Soviets had a guided missile system as good as, or even better than, the Ajax Nike? Where would this leave British and American nuclear bombers on missions to the Soviet Union?

On 1 May 1960, a day etched in the memory of Cold War historians, a U-2 spy plane flying a 2,900-mile intelligence-gathering mission from Peshawar, Pakistan, to Bodø, Norway, across Soviet airspace on behalf of the USAF and the CIA, was shot down over the Sverdlovsk Oblast on the western slopes of the Urals. Asked in 1962, when he was safely back in the US, how high he had been flying when he was intercepted, the U-2's pilot Gary Powers quipped, 'Not high enough.' While the facts remain a little unclear, Powers would probably have been at 70,000 feet or a little over when the V-750VN missile fired from an S-75 Dvina air defence system struck his U-2. And even if the former USAF captain, now a pilot for the CIA, had been able to fly at 80,000 feet, the Soviet missile would still have got him.

The incident was a huge blow both to American prestige and to the very idea of NATO nuclear bombers flying into Soviet-controlled airspace. But if not easy to divine, the warning had been there. On 7 October 1959, a Taiwanese Martin RB-57D reconnaissance Canberra flying at 65,600 feet had been brought down near Beijing by a V-750 missile. To keep the new S-75 missile programme secret, a Chinese fighter was credited with the hit. But how credible was this claim? What Chinese fighter at the time, short of having a dragon in its tail, could fly so very high?

The S-75 and its V-750 missiles had been designed starting in 1953 by a team at MKB Fakel, founded that year at Khimki near Moscow. Pyotr Grushin, an aeronautical engineer, was the head of the programme. Paraded through Red Square on May Day 1957, the S-75 was by then ready to defend the Motherland. By 1964, when V-Force was at its height, there may have been as many as a thousand S-75 sites embedded along the Soviet Union's western border, with more in East Germany. The S-75 was also to be used to great effect in Vietnam, encouraging the Americans to develop increasingly improved electronic countermeasures (ECM). In turn, the Vietnamese responded with salvos of missiles while fabricating decoy S-75 launch sites from painted bamboo, to fool US fighter-bombers aiming to destroy the real McCoy. On 27 July 1965, six US Mach 2 Republic F-105 Thunderchiefs and five pilots were lost for the sake of two fake S-75 sites.

While SAM and ECM played lethal cat-and-mouse games with one another, the debate over just how fast and how high a military aircraft would have to fly to escape ground-to-air missiles intensified. The answer was provided by the sensational Lockheed SR-71 Blackbird, a Mach 3.2 USAF reconnaissance plane. Its design was led by Clarence 'Kelly' Johnson, mastermind of the U-2 and such special machines as the fast, twin-boom Second World War P-38 Lightning piston-engine fighter; the first US fighter jet, the P-80 Shooting Star; the F-104 Starfighter, which was the first US Mach 2 fighter; and the much-loved Constellation piston-engine airliner.

In a career longer than thirty years, the stealthy SR-71 is said to have escaped nearly 4,000 missiles aimed its way. It could fly at up to 85,000 feet and was stupendously fast. If attacked by Mach 3 missiles, its pilots could accelerate away from them. The SR-71, though, was a very particular aircraft. Made of a titanium and polymer composite, it was not cheap. Quite remarkably, the titanium came from the USSR, shipped to the US largely by bogus companies in developing countries. The Blackbird was also expensive to maintain. There was no possibility of a bomber spin-off.

The SR-71's evasive qualities were second to none. Flying missions to the Baltic states from RAF Mildenhall, Suffolk, for example, it had to negotiate the narrow air passage between Denmark and Sweden. If it entered Swedish airspace, it would trigger Mach 2 delta-wing Saab Viggens of the Swedish Air Force, and when over the Baltic, Mach 2.8 Soviet MiG-25s from Finow Air Base in East Germany. It could, though, outpace and outclimb both these otherwise highly effective supersonic interceptors.

Short of investing in some fabulous Mach 3 bomber that could fly higher than a Soviet ground-to-air missile, the British were to push forward the idea of missiles fired from the V-bombers, allowing the aircraft to keep as far from their targets as these would allow. The first choice of weapon – and the one Victors and Vulcans would carry throughout their nuclear deterrent years, as we have seen – was Blue Steel. But an alternative train of thought, nurtured at the same time as the Blue Steel programme, was for a ground-based medium-range ballistic missile (MRBM) carrying a nuclear warhead launched from Britain against Soviet targets. This was Blue Streak. The idea was that it would either complement V-Force or replace it altogether.

The project had emerged from a proposal put forward in April 1954 for a joint US-British ballistic missile programme. For their part, the Americans would offer the SM-65 Atlas ICBM with a range of 5,000 nautical miles, with the British developing a 2,000-nm MRBM. In 1955, the contract for the British missile was made with de Havilland Propellers. Rolls-Royce supplied the liquid-fuelled engines – RZ.2s, with a combined 137,000-lb thrust – and Sperry Gyroscope the guidance system. The stainless-steel fuselage was fabricated by Firth Vickers. The missile, with its licensed US technology, was 60 feet high with a diameter of 10 feet.

As a weapon, Blue Streak was not a success. Its key problem was that it took too long to fuel with liquid oxygen. By the time it would have been ready for launch, Soviet bombers and missiles would have struck their British targets. Blue Streaks themselves were housed in silos designed to withstand nuclear blasts, and finding the right sights for these was not easy. Geological conditions had to be just so, and subsidence was the key issue. RAF Upavon, Wiltshire, and the former Royal Navy Air Station Crail, near Fife on the east coast of Scotland, were marked out as the first Blue Streak launch sites, although construction on a full-scale site finally took place at RAF Spadeadam, Cumberland, where the missile was first tested. As it was designed to work in pairs, a system was developed by which one Blue Streak, prepared for launch, was to be kept on standby, while a second was to be fuelled as and when necessary.

The cost of the Blue Streak programme rose from £50 million in 1955 to £300 million four years later. It was expected to peak at £1.3 billion, a colossal sum at the time. As the cost rose, Lord Mountbatten, First Sea Lord (1955–59) and Chief of the Defence Staff (1959–65), campaigned for a complete change of course. Britain's nuclear deterrent should be switched from RAF aircraft and missiles to Royal Navy submarines. Mountbatten's logic was sound, and Blue Streak was cancelled in April 1960. While the missile went on to serve with the European Launcher Development Organisation (ELDO) – a precursor of the European Space Agency – as the first stage of its carrier rocket Europa, this project was also cancelled, in 1972. However, this was not the fault of Blue Streak itself, which had proved to be a reliable rocket in non-military service.

One further possible future for Blue Streak, made in a proposal by Hawker Siddeley Dynamics in 1972, was as a British space rocket capable of delivering satellites into orbit. The missile would form the first of the rocket's two stages. This, though, was another over-ambitious project and vanished as quickly as a cloud of liquid oxygen.

More than sixty years on, even faint ghosts of Blue Streak are hard to find. The most haunting site associated with Britain's MRBM is RAF Spadeadam, set in the remote marshland and peat bog north of Hadrian's Wall. I went there years ago, not knowing quite what the site was. Driving along the Big Dipper–like 'Military Road' B6318 through Heddon-on-the-Wall in Northumberland to Greenhead on the Cumbrian border, I stopped at the Samson Inn at Gilsland. Here, I learned about the RAF site close by, and Blue Streak.

Curiosity sparked, I threaded my gunmetal Jag Mk 2 up past the village's lonely Gothic church, a Victorian design by James Stewart of Carlisle, before stopping at an MOD sign that made it clear it was unwise to carry on. If I had, I might have seen the Brutalist-like concrete structures associated with Blue Streaks, evidence of a concrete silo, and the carcasses of Cold War military jets – including, I learned later, Soviet MiGs and Sukhois. I might also have been escorted out. What I did see was a landscape of grave beauty, and red squirrels darting from conifer to conifer.

Today, much, if not all, of Spadeadam is visible on Google Maps. It remains an active military site and the RAF's largest base, offering occasional public tours. Odd to think that as many as sixty Blue Streak launch pads with their associated concrete silos and other brutally functional structures might have been built here and elsewhere across Britain. They would, at least, have been more discreet than our sprawling, two-fingers-up-to-the-landscape twenty-first-century housing estates.

As it turns out, Blue Streak was not the first nuclear missile to operate from British soil. In March 1957, Harold Macmillan, Britain's new prime minister, met US president Dwight D. Eisenhower in Bermuda. Tensions that had arisen between Britain and the United States during the Suez Crisis the previous year were eased as the two men wined and dined at the Mid Ocean Club. From 1942, Macmillan had been the British Resident Minister in Algiers – then newly liberated from occupying German and Italian forces – reporting directly to Winston Churchill and liaising closely with General Eisenhower, Supreme Allied Commander in the Mediterranean. The two men had forged a good working relationship.

At the Bermuda Conference, Macmillan was keen to get the US to share nuclear information and to reignite the 'special relationship' between the wartime allies. Eisenhower agreed on condition that Macmillan's government was willing to allow U-2 spy planes to operate from British airbases and – the crux of the matter – to deploy American Thor intermediate-range ballistic missiles (IRBMs).

On his return to Britain, Macmillan addressed the House of Commons on 1 April:

> The [Thor] rockets will be the property of Her Majesty's Government, manned by British troops who will receive their prior training from American experts. The rockets cannot be fired by any except the British personnel, but the warhead will be in the control of the United States – which is the law of the United States – and to that extent the Americans have negative control; but it is absolutely untrue to say that the President and not the British Government will decide when these missiles will be launched and at whom. So long as we rely upon the American warheads, and only so long, that will remain a matter for the two Governments.

Manufactured by the Douglas Aircraft Company in Santa Monica, California, Thor had its roots in von Braun's V-2.

Work on the IRBM had been initiated in 1954, but then it was rushed through development and testing in 1957, when news of the launch of the Soviet R-7 Semyorka heralded the era of the ICBM. Slightly modified, the R-7 took Sputnik, the world's first artificial satellite, into orbit in October 1957. In April 1961, a derivative of the R-7, Vostok, lifted Major Yuri Gagarin, the first human in space, into orbit around the Earth.

The Soviets had got there first. By the time of the Bermuda Conference in 1957, the Americans were all too aware that they had been slow off the mark. Wernher von Braun and Walter Thiel must surely have said so well before then. In early 1945, tests had been made at Peenemünde on the German Baltic coast with the engine of the A9/A10 Project Amerika ICBM. Designed to hit Washington and New York, the missile – first thought up as early as 1940 – was in a very early phase. The lack of an advanced guidance system, for example, meant that it would have had to be piloted across the Atlantic. Pilots were unlikely to have survived such unprecedented missions. Undeterred, von Braun and his team were also working on a four-stage A12 rocket designed for orbital space flight.

As the SM-65 Atlas, the first American ICBM, was not to enter service until September 1959, Thor IRBMs based in a friendly Britain seemed a realistic temporary fix to the perceived 'missile gap' widening between the US and the Soviet Union. Through the innocent-sounding Project Emily, sixty complete Thor missiles were flown from the

US to RAF Lakenheath, Suffolk, in the capacious fuselages of piston-engine Douglas C-124 Globemaster IIs and turboprop Douglas C-133 Cargomasters. Equipping twenty dedicated RAF launch sites in eastern England – spread across Lincolnshire, Suffolk, Norfolk, Rutland and East Yorkshire – the combined force of the Thors was said to be equal to that of seven and a half squadrons of V-bombers. On Saturday, 27 October 1963, fifty-nine of the sixty 65-foot nuclear-armed missiles – garbed in white and adorned with RAF roundels – were ready and prepared for launch against Soviet targets.

To achieve this level of readiness was no simple matter. Because Operation Emily was a joint US–UK affair, Thors could only be launched with both authorized RAF and USAF personnel present. The RAF would initiate the missile launch process with one dedicated key, while the USAF would arm the nuclear warhead with another. RAF missile crews had been trained in the operation of Thors in California and Arizona, a far cry from the farmlands and rural settlements in the east of England where the gleaming white missiles were now based. Period photographs show heavy American military low-loader lorries shouldering complete Thor missiles to their sites at walking pace, through narrow town and village centres with a single motorcycle escort. Nuclear warheads were transported independently by road in the middle of the night from a central store at RAF Faldingworth, Lincolnshire – which also held nuclear weapons for V-Force – with just the one military policeman and dog as escort.

Thor missile in the village of Weldon, threading its way to
218 Squadron at RAF Harrington

The purpose-built Thor bases featured retractable hangars for the missiles, which were stored horizontally on trans-porter-erector trailers. They were drawn out to launch pads, raised vertically, and then fuelled and prepared for launch if and when the order came. The entire sequence took approximately fifteen minutes, the missiles rising incongruously over remote and venerable English farmland.

Thor crews could certainly be quite isolated. At RAF Catfoss in the East Riding of Yorkshire, members of 226 Squadron kept pigs in the old control tower, while at nearby RAF Full Sutton, 102 Squadron boasted a flock of geese. Norse and old German gods might only know what these animals would have made of a Thor launch. With a thrust of 150,000 lb from its Rocketdyne engine, the thunderous missile would punch its way 300 miles into space, accelerating to a maximum speed of 11,020 mph on its blazing flight from bucolic English farmland to Soviet cities, airbases and missile launch sites, where the Communists might or might not keep pigs and geese.

On loan to Britain and RAF Bomber Command, the Thors were due to be returned to the United States in November 1964, yet with the Atlas ICBM now in service, capable of striking Moscow from US launch sites, the British-based IRBMs were stood down in September 1963 – by which time Victor and Vulcan squadrons were equipped with Blue Steel. What V-Force needed, however, was a more potent missile that could be launched much further from targets than Blue Steel, allowing the bombers to keep as far away as possible from their targets, and thus from Soviet missiles and fighters.

In May 1960, Douglas Aircraft unveiled its GAM-87A Skybolt. The promise was that this solid-fuelled rocket-powered missile could be unleashed from under the wings of nuclear bombers 1,000 miles from the target. This would make bombers competitive with ICBMs. The USAF B-52s were to carry four 38-foot-long, 15,000-lb Skybolts; the RAF Vulcans only two (the Vulcan B.3, which never got beyond the drawing board, would have managed six). Skybolt, however, could not be fitted to the Victor, for two reasons. The first was the problem of ground clearance; the second was that the missile's back-up 'star tracker' navigation system was unsuited to the Victor's wing. Although only the Vulcan would be able to carry the missile, Harold Macmillan's government decided to put all its nuclear eggs into the Skybolt basket. There was no plan B.

Macmillan met Eisenhower at Camp David, Washington DC, in March 1960. The upshot was that the British would be allowed to buy Skybolts if US submarines could be based at Holy Loch, Scotland. As the prime minister and president jawed, the new USS *Washington* nuclear submarine was preparing to launch the Polaris A-1 ballistic missile from underwater. Macmillan sought and received formal approval from his government for the cancellation of Blue Streak. In May, Britain placed a formal order for 100 brand-new Skybolts.

This would prove unwise. Because the RAF planned to tip its Skybolts with the heavier British Red Snow nuclear warhead instead of the lighter American W47 (the British questioned the latter's safety), Vulcans would be unable to launch them until 600 miles from the target, meaning they would need to cross the Soviet coastline to attack Moscow. This rather defeated the point. The same would have been true if, as was seriously considered, Skybolts were carried by militarized versions of the up-and-coming Vickers VC10 airliner.

In January 1961, a Vulcan, flown to the Douglas factory at Santa Monica, was test-fitted with Skybolts. The first five trials conducted at home in Britain were failures. The sixth, on 19 December 1962, was successful, but its timing was not good. Skybolt costs were rocketing, and Robert McNamara, the bombastic US Secretary of Defense, was set against the project. In November 1962, he let the British government know through a briefing with David Ormsby-Gore, British ambassador to the United States, that the cancellation of Skybolt was in the offing.

This promoted heated discussions in the House of Commons. Jo Grimond, leader of the Liberal Party, asked, 'Does not this mark the absolute failure of the policy of the independent [British] deterrent? Is it not the case that everybody else in the world knew this, except the Conservative Party in this country?' In December, President John F. Kennedy cancelled the programme, leading to the 'Skybolt Crisis'. Without Skybolt, Britain would have no credible long-term nuclear deterrent. This was deeply humiliating for Macmillan. Something needed to be done, and urgently so.

Kennedy, Macmillan and their respective advisors met for three days at Nassau in the Bahamas. While the Nassau Conference was not plain sailing, an agreement was reached on 21 December. By coincidence or not, the next day the USAF carried out its own successful Skybolt test, much to Kennedy's annoyance. Macmillan kept calm, trusting that Skybolt had been 'cancelled on good general grounds' – which it was, officially, on 31 December – and 'not merely to annoy us or drive Great Britain out of the nuclear business'. The surprising and positive upshot was that Britain would be supplied with Lockheed Polaris missiles, to be equipped with British nuclear warheads and installed in Royal Navy submarines with the proviso that the missiles could be launched independently of Washington only when 'supreme national interests' allowed no option.

Polaris sealed the fate of V-Force. The idea of using nuclear-powered submarines to carry long-range nuclear missiles that could be launched from underwater had been gathering momentum rapidly from the mid-1950s. The proposition was compelling. Such submarines would be all but immune from detection and attack. Four *Resolution*-class nuclear ballistic submarines were ordered in May 1963. An option for a fifth was cancelled by Harold Wilson's Labour government in February 1965. Laid down in February 1964, launched by Queen Elizabeth The Queen Mother in September 1966, and commissioned in October 1967, HMS *Resolution*, the first of the class, test-fired a Polaris A-3 off Cape Kennedy, Florida, on 15 February 1968. That June, *Resolution*, armed with sixteen Polaris A-3s, set sail on its first patrol from HM Naval Base Clyde, sited at Faslane on Gare Loch on the west coast of Scotland.

The speed at which *Resolution* and her sister ships were built was impressive. This was a new type of British submarine – nuclear-powered and equipped with a US nuclear armoury. It had taken 10,000 drawings and 500,000 work hours to design and build *Resolution*. The 425-foot-long sub proved to be fast underwater (25 knots, or nearly 30 mph), with the power required delivered near-silently by a Rolls-Royce pressurized water nuclear reactor feeding high-pressure steam to a 27,500-shp English Electric turbine. The sub's indefatigable reactor could, said the navy, power an entire town.

The range of the submarine was limited only by the amount of food it could store. In practice, its 143-strong crew would be served three hot meals a day in a dedicated dining room throughout regular two-month missions. With two separate crews, known as 'Port' and 'Starboard', the *Resolution*-class

subs would be able to sail almost continuously, with one reliev-
ing another at regular intervals.

Unlike an RAF bomber, the subs offered proper lavatories.
Showers, too, with unlimited hot water. Even a laundry. Each
crew member had a dedicated bunk of their own. Running
stealthily, and as deep as 900 feet, SSBNs (ship, submersible,
ballistic, nuclear) sailed undetected around the world despite
the best attempts of the Soviet Navy and Russian government's 'willing fools' to find them. Were a *Resolution*-class sub
to be detected, it could defend itself underwater with long-
range, high-speed Tigerfish torpedoes. And should power be
lost, a diesel-generator would kick in to keep it on the move.
The first Soviet nuclear submarine, armed like for like with
sixteen nuclear ballistic missiles, slipped into service in 1967.

The submarine's missile compartment housed two rows of
eight Polaris A-3 missiles. These 31-foot, 28,000-lb weapons
of mass destruction had a range of 2,500 miles. Launched
underwater by powerful jets of steam, the engines would
ignite as the missile surfaced. Small wonder Royal Navy
crews knew the nuclear subs of 10th Submarine Squadron as
'the bombers'. 'The fighters' were the conventionally armed
hunter-killer subs of 3rd Submarine Squadron, also based
at Faslane. The Polaris quartet served reliably and well until
replaced in 1996 by four *Vanguard*-class submarines. The
latter were armed with new 6,000-mile-range Trident II
missiles acquired from the US in March 1982 following cor-
respondence between Prime Minister Margaret Thatcher and
President Ronald Reagan.

Given the superiority of Polaris to both ground-to-air and air-launched missiles, it might seem odd that it appeared to arrive so late in the nuclear day and after so much toing and froing over the best way to invest in and operate a credible nuclear deterrent. The Royal Navy had, in fact, suggested a seagoing nuclear role for itself as early as 1945. While this was to be first realized in 1962 with the arrival of the aircraft-carrier-borne subsonic Blackburn Buccaneer, a twin-engine strike jet designed to fly below radar, a nuclear missile that could be fired from below water was at the time a demanding technical proposition. That position changed steadily, beginning with the launch of the US Navy's first nuclear submarine, *Nautilus*, in January 1955.

With Lord Mountbatten's appointment as First Sea Lord in April that year, the Royal Navy had a champion who, in discussions with US Navy chiefs, campaigned hard to ensure the technology underpinning *Nautilus* was transferred to Britain, officially through the 1958 US UK Mutual Defence Agreement. Meanwhile, during the Project Nobska anti-submarine warfare conference organized by Mountbatten's friend Admiral Arleigh Burke, US Chief of Naval Operations, and held in Cape Cod in summer 1956, an off-agenda discussion took place regarding what would become the Polaris missile project. The main protagonists were Edward Teller, 'Father of the Hydrogen Bomb', and J. Carson Mark of Los Alamos Scientific Laboratory. It was agreed that by 1963 a small nuclear warhead could be made for the US Navy's Mark 45 torpedo – and that this, in turn, could be fitted to a US

Navy missile. Its yield, Mark suggested, would be something like thirty times that of Little Boy. Now, imagine a warship or even a nuclear submarine with global reach, armed with a dozen or more solid-fuelled nuclear fission warheads.

Work on the Lockheed Polaris began in 1956, with a Royal Navy liaison officer included in the team. The missile was first fired from the nuclear submarine USS *George Washington* on 20 July 1960. The sub sent a message to President Eisenhower. 'POLARIS – FROM OUT OF THE DEEP TO TARGET. PERFECT.'

In Britain, despite Mountbatten's urging, the project was delayed by indecision. The Air Ministry argued that Polaris would have less accuracy and a smaller warhead than Blue Streak while costing twenty times as much. The Chiefs of Staff Committee recommended Skybolt as the navy pressed for Polaris. Understandably, there was a certain degree of posturing involved in the tangle of official meetings held in Britain. The RAF was loathe to hand over the country's nuclear deterrent, while the Royal Navy was keen to reassert its senior service role. It all became immensely complicated, submerging for some time into the murky and treacherous depths of politics.

By 1966, however, the staff of Britain's Polaris Executive (formed four years earlier) had grown to 504, with 38 at its London office, 5 at the Ministry of Aviation, 430 in Bath and 31 in Washington DC. A justified concern was raised in parliament concerning the development of the Poseidon missile, a US replacement for Polaris. Was Britain in danger of buying sight unseen? Not so with the latest, A-3, version of Polaris, which became operational in September 1964, the month before China conducted its first nuclear test. In any event, Poseidon would not be in service with the US Navy until 1972.

Possibly the most bizarre turn of events faced by the Polaris Executive had come in April 1963, when Vice-Admiral Sir Hugh Mackenzie DSO & Bar, DSC, a distinguished Second World War submarine commander and newly appointed head of the organization, received 'a proposal from the Secretary of Defence [that] threw my very existence into the melting pot. It suggested that I personally be replaced by Dr Beeching who had recently acquired fame, or infamy, for his reorganisation of British Rail[ways].'

Perhaps Peter Thorneycroft, the minister in question, thought that drastic cuts in costs were needed. In any case, Thorneycroft's baffling proposal was overruled. Given what Beeching did to the railways, what might he have done to the navy? Mackenzie and his dispersed team went on to complete the project on time and within budget – 'an unprecedented feat in British naval history', barked the *Daily Telegraph*. One can almost hear the band striking up 'The Roast Beef of Olde England' and see the port being passed to the left in some celebratory officers' mess.

On 14 June 1969, Commander Henry Ellis of the RN's Plans Division was charged with formally notifying the RAF that the Royal Navy was now in command of Britain's nuclear deterrent. The new *Resolution*-class submarines were named after historic capital ships, battleships and battlecruisers that could trace their ancestry back to Elizabethan fifty-gun galleons and Britain's one-time command of the High Seas. They also happened to be the names of ships Lord Mountbatten had served on.

John Major, the Conservative prime minister, was to give a speech at Faslane on 28 August 1996, at a ceremony marking the decommissioning of HMS *Repulse*, last of the *Resolution*-class submarines, and the end of the Polaris programme.

> The debt we owe is very large. For the last twenty-eight years this Force has mounted continuous patrols that have been vital to ensure this country's peace and security. Because of these patrols any possible aggressor has known that to attack the UK would provoke a terrible response. In particular, we are here today to pay tribute to the last of the four Polaris submarines, HMS *Repulse*, which returned from her sixtieth and final deployment in May. But not only *Repulse*, of course. I pay tribute, too, to the other three boats and their crews in her Class: the *Resolution* herself, *Renown* and *Revenge*. Each has made its own unique and invaluable contribution to the remarkable record of maintaining a Polaris submarine at sea, on deterrent patrol, undetected by friend or foe, every day, of every year, from 1969 until May this year.

Polaris marked the end of V-Force as Britain's nuclear deterrent. It is not hard to understand why. Over a 28-year operational life, *Resolution*-class submarines and the Polaris programme cost 1.5 per cent of Britain's annual defence budget compared to the 6 per cent spent each year on V-Force. V-bombers and their bases were vulnerable to attack; Polariis submarines, impervious to weather, lurked stealthily and undetected in the global depths, each armed with sixteen 2,800-mile-range Polaris A-3s. V-Force had more than met its match.

Launched from underwater: Polaris A-3 bearing
three nuclear warheads

SIX

Impact

V-Force might have lost its nuclear deterrent role, yet who in 1969, when the Royal Navy's *Resolution*-class submarines took over, could have ever imagined V-bombers as cuddly toys? Such has been the enduring appeal of the Vulcan, especially, that in 2025 it is possible to buy Vulcan kits, models, jigsaw puzzles, tea towels, key rings, lapel badges, fridge magnets, bottle stoppers, brooches, earrings, ice scrapers, sweatshirts, watches, phone stands and plush soft toys. Is it odd for children to cuddle up with a nuclear bomber at night? These bedtime toys are an unusual yet pertinent reminder of how, in its heyday, V-Force occupied – as it still occupies – both light and dark sides of the popular imagination.

The V-bombers were hugely popular attractions at air shows – hugely popular, too, as the subject of children's comics. However peculiar this might seem from the perspective of the second quarter of the twenty-first century, V-Force reached the peak of its terrifying destructive capability at the same time as pop culture – music, fashion, art, design, shopping for the fun of it, and comics – boomed; when satellites, space rockets and jet aircraft were glamorous and exciting.

If radios had been left playing when Pilot Officer Peter West and his fellow crew members rushed to their Vulcans at RAF Coningsby on Friday, 26 October 1962, soon enough the distinctive sound of the science-fiction-inspired instrumental 'Telstar' – No. 1 in the UK charts that week – would have bleeped and whirred from their speakers. Written and produced for the Tornados by Joe Meek, an inventive English sound engineer, producer and songwriter then in his early thirties, 'Telstar' was Britain's bestselling record of 1962.

Catching and expressing something of the excitement of the new Space Age (the young US president John F. Kennedy gave his 'We choose to go to the Moon' speech at Rice University that September), 'Telstar' also went to No. 1 in the US charts, making the Tornados the first British group to reach that covetable position. The Beatles were next in February 1964, when V-Force reached its zenith, with 'I Want to Hold Your Hand'.

No one buying 'Telstar' would have known that Meek had overdubbed this offbeat yet catchy instrumental in a makeshift studio in a flat above a leather shop on London's Holloway Road. The sound of a rocket heading into space was, according to the *Observer Music Monthly*, that of Meek's flushing lavatory played backwards. The actual Telstar, launched into orbit by a NASA Delta rocket from Cape Canaveral on 10 July 1962, was a tiny communications satellite created at Bell Laboratories by the American engineer, inventor and popular science-fiction author John Robinson Pierce. Operating in tandem with AT&T, the British GPO (General Post Office) and France's Direction Générale des Télécommunications, Telstar relayed telephone calls and the first live television feeds between Britain and the United States. Long-defunct, the epoch-making satellite continues to spin in orbit above the Earth.

In 1962, Telstar captured the public imagination, while the 45-rpm 'Telstar' saw the Tornados outselling chart favourites Adam Faith, Cliff Richard, Shirley Bassey, Acker Bilk and The Beatles, a budding group from Liverpool whose first single 'Love Me Do' was No. 41 in the UK charts at the time of the Cuban Missile Crisis. The US No. 1 in October 1962 was 'Monster Mash', a novelty number by Bobby 'Boris' Pickett and the Crypt-Kickers, a daft way to play out what had seemed to many the end of the world. Released ahead of Halloween, 'Monster Mash' edged 'Sherry' by the Four Seasons from the top spot.

Of course, there were warnings – had been warnings – of the dangers of nuclear weapons and the headlong rush into space. And who could know that fearful October whether there would be any humans left to venture much beyond a bunker or a cave? This understandable paranoia was reflected in pop, folk and rock songs throughout the decade as V-Force stood guard. In 1969, Pete Sinfield wrote 'Epitaph' for King Crimson, the inventive prog rock band who took to the stage ahead of the Rolling Stones at a free open-air concert in Hyde Park in the summer of 1969. The song concerned the fear instilled by nuclear weapons. The Summer of Love (1967), a short flowering of peace and love, was over as the Cold War continued to haunt the collective imagination.

And yet, throughout the Cold War and as if in equal measure to the terrifying dangers it posed, popular culture had a habit of popping up smiling and making this daunting new era glamorous and even fun. Soon after Count Basie released his new album, *Basie*, in 1958 with a cover sleeve depicting a mushroom cloud from one of the previous year's Operation Plumbbob nuclear bomb tests in Nevada, 65 miles from Las Vegas, its name was quickly changed to *The Atomic Mr Basie*. By all accounts, the recording had been a blast – as was Operation Plumbbob itself, set up to test how soldiers would cope on a tactical nuclear battlefield. Twelve hundred pigs stood in for infantry, some in raised cages dressed in suits of different materials, others trapped in pens waiting to be hit by fast-moving debris.

Days after the much-publicized US atomic bomb detonations made in the mid-Pacific at Bikini Atoll over and under water in July 1946, as part of Operation Crossroads, the French automotive engineer and fashion designer Louis Réard revealed the bikini, his daring two-piece bathing costume with a G-string back. It was modelled that summer day at the Art Deco Piscine Molitor by 18-year-old Micheline Bernardini, a nude dancer from the Casino de Paris. 'Like the bomb,' Réard purred, 'the bikini is small and devasting.'

Réard hired skywriters to fly over the French Riviera with the message 'smaller than the smallest bathing suit in the world'. In an advertising campaign, he said that a two-piece swimsuit was not a genuine bikini 'unless it could be pulled through a wedding ring'. On either side of the Atlantic, the press was enraptured. Writing for *Harper's Bazaar,* the Paris-born American fashion columnist Diana Vreeland opined 'the bikini is the most important thing since the atom bomb'.

The pigs, goats, guinea pigs, rats and mice that died needless and agonizing deaths tethered and otherwise trapped on board target ships anchored in Bikini Atoll during Operation Crossroads were unable to speak or read. If they could have, they might well have disagreed with Vreeland and found Réard absurd. Wretched creatures, those that survived the atomic blast and fallout were subjected to medical tests and then destroyed. Plants and wildlife on Bikini Atoll were wiped out.

When US troops had overrun the atoll in 1944, the remaining five Japanese soldiers there committed suicide. For all its beauty, this was a deathly place. Despite attempts at resettlement since Operation Crossroads, Bikini Atoll, infused with strontium-90 and caesium-197, has been uninhabited for the past forty-five years.

Unintentionally, Operation Crossroads highlighted the bizarre conflation of high glamour and hellish destruction. The A-bomb dropped by the B-29 *Dave's Dream* – the same Superfortress, formerly known as *Big Stink*, that had flown Leonard Cheshire and William Penney to Nagasaki the previous August – was called 'Gilda' after the character played by Rita Hayworth in the 1946 film noir of the same name. 'The producers,' noted *Variety*, 'have created nothing subtle in the projection of her s.a [sex appeal].' A raunchy illustration of Hayworth as Gilda adorned the bomb. The underwater bomb exploded in the tests was named 'Helen of Bikini', a play on Helen of Troy, in legend the world's most beautiful woman; the face that, in the playwright Christopher Marlowe's words, 'launched a thousand ships' and began the Trojan War.

Robert Oppenheimer was in no two minds about the Bikini Atoll tests, which he said were a waste of time. The research could have been conducted in a laboratory. Perhaps all thinking Americans could do was laugh. The very title of *Mad* magazine, founded by US publisher William Gaines and editor Harvey Kurtzman in 1952, reflected the craziness of the nuclear age. Although the acronym MAD (Mutual Assured Destruction) would not be coined – by Donald Brennan, a strategist at the Hudson Institute – until ten years later, *Mad* proved as adept at lampooning the neuroses and idiocies of the atomic era and the Cold War as *Private Eye*, launched in October 1961, was to do in Britain.

Children joined in on the fun, too. A 1953 US advertising jingle, 'You'll wonder where the yellow went when you brush your teeth with Pepsodent', was translated in schoolyards as 'You'll wonder where your mouth has gone when you brush your teeth with Atom Bomb'. As we've seen, Britain tested its very own H-bomb, dropped from a Vickers Valiant, over Christmas Island in May 1957. British schoolchildren, most from booming nuclear families, were soon singing:

Ten Little H-bombs hanging from the wall
Ten Little H-bombs hanging from the wall
And if one little H-bomb should accidentally fall
There'll be no little H-bombs and no blooming wall

Playful, and even plain daft, contemporary commercial references to atomic bombs seem – in hindsight – like awkward distractions from the unspeakable horror of nuclear war. These went ballistic after the detonation of the first H-bomb, an 82-ton device the size of a small building, at Enewetak Atoll in the Marshall Islands, on 1 November 1952. The Ferrara Pan Candy Company of Forest Park, Illinois, responded with its Atomic Fireball – 'Burns So Good' – a toothsome kickshaw comprising sugar and 'Less Than 2% of the Following: Modified Food Starch (Corn), Artificial Flavor, Carnauba Wax, Acacia (Gum Arabic), Titanium Dioxide (Color), Red 40 Lake'.

A year after the Cuban Missile Crisis, and under the banner 'Be the Ace of your own Air Corps', Marx Toys offered the Strategic Air Command Play Set – '179 pieces for $9.99' – including an 'Atom Bomber with automatic metal bomb release'. Prop-driven, it resembled a Superfortress. This might be added to a child's collection of earlier Cold War toys like Ideal's 1958 Atomic Cannon. Founded in Brooklyn in 1903 by Morris and Rose Michtom, Ideal's first product was the less threatening Teddy's Bear endorsed by US President Teddy Roosevelt. Business had boomed then with cuddly bears, just as it did half a century on with toy nuclear weapons. 'Get Mum to get your Ideal Atomic Cannon at your nearest toy department.' If she did, this near 4-foot-long device was surely ideal for vaporizing annoying siblings or family pets.

Why Mum? Perhaps Dad was too busy thinking about the next family car. What about the exciting '58 Ford Nucleon? With twin steam turbines powering a uranium fission reactor mounted cautiously some way behind the passenger cabin, the Space Age Nucleon, styled by 24-year-old Jim Powers of Ford's Advanced Design Studio, promised a range of 5,000 miles before the reactor needed replacing – something easily done, said Ford, at local service stations. American Dad could only dream. Like so many other nuclear vehicles of the future, the Nucleon was a chimera. If it had been real, it would have required a thick lead shield set between Mum, Dad, the kids and that uranium fission reactor. As this device would have weighed Ford only knows how many tons, the Nucleon would have needed to be improbably powerful. Powers went on to shape the sleek, long-tailed 1961 Ford Thunderbird, which – though making do with a 390-cubic-inch V8 internal-combustion engine rather than a nuclear reactor – had more than something of the Nucleon about it.

Marx Toys' subsidiary Linemar – its products made under licence in Japan – included a steam-driven Atomic Reactor. British children flocking to the wondrous toy department at Gamages, a much-missed department store on London's Holborn, dreamed of Father Christmas bringing them Marx and Ideal toys from across the Atlantic, although the British selection could be magical, too. During the First World War, Gamages had stocked the Leach Trench Catapult designed to sling a 2-lb bomb from your trench across no man's land into the Huns. Ideal for those challenging occasions when the vicar or appalling relatives came to tea.

Model construction kits of V-bombers were popular in Britain. By 1958, Frog ('Flies right off the ground') had the Valiant, Vulcan and Victor in production in 1:96 scale. Curiously, when Frog went out of business in 1976, moulds for its kits were sold to the Soviet Union. Sales of kit warplanes soared, as did that of Britfix-77 polystyrene cement (*the* glue for kit modellers), together with weekly comics in which warfare, weaponry, warplanes and new technology played leading roles.

British Cold War action-adventure comics, aimed mostly at boys, thrived in the 1950s and '60s. Among them were D. C. Thomson's *Victor*, first published in January 1961, and Fleetway's rival, *Valiant*, making its appearance in, of all months, October 1962. The short-lived IPC Magazines' *Vulcan* was launched in 1975 and merged with *Valiant* the following year. All three V-titles focused on stories – fictional or real – set in the Second World War. None was a patch, editorially or pictorially, on the legendary *Eagle*, an impressive comic published by Hulton Press from April 1950 whose launch issue sold close to a million copies. *Eagle* majored on the future. Its acclaimed front-page and lead strip, *Dan Dare: Pilot of the Future*, set the tone for what was a distinctive, much pored over and influential comic. Dan Dare was originally to have been Lex Christian, a space padre, and while Colonel Dan Dare of Space Fleet proved to have immense sales appeal, his character was Christian through and through, and very unlike the machine-gun-toting, no-hostages-taken daredevil action heroes of *Victor, Valiant* and *Vulcan*. The names of these titles were, of course, linked to the names of the V-Force bombers, which very few boys, or girls, were unaware of.

Each issue of *Eagle* featured a double-page cutaway drawing, mostly in colour, of one fascinating mobile machine or another, some from a near future that never quite came to be. Two-thirds of the 960 cutaways published between 1950 and *Eagle's* demise in 1969 were drawn by Leslie Ashwell Wood, a draughtsman and technical illustrator for Fairey Aviation in the 1930s who had then worked for the Ministry of Information during the Second World War. Atomic vehicles and machines were popular subjects among the latest jet aircraft, rockets, satellites and spaceships. The accuracy of Wood's drawings led to investigations by guardians of the Official Secrets Act. Wood was asked to prove that his cutaway of the English Electric P1B – prototype of the RAF's Mach 2 Lightning interceptor – had not been based on official documents.

Atomic subjects included a submarine, a future aircraft carrier, the Dounreay Nuclear Power Development Establishment on the Caithness coast, and a 4-8-4 railway locomotive powered by a uranium-235 fission reactor supplying superheated steam to turbines – complete with a 'streamlined cab casing on aircraft principles', and a driver and his 'deputy' in smart, peak-capped uniforms. There was even a nuclear-powered steam whistle.

It was hardly surprising that 'spooks' would have been knocking on the door of *Eagle's* editor given that the Cold War was famously an era rampant with spies. While spies have long existed, there was something about the Cold War, with its numerous new and often experimental weapons and the ever-present threat of global destruction, that made the world of international espionage perilously exciting. Glamorous and well-dressed, too, if only in fiction. There was, of course, James Bond with his black-tie dress code, shaken-not-stirred dry martinis and even drier wit, svelte Aston Martins and gorgeous young women. The first Bond film, *Dr No*, premiered at the London Pavilion on 5 October 1962. Good timing. The bikini featured, too – and sensationally so – with Honey Ryder, played by Ursula Andress, stepping from the sea onto a beach in Jamaica like a modern Botticelli's Venus. Bikini sales soared.

From the time of *Dr No*, spy films were reeled out at a rapid rate on both sides of the Atlantic. Off the top of my head, I can think of *The Manchurian Candidate* (1962), *The Ipcress File* (1965), *The Spy Who Came in from the Cold* (1965), *The Quiller Memorandum* (1966), *Funeral in Berlin* (1966), that year's Pop spoof thriller *Modesty Blaise*, and *Ice Station Zebra* (1968)... films based on novels by writers who were or soon would be household names, among them Ian Fleming, Len Deighton, John le Carré and Alistair MacLean.

Spy shows made their way onto the small screen: *Danger Man* (1960–68), *The Avengers* (1961–69), *The Man from U.N.C.L.E.* (1964–68), *Mission: Impossible* (1966–73), *The Prisoner*

(1967–68). Whether earnest like *Danger Man*, witty like *The Avengers* or philosophical and surreal like Patrick McGoohan's *The Prisoner*, and whether or not the Soviets played a role in them, they commanded large audiences and developed cult followings. Like Tu-16s and B-52s, they continued to perform long after the Cold War appeared to thaw.

Films and TV shows revolving around nuclear Armageddon or alien invasions and infestations (for which read the Soviet threat, or Red Menace in general) were popular, too. On the big screen, these ranged from *The Day the Earth Stood Still* (1951) – directed by Robert Wise, best known perhaps for *West Side Story* (1961) and *The Sound of Music* (1965) – to Stanley Kubrick's *2001: A Space Odyssey* (1968). Both of these films concern human destiny. In Wise's, an alien arrives in Washington DC to warn humans that their new-found destructive powers are being monitored from outer space and that they must learn to live peacefully. The alien's task proves difficult. In *2001*, humankind is drawn slowly to a wholly new condition of life beyond machines, to something altogether incorporeal. The final enigmatic scene shows what was an American scientist-astronaut, transformed by some higher intelligence into a newly born 'Star Child' gazing lovingly at the Earth. In Arthur C. Clarke's novelization *2001: A Space Odyssey*, written concurrently with the production of Kubrick's film and published soon after its release, we learn that the first thing the Star Child does is to detonate an orbiting nuclear warhead to protect the planet, and presumably the lives of those living on it.

Quintessentially British films of the era included *Seven Days to Noon* (1950) and *The Day the Earth Caught Fire* (1961). The former, made by the Boulting brothers, concerns a British scientist who steals a powerful yet small atomic bomb – he carries it in a Gladstone bag – and threatens to blow up central London unless the government assures him it will put an end to the production of nuclear weapons. The latter features a *Daily Express* journalist investigating the story of how US and Soviet nuclear bomb tests have tilted the Earth to the extent that not only are cities threatened with destruction, but the planet is also spinning ever closer towards the sun. Will a plan to explode further bombs in Siberia rebalance the imperilled Earth? The final scene displays alternative covers of the *Express*: 'Earth Saved'; 'Earth Doomed'. How could Fleet Street know? This was a brave and original film that its director, Val Guest, found hard to place. Finally, he put up profits from his 1959 hit *Expresso Bongo* (starring a nineteen-year-old Cliff Richard) as collateral, and British Lion took the bait. The film was an unusual one for Guest. He had made his name as a director of light comedies. Old habits were to die hard. Among his later films were *Au Pair Girls* (1972) and *Confessions of a Window Cleaner* (1974). The fear of nuclear devastation, however, was hardwired in the public consciousness, and evidently even a director of lightweight films felt a burning need to explore it.

Meanwhile, on the distant fictional planet Skaro, a thousand-year war between two races, the Thals and the Kaleds, had at some point involved the use of nuclear weapons.

Surviving Kaleds were genetically modified into compassionless squid-like creatures housed in robotic shells, with a mission to exterminate other races at will. These were the Daleks, science-fiction characters who grabbed the imagination of a generation – and beyond – of British children through the long-running BBC TV series *Doctor Who*. Beginning in 1963, viewing figures for *Doctor Who*, normally in the range of 6–9 million, rose whenever the Daleks appeared. In primary school playgrounds up and down the country, energized by small bottles of free milk, boys – mostly – fought countless Thals-vs-Daleks playtime battles as girls skipped, hula-hooped and ignored them.

Despite nuclear war references, the Daleks were more Nazi than Soviet-like. In Britain, the experience of the Second World War remained fresh in the collective memory. That had been a total war – in one way or another, pretty much everyone had served in it. In popular culture, the Nazis remained public enemy number one, and the war against Germany was refought relentlessly in comics, books, films, TV series and those same school playgrounds. The Daleks added a new twist.

But what to do if there was a real nuclear war, with V-Force bombers straining at the leash, missiles streaking towards Britain and air-raid sirens wailing? Run from the playground to your classroom. Hide behind the sofa at home. Pedal to the library and back as fast as you could to pick up an informative leaflet on how to survive a nuclear attack. Find a local authority bunker. Tape up the windows. Pull the curtains, and make sure you go to the lavatory before the Soviet missiles hit home.

Going to the lavatory was a serious issue. In the event of a nuclear attack, HM Government advised, it was important to stay indoors at all times. Should you not be killed immediately, atomic radiation would be lurking outside your home. And it would kill you. The 1961 Census, however, revealed that in old British industrial cities many homes lacked indoor lavatories. The figure for Sheffield was one in five. In rural areas, especially in Norfolk, Suffolk and central Wales, as many as half of all homes lacked inside lavatories, and this at a time when sophisticated V-bombers were flying from East Anglian bases to drop H-bombs on Soviet targets. Still, in comparison the all but non-existent sanitary arrangements in V-bombers were primeval.

In theory, a much-vaunted official four-minute warning system would get the population of 1960s Britain to safe places, home or otherwise. If and when early warning stations – principally RAF Fylingdales, operational from 1963, with its eye-catching golf-ball radomes set on a crest of the North Yorkshire Moors – picked up Soviet IRBMs and ICBMs, microwave messages would be relayed to the UK Warning and Monitoring Organisation HQ at RAF Booker near High Wycombe, where the comic airfield scenes of *Those Magnificent Men in Their Flying Machines* (1965) were filmed. The BBC would be alerted, and air-raid sirens would sound their unsettling waxing and waning wail. Most of these had been manufactured, from 1938, by Gents of Leicester, for service in the Second World War. While audible in towns, suburbs and cities, there were extensive patches of rural Britain where church bells or trained cockerels would have been more effective. The government's policy was for local postmasters, police officers, parish priests, publicans, magistrates and other responsible private citizens to operate hand-powered sirens. Whistles and rattles might also be used. And all this flurry of activity executed in just four minutes max.

Politicians, civil servants and assorted royals and VIPs would be sped to top-secret concrete shelters, whether beneath central or suburban London or rural Wiltshire. How they would do this within four minutes remains a mystery. The truth is that, should Britain have come under nuclear attack, there would have been precious little hope for the vast majority of people. No amount of sticky-back plastic, blackout curtains, upturned tables or DIY concrete bunkers would have kept citizens safe. And for those seemingly lucky enough to scramble into the depths of a VIP bunker, it would have been a very long time – who could know how many years – before it was safe to climb back up to the surface in the hope of breathing uncontaminated air. And then what?

The apparatus of the four-minute warning system was dismantled from 1991, at the end of the Cold War. Air-raid sirens had gone by 1993, although examples remain in use to warn of floods and escapes from Broadmoor, the high-security Berkshire psychiatric hospital. The Cold War also left a legacy of buildings and structures other than bunkers, including radar stations, nuclear bomb stores, missile launch sites, and various forms of listening devices and relay stations. Most of these were ruggedly functional, yet occasionally they exhibited an elemental beauty that enhanced rather than detracted from local landscapes. One such was the 1,443-foot-diameter antenna array at RAF Chicksands, an intelligence-gathering base subleased to the USAF from 1950 to 1995. Looking, for all the world, like some futuristic or alien interpretation of Stonehenge, this listening device was built from components – Douglas fir frames, steel lattices, steel antennae – shipped from the States and re-erected in concentric rings around a small central circular control hut in rural Bedfordshire.

One of eight identical antenna arrays erected in Alaska, England, Germany, Italy, Japan, Philippines, Thailand and Turkey, each with a high-frequency signal range of 4,000 nanometres, Chicksands was an integral part of a global intelligence-gathering system. Superseded technologically by solid state phased array radar systems, it was dismantled in 1996. The architectural virtues of the design were not wholly overlooked, however. The redundant Philippines antenna was converted into a 35,000-seat fabric-covered auditorium for the 1998 Expo Pilipino.

The link is not explicit, yet the Brutalist architecture of the 1960s and '70s – witnessed in the design of British shopping malls, churches, multistorey car parks, high-rise housing, theatres and art galleries – had much in common with the design of Cold War structures. On a purely aesthetic level, both appeared to have been inspired by the Atlantic Wall defences built in Normandy between 1942 and 1944 by the

German Organisation Todt. But while there is more than a grain of truth in this, Britain's Cold War military architecture was mostly an example of practical materials used in unassuming and matter-of-fact fashion, while civil Brutalism was a period style amid an explosion of Pop design, art, fashion, social attitudes and architecture resounding to a backbeat of pop and rock music.

In post-war Britain, planners and politicians helped to destroy venerable areas of London more effectively than the Luftwaffe had been able to. This wanton destruction of historic architecture in the 1950s and '60s encouraged protest. When, from December 1961, the Greek Revival–style Euston Arch in London was demolished for no good reason, the architectural conservation lobby grew in strength and righteous anger. How dare the prime minister, Harold Macmillan, have approved this blatant act of contemporary barbarism. This, after all, was the very same Harold Macmillan who had spent much of an entire day as a young army officer reading Aeschylus in ancient Greek, while badly wounded and waiting to be rescued from a slit trench during the Battle of the Somme.

Of course, the 'bomb' was a much greater threat altogether. And there were those that believed it should be stopped. No ifs and buts. Ban the Bomb. The first gathering of the Campaign for Nuclear Disarmament (CND) took place in November 1957, a month after a disturbing accident at the Windscale atomic energy plant near Seascale, on the Cumberland coast. The plant's purpose was to provide material for Britain's nuclear bombs. From 10 October, a fire at one of the reactors

Easter 1962 Aldermaston march poster designed by Ken Garland

burned for three days. Leakage of radiation spread across Britain and Europe. Reports were censored. Harold Macmillan was concerned that the incident would harm UK–US nuclear relations.

The first CND march, a four-day slog from London to the Atomic Weapons Research Establishment at Aldermaston, Berkshire, 52 miles away, took place over the 1958 Easter weekend. Marchers sported CND's newly adopted symbol, designed the previous year by Gerald Holtom. A crowd of 8,000 gathered at Trafalgar Square – the future left-wing politician Tony Benn, champion of Concorde, and Michael Foot, editor of the socialist *Tribune* newspaper and later leader of the Labour Party, among them – thinned out over a duffle-coat march made in the coldest, wettest, slushiest Easter weather in decades. The majority of the demonstrators rallied, one way or another, at Aldermaston on the final day. The organizers originally wanted the march to be made in monastic silence. Had they ever marched before? Marchers certainly did sing. Accompanied by skiffle and jazz bands, choirs and protest singers, they belted out 'We Shall Overcome' and 'The H-Bomb's Thunder'. And, they chanted, 'Oh no no, not in my name.'

The CND had insisted that if there was to be singing, then a song list must be approved. It had its reasons. Colin Irwin, writing in the *Observer* in 2008, recalled that 'the most forceful voice... belonged to Ewan MacColl... By the 1950s, he was writing numbers such as "The Ballad of Ho Chi Minh" and "The Ballad of Stalin".' Already a key figure in the burgeoning folk music movement with his Ballad & Blues club at the Princess Louise pub in Holborn, MacColl 'wrote characteristically volatile songs about the threat to peace, notably "Against the Atom Bomb"... Certain songs were banned, not necessarily because of their content, but because they were sung by communist sympathisers like Pete Seeger. Among those subject to embargo... were "Down By the Riverside" and "If I Had a Hammer".'

Fifteen thousand protestors marched in the opposite direction the following year – headed by Jacquetta Hawkes, wife of J. B. Priestley, the omnipresent novelist, playwright, screenwriter, broadcaster, social commentator and founding CND committee member. According to Irwin, Hawkes 'presented a Ban the Bomb charter at 10 Downing Street wearing a crimson stetson and yellow ankle socks as protesters filed silently through Whitehall accompanied only by the beat of a single drum, spelling in Morse code the letters N and D – nuclear disarmament'.

In 1960, it was estimated that 100,000 gathered at the climax in Trafalgar Square. 'In songwriting terms,' recalled Irwin, 'Aberdonian Ian Campbell raised the bar with his shockingly vivid "The Sun is Burning in the Sky", which became a new Aldermaston anthem and was later recorded by Simon & Garfunkel.'

'For many of us of that period and generation,' Michael Foot was to recollect, 'it was CND that best expressed the response which the human race must make to the bomb: the moral outrage that such an instrument should ever have been invented, the awareness that a new kind of politics would be needed to bring it under control, the determination to act together at once, whatever the cynics or sceptics might say.' He described the first Aldermaston march as 'bigger than any of us had expected, with so many people from all generations, from all walks of life and from all over the country showing the strength of feeling about the horrors of nuclear war'. The Aldermaston marches marched on until 1965.

Whatever governments, the military and nuclear establishments thought of it, CND was not to be dismissed. Its president was Sir Bertrand Russell, the renowned philosopher, its chairman John Collins, Anglican priest and former Second World War RAF chaplain, and its general secretary the noted campaigner Peggy Duff. At the time of the first three marches, the three main parties at Westminster were officially in favour of an independent nuclear deterrent. This was, as Winston Churchill had said in 1954 when his Conservative government approved the British H-bomb, 'the price we pay to sit at the top table'. Addressing the House of Commons the previous year, Churchill had spoken of how if 'the advance of destructive weapons enables everyone to kill everybody else, nobody will want to kill anyone at all'.

When left-wing members of the Labour opposition called for unilateral disarmament at the party's Brighton conference in October 1957, Nye Bevan, the avowedly socialist shadow foreign minister, reprimanded them in no uncertain terms:

> I know that you are deeply convinced that the action you suggest is the most effective way of influencing international affairs. I am deeply convinced that you are wrong. It is therefore not a question of who is in favour of the hydrogen bomb, but a question of what is the most effective way of getting the damn thing destroyed. It is the most difficult of all problems facing mankind. But if you carry this resolution and follow out all its implications and do not run away from it you will send a Foreign Secretary, whoever he may be, naked into the conference chamber... You call that statesmanship? I call it an emotional spasm.

In the media, the *Manchester Guardian* supported an independent British deterrent but thought this should be borne by missiles rather than the V-bombers currently in production. The *Economist* supported deterrence but believed the US should foot the bill, as did the *New Statesman*, the magazine founded by Beatrice and Sidney Webb and George Bernard Shaw and edited for thirty years by Kingsley Martin, Stalin's 'willing fools' all four. In 1932, the Webbs had enjoyed a too, too marvellous official tour of the Soviet Union, either wholly ignorant of or simply willing to dismiss Stalin's mass shooting and then starvation of millions of Ukrainian kulak farmers and their families. *Manchester Guardian* journalist Malcolm Muggeridge – whose wife Kitty happened to be the daughter of Beatrice's youngest sister, Rosalind – was in the Soviet Union at the same time as the Webbs. Making his own way through the country as best he could, he reported honestly on the horror unfolding in Ukraine, describing it as 'the most terrible thing I have ever seen'.

In her diary, Beatrice Webb noted 'Malcolm's curiously hysterical denunciation of the USSR and all its works'. She had gone to see the Soviet ambassador Ivan Maisky about it, 'and I realize that he's [Muggeridge] got it absolutely wrong'. In his now famous diary, 'Chips' Channon, the US-born Conservative MP, described the well-connected and convivial Maisky as the 'ambassador of torture, murder and every crime in the calendar'. On Muggeridge's last visit to Beatrice – she died in 1943 – she showed him a portrait of Lenin set up 'as though it were a Velázquez, with special lighting coming from below'. In the 2020s, left-wing Labour politicians could still be seen sporting Lenin-style 'worker' caps in honour of their murderous Rolls-Royce–owning hero. With this strange history in mind, it is not too hard to understand why a sizeable number of left-wing Labour MPs were in favour of unilateral nuclear disarmament at the time of those first CND marches. Nuclear weapons were best left in the hands of the Soviet Union and the United States.

The general election held in October 1964, the year V-Force was at its strongest in terms of the number of bombers in service, witnessed the Conservatives, now led by Sir Alec Douglas-Home, campaigning on behalf of both the British deterrent and a limited nuclear test ban. While CND was unable to ground V-Force, it did have some effect on government thinking in both Britain and around the world. If it was impossible to ban the bomb altogether, at least the sheer number of nuclear weapons could be reduced and international treaties signed to this effect. In the name of self-preservation, politicians on either side of the Iron Curtain were well aware of the madness of ever-increasing stockpiles of nuclear bombs, yet fear that the enemy might strike first whatever the cost kept 'the bomb' in dark play. In Britain, the Labour opposition, with Harold Wilson at the helm, sniped at the 'Tory nuclear pretence' – neither truly independent nor effective, he said – while Wilson positioned himself as a champion of domestic issues. An economic downturn in 1960–61 had not helped Douglas-Home's prospects at the ballot box, and Labour won the election with a majority of four seats. It is fascinating to see how concerns for national security and worries about the bomb were in balance with the siren call of consumerism and, not unnaturally, fears for the state of the economy. And it had been even more fascinating – positively titillating – for the British public to follow a sexual scandal that helped bring the Conservatives down.

From July 1961, John Profumo, Secretary of State for War, had conducted an extramarital affair with nineteen-year-old model Christine Keeler, who was also sleeping with Captain Yevgeny Ivanov, a Soviet naval attaché and spy. What might pillow talk have revealed? Had Profumo's affair been a security risk? Possibly not, yet the scandal made the government look ridiculous at the height of the Cold War.

From November 1962 to December 1963, and with a regular audience of 12 million, the BBC's Saturday-night *That Was the Week That Was*, devised by Ned Sherrin and presented by David Frost, lampooned the Tories (mostly), and justifiably so. Scriptwriters including John Cleese, Peter Cook, Graham Chapman, John Betjeman and Richard Ingrams, editor of *Private Eye*, had a field day, too. In New York, a comedy satire highlighting the Profumo affair, *Fool Britannia*, was recorded live late at night on 6 August 1963. Devised and written by actor and songwriter Anthony Newley and composer and lyricist Leslie Bricusse, it was performed by, among others, Joan Collins and Peter Sellers, who also worked that year on *Dr Strangelove* with Stanley Kubrick.

For well-informed consumers of satire, the government was also made to look foolish late in 1962 with the US cancellation of the Skybolt missile programme, leaving Britain, or so it appeared, without a credible nuclear deterrent and threatening the purpose and future of V-Force. The House of Commons was in uproar. So many British military projects had been cancelled in favour of the American Skybolt. Such was the 'special relationship' between Britain and the United States.

While the issue was resolved in terms of national and global security with the Nassau Agreement made between Harold Macmillan and President Kennedy in December 1962, Britain came out of the agreement very much as the junior partner. And that was the year that was a tightrope walk, or so it seemed, between life and death on an unimaginable scale – and also between government expenditure on hugely costly weapons of nuclear war and consumer expenditure on new comforts and delights: winklepicker shoes; Dick Francis's first novel, *Dead Cert*; the Ford Cortina, styled by the Canadian-American Roy Brown and complete with 'Ban the Bomb' tail lights; the first flavoured crisps, Golden Wonder Cheese and Onion; and *Z-Cars* on TV. Smog in December reduced visibility in central London to next to zero, resulting in children walking to school tied to one another by scarves. A stench of sulphur, and something like 700 deaths. Life went on.

SEVEN

Swords Into Ploughshares

Could bombers make good airliners? This question arose early in the development of V-Force. While the Second World War had been good for business, Britain's leading aircraft manufacturers knew that they would need to stretch their wings in a new era when orders for military aircraft would fall. New jet bombers and fighters were in demand, but their numbers would never be remotely as high as they had been, for example, with the Avro Lancaster. Between 1942 and 1946, beginning with an initial order of 1,070, Avro built 7,337 Lancasters. Between 1956 and 1965, the company would produce 134 Vulcans. Would it have made commercial sense for Avro, Vickers and Handley Page to have developed and manufactured civil versions of their V-bombers? To answer this complex question, we might begin by imagining a June morning in 1965 at London Airport, and let the story unfold from there...

The Queens Building, designed by Frederick Gibberd, architect of Harlow New Town, and opened by Her Majesty in 1955, embraces the public at ten o'clock. With its runway viewing

187

...*an aircraft of outstanding importance*

VICKERS 1000

FOUR ROLLS-ROYCE CONWAY BY-PASS JET ENGINES

VICKERS-ARMSTRONGS (Aircraft) LIMITED · WEYBRIDGE · SURREY

Advert for proposed Valiant-derived Vickers 1000
RAF support aircraft

platforms and roof garden, the Queens Building is a magnet for plane spotters, passengers with time on their hands, parties of visiting schoolchildren and those who simply enjoy watching so many different types of aircraft landing, taxiing and taking off. Heathrow will be abuzz today with short- and medium-haul turboprop Viscounts, Vanguards, Argosys and Friendships, as well as turbojet airliners, among them Pan Am Boeing 707s, Air Canada Douglas DC-8s, BEA Hawker Siddeley Tridents, BOAC Vickers VC10s and Aeroflot's Tupolev Tu-104. The Tupolev, which first flew into London in March 1956, is derived from the Soviet Tu-16 strategic bomber – or at least its wings, engines and tail surfaces are, as is its distinctive glazed 'bomb aimer's' nose.

You hold that thought in mind as, with permission for an early morning visit to the Queens Building viewing platforms, you catch sight of the arrival of a transatlantic flight. No one with the remotest interest in aviation can fail to recognize the profile of the BOAC airliner coming down to land. That delta wing gives the game away. It is, of course, one of the charismatic Avro Atlantics. Across the Atlantic in five hours.

The Atlantic spools to a stop, resplendent in the latest BOAC colours, introduced this year. Deep navy blue, white and silver-grey, bold gold lettering and a gold Speedbird on its wingless fin. That Speedbird is the oldest aspect of this futuristic airliner. The striking motif was created more than thirty years ago by the English artist (David) Theyre Lee-Elliott for Imperial Airways. Lee-Elliott had been inspired by Edward McKnight Kauffer's 'Soaring to Success . . . the Early Bird' poster designed for the launch of the *Daily Herald*, which first went to press in March 1919. This in turn was adapted from a Vorticist-style woodcut of 'speedbirds' the American graphic artist had made in 1917 – after, he said, watching birds flocking over a Berkshire cottage he had stayed in soon after his arrival in Britain from New York.

Groomed passengers step down from the Avro Atlantic, having enjoyed the benefit of its generous dressing rooms. Their journey has been swift and stylish. We can only daydream today. Of course, the Avro Type 722 Atlantic, a civil airliner version of the Vulcan bomber, was never actually built. It made it only as far as the designers' drawing boards, enticing 1:24 see-through scale models and detailed cutaway drawings in *Popular Mechanics*. These showed the Vulcan remodelled as an airliner seating between 76 ('Luxury') and 113 ('Tourist') passengers. In military fashion, the seats faced rearwards. Exhausts from the four Bristol Olympus or Rolls-Royce Avon engines were behind the cabin. The Avro airliner promised a quiet and smooth flight. There was a cocktail 'lounge' bar at the front of the aircraft and, beyond that, a spacious cockpit accommodating a crew of five. Drawings from 1953 show the 'engineering officer' sat on a swivel-chair at a full-scale desk. Cruising at 600 mph at 40,000 feet, the Type 722 was to have entered transatlantic service with BOAC in 1958, the year that what was to be the all-conquering Boeing 707 made its debut with Pan Am.

Avro worked hard on the Atlantic. In 1955, a revised concept showed the airliner fitted with the more efficient kinked delta wing of the Vulcan B.1. One of my favourite impressions of

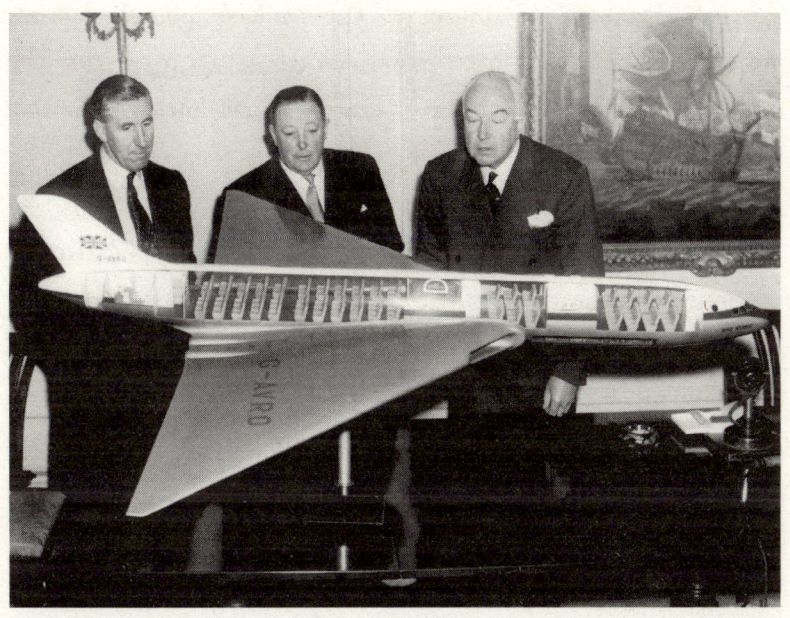

Model of Avro Atlantic shown to press (Stuart Davies, right),
June 1953

what would surely have been a thrilling aircraft to have flown on is from the *Jeff Hawke* comic strip, drawn by Sydney Jordan for the *Daily Express* between 1954 and 1974. Jordan had trained for a spell as an aero engineer with Miles Aircraft. In a 1955 strip, 'The Threat to the Past', Jordan depicted an Avro Atlantic shooting through the night as Wing Commander Jeff Hawke hurries from London to New York on some world-saving mission. How one longs to have been on such a flight.

Jeff Hawke was encouraged and promoted by Max Aitken DFC, DSO, son of Lord Beaverbrook, the press magnate and Winston Churchill's indefatigable wartime Minister of

Aircraft Production. Rising to the rank of group captain, Aitken had been a high-scoring RAF ace who fought from the cockpits of Bristol Blenheims, Hawker Hurricanes and Bristol Beaufighters. He would have relished the idea of flying the Atlantic on board a delta-wing Avro...

The need for Britain's competing and cash-strapped aircraft companies to succeed in the civil market now that wartime contracts had ceased mirrored the situation they had found themselves in in the aftermath of the First World War. In 1919, for example, Vickers had only recently invested in its Vimy heavy biplane bomber. Although this did go on to serve with the RAF throughout the 1920s, the company needed an insurance policy. The one it created for itself was in the guise of the FB.27 Vimy Commercial, first flown in April 1919. With a spruce plywood cabin providing ten wicker armchairs, it had a service ceiling of 7,000 feet and a top speed of 100 mph.

Like Concorde, the bulkhead of the passenger cabin boasted an altimeter and speed indicator. Unlike Concorde, which was 1,250 mph faster, the crew of the Vimy sat in an open cockpit, battling the elements on such demanding routes as London to Cairo and Cape Town. Designed by Rex Pierson, son of a Norfolk rector – to whom we owe both the Wellington bomber, with its Barnes Wallis geodesic fuselage, and the post-war Viscount turboprop airliner – the Vimy Commercial was of a very different era indeed from that of the streamlined airliners operating within just fifteen years of its maiden flight.

On 12 January 1931, an FB.27 flown by night from the Vickers factory at Brooklands, Surrey, with the aim of reaching Digby, Lincolnshire, crashed into a ploughed field at Westwoodside, South Yorkshire. The Vimy upended on its nose. Three of the four-man crew led by Flight Lieutenant Geoffrey Shaw were killed. The survivor, Aircraftman Cecil Jones, told the inquest into the accident that the crew had lost its way. They had dropped low in bad light to try to read the name of a railway station, and then, attempting a landing in what they took for a green field, had hit a ridge-like sillion. Reading the name of a railway station! How close to the ground were they flying? It was fortunate, perhaps, that this was a flight made by the RAF with no fare-paying passengers on board.

Frederick Handley Page did, however, pack a party of forty passengers – mostly journalists – into the fuselage of one of his massive four-engine V/1500 bombers designed by George Volkhert to bomb Berlin from East Anglia. The occasion was Handley Page's thirty-third birthday. The V/1500 predated the Atlantic-conquering Vimy by a year and was pretty much twice its size. Volkhert went on to design the Halifax, the first of the RAF's three heavy four-engine Second World War bombers.

From 1945, both the Halifax and the Avro Lancaster were made available as civil airliners. These were the Halton and the Lancastrian. Cramped, they offered few seats and virtually nothing in the way of creature comforts. Only the hardiest flyer would have relished a trip from London to Buenos Aires on board a Lancastrian. This, though, was the route of British South American Airways, whose Lancastrian *Star Light* was the first commercial aircraft to depart the new London Airport, on 1 January 1946. The journey might have been uncomfortable, but at least there was little chance of getting lost or of the crew trying to read the names of Argentinian railway stations. The Lancastrian's captain was 35-year-old retired Air Vice Marshal Don Bennett DSO, who had led the RAF's Pathfinder Force with great daring and success between 1942 and 1945.

There was at least one example of a 1930s airliner being converted into a Second World War bomber. This was the elegant 26-seat Focke-Wulf Fw 200 Condor designed by Ludwig Mittlehuber for transatlantic crossings, operated by Deutsche Lufthansa and in production from 1937 to 1944. But while the Condor was a capacious bomber, the Handley Page Victor V-bomber was not an ideal model for a spacious airliner. Like Avro, however, Handley Page responded to the Ministry of Supply's October 1952 Air Specification C.132D for a 'long-range jet transport'. This included both airliners and a transport aircraft for the RAF that, in the first instance, would offer a complete back-up service to V-bombers dispatched overseas.

Handley Page's HP.97 design for an airliner was essentially that of a Victor fitted with a double bubble fuselage. This was to allow space for between 96 ('Luxury') and 150 ('Tourist') passengers accommodated on an upper deck. The lower deck, reached by a central spiral stair, offered a cocktail 'lounge' bar, storage for hats and coats, ladies' and gents' dressing rooms, lavatories and a baggage compartment.

An artist's impression of the proposed Victor-based HP.111
RAF support aircraft

Despite those remarkable crescent wings, that high tailplane and those well-concealed engines, the HP.97 lacked the design charisma of either the Victor bomber itself or Avro's Atlantic. The double bubble fuselage gave it a slightly dumpy and unre-solved appearance. Should it have been built, however, it would have offered fast, comfortable and exciting long-distance flight. This might have been the Aston Martin of passenger flight, as opposed to the cushioned Chryslers of Boeing and Douglas. A see-through scale model of the HP.97 was on show at the 1952 Farnborough Air Show. Given that the Victor had proved capable of breaking the sound barrier, might the HP.97 have been the world's first supersonic airliner?

Handley Page continued to have hopes for the project after the cancellation in November 1955 of the Vickers V1000, a military transport version of the Valiant, and soon afterwards that of the V7 airliner derivative. With these aircraft out of the running. could Handley Page make it back in with a slightly larger version of the HP.97, especially now that BOAC had been given the go-ahead to order an unspecified new British airliner along with fifteen Boeing 707s? Given a choice, BOAC would have preferred to buy more Boeings. Government restrictions on foreign currency purchases, however, forced the airline to look to British manufacturers.

In 1957, Handley Page proffered what had now become the Civil Victor, also known as the Commonwealth. Bigger than the HP.97, the double-bubble Civil featured a pair of spiral stairs, and dressing rooms and lavatories on both decks. A galley on the lower deck was linked by a lift to an upstairs service counter. The *Eagle* published a cutaway drawing in its 26 July issue.

After Vickers won the battle for the next big British jet airliner with its VC10, Handley Page cracked on with a third version of its commercial Victor. This was the wide-bodied HP.111, a proposal from 1958 intended as a multi-role trans-porter suitable for both civil and military aviation. The RAF was impressed, yet the HP.111 was rejected by the Air Ministry – George Ward, a wartime RAF group captain, was Secretary of the State for Air at the time – because, in accordance with government policy, it could only work with either one of the two newly consolidated major manufacturing companies,

Hawker Siddeley and BAC. Sir Frederick Handley Page, who had set up his aviation business in 1909, refused steadfastly to join either. He wished his company to remain independent.

This was a sorry affair, as not only did the RAF not get the jet transporter it wanted – it got what became the decent but much slower turboprop Short Belfast instead – but also Handley Page was nudged towards liquidation. Disquietingly for Handley Page, Short Brothers was not a part of either BAC or Hawker Siddeley. Northern Ireland, though, needed an economic boost, and with the 1959 general election looming – an increased majority for the Conservatives as it turned out – it must have seemed a wise idea to award Shorts the contract.

The mergers in the aviation manufacturing sector were part and parcel of the Macmillan government's 1957 Defence White Paper, 'Outline of Future Policy', drawn up in 1957 by the defence minister Duncan Sandys. This aimed to trim £100 million from Britain's defence budget. Among its controversial proposals was for Bloodhound ground-to-air missiles in place of new RAF jet interceptors, leading to the cancellation of several promising designs (notably the Avro 730 and the Fairey Delta 3 long-range interceptors), the loss of 70,000 skilled jobs, and the expansion of Hawker Siddeley (comprising Hawker, Gloster, Avro, Folland, Blackburn and de Havilland) and BAC (English Electric, Vickers-Armstrongs, Bristol and Hunting). Handley Page shut up shop in 1970, but not before its design team had come up with several intriguing proposals, among them the futuristic blended-wing HP.134

'Aerobus' of 1965 and both civil and military versions of the evolving all-wing HP.117.

The all-wing, or 'flying wing', concept has been a darling of aero-engineers and aviation enthusiasts since the 1920s. While never taken up in other than very small numbers, Northrop Grumman is at work as of 2025 on the B-21 Raider, a flying-wing stealth bomber that may well replace all three US long-range bombers – the Northrop Grumman B-2 (also a flying-wing), the swing-wing Rockwell B-1 Lancer and the long-lived Boeing B-52.

Of the three V-Force bombers aiming to cross the divide into the civil aviation market, only one – the Valiant – almost succeeded. When its airliner derivative, the VC7, was cancelled, Sir George Edwards, Vickers-Armstrongs's MD, said, 'We have handed to the Americans, without a struggle, the entire world market for big jet airliners.' To an extent, this was true. While the cancellation of the VC7 led to BOAC buying Boeing 707s, it also encouraged the development of the gracious VC10 – a fast, powerful airliner equally at home flying the Atlantic, taking off with aplomb into thin air from the high-set airports of East Africa, or serving with the RAF as a transporter and air-to-air tanker.

Vickers had been very keen on the jet transporter-airliner idea. Both the RAF and BOAC appeared to want it to succeed. The similar designs for the military V1000 and civil VC7 did, however, mean a major reworking of the Valiant itself. A nicely rendered artist's impression of the V1000 commissioned for a 1955 promotional advert in *Flight International* depicts a much leaner machine than the Valiant. It has the Valiant's wing and engine arrangement, but the wing is lower and the nose and fuselage are more like those of the de Havilland Comet. It was certainly a good-looking aircraft.

An earlier proposal for a VC5 airliner – a stretched Valiant complete with shoulder-mounted wing – was less convincing. The wing position spelled rows of seats without windows. True, in the 2020s, many passengers pull window blinds down completely in daytime, immediately after the captain switches off the seatbelt warning lights, presumably to keep glare from their sacred digital screens – and, it is hard not to feel, in a selfish ploy to annoy fellow passengers. Yet, once upon a time, and certainly in the 1950s and '60s, passengers enjoyed the daylight – the blinds used as and when appropriate, to deflect or cut out glare – as well as the views of cloudscapes, mountain peaks, coasts, the changing colours of landscapes, the contrails of passing aircraft, and the meandering paths of great rivers far below them.

The V1000 was given the green light in June 1954, but cancelled the following year. Costs were rising fast, while the design was gaining weight with the need for a more powerful version of the new Rolls-Royce Conway turbofan jet engine. Rather gallingly – for Vickers if not for Rolls-Royce – the first 707s flew into London powered by the uprated Conway they had wanted for the V1000. Both Boeing and Douglas, meanwhile, had taken a long and hard look at the VC7 before finalizing the designs of what proved to be the immensely successful 707 and DC-8.

Several arguments were put forward in favour of cancelling the VC7, none of which was particularly convincing. Some at BOAC said the upgraded Rolls-Royce Conway would be unhappy installed in the VC7's wing, although they proved to be quite content when installed in the wings of Victor B.2s. If the VC7 had gone into production, BOAC would have needed this one type of airliner alone rather than both the 707 and the later VC10. The Boeing, a transatlantic cruiser, was unsuitable for the airline's Commonwealth routes, especially with its high-altitude airports. Eventually, it was possible to get 707s and DC-8s into the airports along these routes and, with its advantage challenged, sales of the VC10 fell. Just 54 VC10s were built between 1962 and 1970, compared with 865 Boeing 707s (1956–78) and 556 Douglas DC-8s (1958–67). A stretched transatlantic VC10 – the Super VC10 – had entered subsonic service with BOAC in April 1965; and that July, BAC announced a 'Super Super' double-decker version of the airliner seating up to 265 passengers. But with the Boeing 747 'Jumbo Jet', first flown in 1969, on the cards, the scheme was dropped.

A heated parliamentary debate followed the cancellation of the VC7. In the House of Commons, George Brown, deputy leader of the Labour Party, asked, 'Does not this decision mean that the American companies, the Douglas and the Boeing, will, in effect, be so far ahead of us in the next development of the pure jet that we shall have 10 or 20 years to make up at some stage afterwards?' Outside parliament, Sir Cyril Musgrave, permanent secretary of the Ministry of Aviation at the time, recalled saying, 'All the major airlines were buying the 707 or the DC-8 and there was no point in developing another subsonic plane. We felt we had to go above the speed of sound or leave it.' Concorde was on the drawing board, and in years to come, Sir George Edwards would lead the British side of the project.

Going back to our imagined scene at London Airport in June 1965, it would have been exciting to watch BOAC VC7s and VC10s in action together alongside the occasional Avro Atlantic, Handley Page Commonwealth and, of course, those flocks of Boeing 707s and Douglas DC-8s – with infiltrations of Soviet and Hungarian Tupolev Tu-104s, French and Finnish Caravelles, Comet 4Bs and 4Cs, Ilyushins, Tridents, a DC-6, a DC-7, a British Eagle Britannia, and a speedy four-engine Convair 990 Coronado in cleanly graphic Swissair colours.

One highly impressive airliner developed from a bomber was a very rare sight indeed at London Airport. This was the Tupolev Tu-114 operated by Aeroflot. The world's largest and fastest passenger airliner when new in 1957, the Tu-114 also boasted the longest range – 10,900 kilometres. It was, too, perhaps the most beautiful of all subsonic airliners. From 1962 to 1976, the Tu-114 flew long-distance routes, among them Moscow to Paris, Tokyo and Havana. What made it quite different from the new jet airliners and jet bomber conversions on drawing boards in Britain, France and the US was the fact that, although it could fly at up to 550 mph, it did so with propellers: four sets of enormous contra-rotating props spun by the Kuznetsov NK-12, the most powerful turboprop yet manufactured. This engine was essentially the work of a team of German engineers taken to the Soviet Union in 1946 through Operation Osoaviakhim and led by former SS Standartenführer Ferdinand Brandner, the Austrian-born aeroengineer who had worked with Junkers on projects including the Jumo 004, the world's first production jet engine, as fitted to the Messerschmitt Me 262 fighter and Arado Ar 234 bomber.

The Kuznetsov engine had been designed for the swept-wing Tupolev Tu-95 nuclear bomber, first flown in 1952, upon which the Tu-114 was based. The airliner's fuselage, though, was entirely new, allowing the Tu-114 to seat up to 224 passengers, although in practice the maximum was normally 170. The Tupolev's wing was set low, unlike the Tu-95's, which resulted in a very tall undercarriage to give sufficient ground clearance for the giant propeller blades. Few airports were equipped with steps high enough to serve the Tu-114, leading to embarrassing diplomatic moments – such as, for example, when Nikita Khrushchev made his first visit to the US in 1959 and had to use the aircraft's emergency escape ladder to reach the ground on landing at Andrews Air Force Base in Maryland.

Although considered noisy – their fuel-efficient 15,000-hp NK-12s spun the props fast enough for their tips to break the sound barrier at cruising speed – the Tu-114 was reliable and safe. Just one was involved in a fatal accident, on the ground at Moscow Sheremetyevo Airport in February 1966. The airliner hit a snowbank while attempting to take off from a badly swept runway. The Tu-114 rarely graced London Airport, but was greeted when it did by those looking out from the Queens Building as the star it undoubtedly was. It was replaced by the Ilyushin Il-62, a four-engine jet that looked so very much like the Vickers VC10 – first flown a year before the Soviet airliner – that there was much talk at the time of industrial espionage. But if the Soviets had got hold of working drawings of the splendid VC10, they must have misread them. Unlike the VC10, and rather oddly for the time, the Il-62 made use of all-manual controls, while its performance – perfectly good in the cruise – could not match that of the thoroughly resolved Vickers.

The twin-engine jet Tu-104 had also first flown in 1955. From 1957 it became a familiar visitor at Heathrow on regular flights to and from Moscow. Aircraft observers were fascinated by the Tu-104s glazed nose cone. Was this a bomber in disguise? Almost. The swept-wing airliner was a commercial play on the Tu-16 bomber, which had entered military service in 1954. It was the second jet airliner (the de Havilland Comet was the first) – and between 1956 and 1958, once the British airliners had been withdrawn after several fatal accidents caused by structural failure, the world's only jetliner. It was, though, itself flawed, with heavy controls, instability in flight and a high landing speed – not what any pilot wants at airports. It was unforgiving in easily induced stalls. Too many Tu-104s were involved in fatal accidents, and in 1979 it was withdrawn from Aeroflot service. The Tu-16 bomber flies on today.

The Tu-135, first proposed in 1958 and championed by the design bureau's Sergei Yeger for a long-range reconnaissance and airborne missile platform resembling the North American XB-70 Valkyrie, was put forward as the basis of a supersonic Soviet airliner. Yeger worked up three proposals for a Tu-135 airliner, but Moscow wanted a more exact Concorde rival, which would become the Tu-144. This was first flown in 1968, two months ahead of Concorde.

Significantly, in 1947 de Havilland had responded to Air Ministry specification B.35/46 with a bomber version of its DH.106 Comet airliner. Designed by a team led by Ronald Bishop of Mosquito fame, the DH.111 would certainly have been a good-looking aircraft. It failed, though, to convince the Air Ministry. De Havilland pushed on with the elegant Comet, the world's first jet airliner. Tragically, within a year of their introduction into service with BOAC in 1952, three Comet 1s were lost in fatal accidents that killed all on board. Metal fatigue. Structural failure. In April 1954, the fleet was grounded. This was a great loss both to BOAC, which was unable to launch its transatlantic jet service between London and New York well ahead of its competitors, and to British aviation engineering prestige. When the Comet returned as the Comet 4 in 1958, it had the transatlantic service to itself for just a few weeks before Pan Am's Boeing 707s began flying the route. The Boeing was an excellent – and bigger – plane. BOAC ordered it. While this seemed impolitic, the airline knew what it wanted and needed.

In those four intervening years, between the grounding of the Comet 1 and the ascent of the Comet 4, Britain had lost ground to the Americans. It was in that gap that Avro,

Handley Page and Vickers might have made a mark. It was not to be. The Americans built the aircraft best suited to civil and military, wanted by airlines and air forces around the world. Beset by government whimsy and ineptitude, the slow machinations of the civil service, and the 'can't do' spirit of swathes of the labour force, British industry offered aircraft like the otherwise excellent Vickers VC10 and the not-so-special de Havilland/Hawker Siddeley Trident designed for narrowly focused markets – mostly, in fact, for BOAC and BEA. There was Concorde, of course, an Anglo-French engineering tour de force, but while it seemed like the future in the 1960s, by the time it flew, only British Airways and Air France took it on. Twenty were built, with just fourteen going into service.

Even so, going back to London Airport in 1965, it would have been exciting to witness such a potentially rich variety of British airliners. I've also chosen 1965 for our morning on the roof of the Queens Building because I like the way BOAC airliners looked that year in their new Golden Speedbird livery, and can imagine the V 'Civils' looking very smart in that colour scheme. Passenger flight was considered glamorous, something to dress up for, an adventure. What an adventure a flight on a V Civil would have been.

That year was marked by moments, both important and seemingly trivial, yet all in their own ways epoch-making and significant in the story of the Cold War – among them the slogan 'Make Love, Not War', soon to be worn by young US soldiers drafted into the hell of Vietnam. January 1965 witnessed the death of Winston Churchill, his funeral attended by legions of international leaders and his coffin taken from Waterloo to Oxfordshire by steam train – the locomotive was a Battle of Britain–class Pacific, 34051 *Winston Churchill* – following a flypast over the River Thames by Lightning interceptors, more than worthy successors to the Battle of Britain Spitfires.

A few weeks later, and thousands of miles behind the Iron Curtain, the USAF began a relentless three-and-a-half-year bombing campaign against North Vietnam, a poor, rural country little bigger than New York state. American aircraft were to drop over 5 million tons of bombs on the sandal-wearing 'Reds' – who, while their Communist government had made fatal mistakes collectivizing farms, hardly deserved to be bombed more than twice as heavily as Nazi Germany had been during the Second World War. In retaliation, the North Vietnamese shot down hundreds of US jets – and, of course, they would go on to win the war.

Conducted mostly underground, Soviet and US nuclear tests proliferated through the year, while beyond the Earth's atmosphere, the Space Race accelerated. Peter Watkins's *The War Game*, a drama-documentary made for TV imagining the aftermath of a nuclear attack on Britain, was pulled from its October scheduled slot on BBC1 and not broadcast until twenty years later, as part of the fortieth anniversary com-memorations of the dropping of Little Boy and Fat Man on Hiroshima and Nagasaki. It was thought to be too frightening, or perhaps too realistic, for the viewing public.

Production of the Vulcan ended in 1965, the year the first metal was cut for the two Concorde prototypes and the year

I would like to imagine us at London Airport watching a Type 722 Atlantic coming in to land on a warm June morning. The Atlantic was never built. The Avro factory itself at Woodford, Cheshire, where all 134 Vulcans were manufactured, was closed in 2011 after the cancellation of the BAE Systems maritime patrol Nimrod MRA4, a turbofan version of the hugely capable Hawker Siddeley Nimrod that, first flown in 1967, was itself a military offshoot of the de Havilland Comet. This being Britain, a housing estate replaced the factory and aerodrome site. This being Britain, when in 2020 the RAF finally took delivery of the aircraft it had wanted the Nimrod MRA4 to be, it was instead the Poseidon MRA1, a military development of the Boeing 737-800 built at Renton, Washington, close to the Pacific Ocean.

An Avro Atlantic in The Threat from the Past, *Jeff Hawke comic strip by Sydney Jordan, 1956*

EIGHT

Rivals – USSR/USA/France

I saw *Diamond Lil*, not knowing the Boeing B-52D Stratofortress's history until then, when I visited the US Air Force Academy at Colorado Springs to see its Mid-Century Modern architecture – and especially its extraordinary Cadet Chapel designed by Walter Netsch of Skidmore, Owings and Merrill, Chicago, completed in 1962 and looking like a row of stainless-steel and aluminium fighter jets stood Gothic-steeple high on their tails. The chapel's interior did not disappoint. Nor did the B-52D, a gate guardian at the academy since 1983.

Painted jet black and two shades of jungle green, *Diamond Lil* retained an air of menace, reinforced by the markings below the cockpit representing more than 200 combat missions flown between 1957, when the B-52 was new, and 1983, when *Lil* was retired. What I had not expected was the menacing tail end of the 157-foot-long bomber. This looked like the stinger of some giant horror-movie insect. There had certainly been a potent sting in *Diamond Lil*'s tail, while tail gunners themselves must have been made of particularly stern stuff,

More than 200 combat missions: B-52 Diamond Lil,
Colorado Springs

or just very good at acrobatics. At Colorado Springs, I was told
that any movement made by the pilot of a B-52 was multiplied
by a factor of six at the back of the long aircraft.

In raids made in 1972 over Hanoi during the Vietnam
War, B-52s had been the very last bombers to have shot
down enemy fighters with tail-end machine guns. These were
finally removed in 1991. The fact that B-52s had rear guns to
fight with in the skies highlights the fact that these bombers
were a product of Second World War thinking – battling over
North Vietnam much like the Flying Fortresses had over
Berlin a quarter of a century before. And yet it was also the
aircraft that, sixteen years before Operation Linebacker II,
had dropped that H-bomb on Bikini Atoll.

The B-52 is certainly a remarkable aircraft – first flown in 1952, in service from 1955, and still going strong as a front-line bomber and nuclear missile launcher seventy years later. The youngest airframe dates from 1964. Upgraded time and again, the remaining B-52Hs are expected to remain on duty until at least their eighty-fifth year; the very last B-52 on active service might just be flying 100 years after the first took to the air. The key to its longevity – resolved design and robust construction aside – has been its adaptability. It proved to be adaptable, in fact, from the very beginning, when it was transformed at a very early design stage from a straight-winged piston-engine machine to a swept-wing jet.

Boeing was always the front runner in the competition to come up with a new long-range heavy bomber at the end of the Second World War. Its Flying Fortresses and Superfortresses had proved their worth time and again. The challenge now was to respond successfully to the Air Materiel Command of November 1945 calling for a bomber 'capable of carrying out the strategic mission without dependence upon advanced and intermediate bases controlled by other countries'.

Boeing's design engineers, led by George Schairer – who had been appointed the Seattle company's chief of aero-dynamics in 1939 at the age of twenty-six – had visited the German Aeronautic Institute at Völkenrode in Lower Saxony shortly before, while working on what would become the B-47 Stratojet nuclear bomber, precursor of the B-52. Studying air tunnel data collected at Völkenrode and having inspected models of swept-wing aircraft at the institute,

Schairer, as we have seen, wired Boeing from Germany: 'Stop the bomber design.'

Like wartime German proposals, the six-engine B-47, first flown in December 1947, featured wings swept back at 35 degrees, and turbojets housed in underwing pods. Although it never saw combat, the handsome B-47, in service from 1951, was the USAF's principal heavy bomber throughout much of the 1950s, continuing its intended role alongside the B-52 until 1965, and then operating in a strategic reconnaissance role for a further four years.

Boeing's long-range nuclear bombers were in continuous development from 1945. The first USAF intercontinental nuclear bomber, however – and the biggest of them all – wasn't a Boeing. This was the Convair B-36 Peacemaker, first flown in 1946 and in service from 1948 to 1959. It dwarfed the outgoing Boeing B-29 Superfortress, and was even to make the Boeing B-52 Stratofortress look small. Designed by a team led by Robert Widmer, the B-36's wingspan was 230 feet (the B-52's was 185 feet), a record for combat planes that stands today. It had a crew of 13–15, six bunks in the aft section, and a dining galley. Crew members pulled themselves from the front to the rear pressurized sections on a trolley mounted on tracks along an 87-foot-long tube.

This Brobdingnagian bomber was powered by no fewer than ten engines – 'six turnin', four burnin''. Six 28-cylinder, 3,800-hp Pratt & Whitney Wasp Major radials, assisted by four General Electric J47 turbojets, each producing a thrust of 5,200 lb. The radials drove propellers at the back of the wing.

The jets were housed in pods outboard of the piston engines. This mixed-generation power made for a cruising speed of 230 mph, which the B-36 could sustain for up to forty hours on end. Based in Greenland and Alaska, the Peacemaker could, theoretically, attack targets in the Soviet Union, with sufficient fuel to return to US bases in Europe, North Africa and the Middle East.

This, though, was more easily said than done. As Lieutenant General James Edmundson, a highly experienced bomber pilot, put it, flying the B-36 was like 'sitting on your front porch and flying your house around'. If it had dropped nuclear bombs, the Peacemaker would have been too slow to avoid their blast. It was, in any case, obsolete from 1950, when US bombers began to face the fast and nimble Soviet MiG-15 jet fighter. The Soviet Union sent MiGs to Korea and China, providing them with seasoned pilots. The first MiG-15 unit in action in Korea was led by Colonel Ivan Kozhedub. With sixty-two victories racked up during the Second World War, he had been the top-scoring Soviet and Allied fighter pilot.

The USAF did have a somewhat quixotic plan for the defence of the B-36 over enemy territory. The bomber was so big that it was possible to fit a small, high-speed 'parasite' jet fighter armed with four 20mm cannons into its capacious bomb bay. This was the McDonnell-Douglas XF-85 Goblin, a tiny machine with a swept-back folding wing. It weighed 5,600 lb when ready for combat – just a little less, that is, than a Mk 1a Battle of Britain Spitfire. Lowered from a bomb-bay gantry, the Goblin – with its Westinghouse XJ34-WE-22 jet engine – was to shoot up to 48,000 feet before swooping down on enemy fighters daring to threaten its host. Just two were built. Would it really climb so high and reach 650 mph in level flight (not that it would do much of that) – and how, in combat conditions, would a regular pilot slowing into its turbulent wake reconnect with a B-36 in order to hook back up inside its bomb-bay gantry? The Goblin would *have* to perform this aerial miracle as, in the quest for lightness, it eschewed landing gear. Understandably, the project was cancelled in 1949.

It is a privilege, though, to be able to walk around both a restored B-36 and a gleaming silver Goblin in the treasure-trove hangars of the National Museum of the US Air Force at the Wright-Patterson Air Force Base, just outside Dayton, Ohio. In October 1948, shortly before the cancellation of the Goblin, senior Boeing engineers led by George Schairer had holed up for a weekend in Dayton's Hotel Van Cleve, with the team working flat out on the design of a nuclear bomber much faster than a B-36 and with a longer range than the B-47. First flown the previous December, the B-47 was not without its problems. Slow to take off, and landing at high speed with the aid of a drag parachute – another technical feature borrowed from wartime Germany – the bomber proved hard work for its three-man, tandem-seated crew. The pilot certainly had his work cut out. While the B-47 was fast, at high altitude there was just a 5-knot difference between cruise and stall. As the automatic pilot was underdeveloped, this called for hands-on precision flying at all stages of a mission.

The high fuel consumption of the B-47 and other early military jets was a particular concern for the Air Staff and Boeing engineers alike. General Howard A. Craig, Deputy Chief of Staff for Materiel, was among those who believed the new bomber would be better off powered by piston engines or the new turboprops than jets. Tried and tested, propeller engines of either kind certainly had the required range. Schairer's team's first presentation to 32-year-old USAF Colonel Pete Warden, chief of the Engineering Division, Bombardment Branch, on Thursday, 21 October 1948 was for a big if conventionally configured bomber with four turboprop engines. Warden, who had studied architecture before taking up aeronautical engineering, was a forward-thinking officer. Highly decorated, too, he had flown fighters for four years in the Pacific theatre during the war against Japan. Aware of Pratt & Whitney's up-and-coming J57 – a powerful turbojet version of the XT45 turboprop the Boeing engineers intended for their bomber – the colonel insisted on jets.

Back at the hotel, Schairer, Art Carlsen and Vaughan Blumenthal were joined by two more Boeing engineers, Bob Withington and Maynard Pennell. The team worked through the night on a turbojet version of the bomber. They were back at the hotel again on the Friday night after Warden said he found the revised design too conventional. Schairer and the team were to spend the entire weekend ensconced in the Van Cleve. While the hotel's celebrated Wagon Wheel and Mayfair restaurants would have kept them well fed with signature dishes like 'Roasted brisket of young steer', 'Broiled Lake Superior Jumbo Whitefish' and 'Sirloin Steak platter', the Boeing engineers more than earned their keep.

On Saturday morning, Schairer picked up balsa wood, glue, carving tools and silver paint from a hobby shop. While the rest of the team worked on critical performance data and technical details, Schairer set to work shaping the form of what would become the B-52. On Monday, the team met with Warden, presenting Schairer's 14-inch scale model, a set of drawings and a 33-page report. With swept-back wings, and eight turbojets in pairs in pods beneath them, the team had come up with not just the B-52 nuclear bomber but pretty much every Boeing airliner since.

B-52H flying on with 2nd Bomb Wing, Barksdale, Louisiana

There was one key change to come after the unveiling of the experimental XB-52 and prototype YB-52 in late 1951 and early 1952. This was the cockpit. General Curtis 'Bombs Away' LeMay, commander of US Strategic Air Command and, like Warden, a keen devotee of the turbojet, insisted on a full-scale cockpit rather than the tandem seating arrangement Schairer and his team had adopted from the B-47.

Thus, the B-52 was born. Sadly, both the XB-52 and the YB-52 were cut up for scrap in the 1960s. A decade of rich creativity yet iconoclastic modernism, it also witnessed the demolition of the Hotel Van Cleve. I had been hoping to stay there on my trip to the air force museum, but it had long gone by then. Given as a gift to the Christ Episcopal Church in 1967, it had closed two years later. Joni Mitchell's 'Big Yellow Taxi', written that year, came to my mind when, thirty years later, I walked down Dayton's West First Street. They truly had paved paradise and put up a parking lot.

The site where the hotel once stood, in front of the Christ Episcopal Church, remains a parking lot. Boeing, meanwhile, went on to build 744 B-52s between 1952 and 1962. Updated over the years, the Stratofortress has served in a wide variety of roles, including dropping nuclear test bombs, carpet-bombing North Vietnam, undertaking low-altitude bombing missions (at 400 feet to avoid detection), flying missions to Iraq, Syria and Afghanistan, and, in recent years, having the ability to launch stand-off and nuclear-tipped cruise missiles.

Between 1959 and 1968, specially adapted B-52s hosted their own 'parasite' – not a fighter like the Goblin, but the stunningly fast XK-15 USAF/NASA hypersonic rocket plane. Launched from the underside of a B-52 wing, this dart-like projectile climbed just beyond the Earth's atmosphere, with one recording a maximum speed of Mach 6.7 (4,520 mph). Among the XK-15's test pilots was Neil Armstrong, the future astronaut and first man on the Moon.

Aerial refuelling allowed the B-52 to fly very long distances indeed. In January 1957, the USAF's Operation Power Flite witnessed three B-52s flying non-stop around the globe at speeds averaging 525 mph, and making a simulated bombing run over Singapore during their epic 45-hour, 19-minute adventure from Castle Air Force Base, California, to March Air Force Base, California. It was proof of sorts that the US nuclear threat could reach anywhere in the world. In January 1962, a B-52H flew a record 12,532 miles without refuelling. Like an airliner, the 'Heavy Brigade' B-52 was designed for steady long-distance flight. Unlike Britain's V-bombers – the 'Light Brigade' – loops and rolls were out of the question. And, yet, with its armoury of air-launched hypersonic missiles, its high availability rate, the promise of laser defences, new Rolls-Royce F130 engines and a global reach, the B-52 remains a formidable combat weapon in the mid-2020s.

In the popular imagination, the B-52 is best remembered as the nuclear bomber on 24-hour patrol at the height of the Cold War, no more than two hours from its targets. This thought leads to Stanley Kubrick's satire *Dr Strangelove*, in which a stray and incommunicable B-52 flies to a Soviet ICBM launching site and drops a nuclear bomb named 'Hi There!' on it – ridden, rodeo-style, by a *waaa-hooing!* Major T. J. 'King' Kong. Kong's H-bomb triggers a Soviet Doomsday machine that, accompanied by Vera Lynn singing 'We'll Meet Again', sets about destroying life on the planet in a chain of nuclear explosions.

The Stratofortress has outlived much faster American bombers. The most significant of these in terms of V-Force history were two exhilarating supersonic machines: the delta-wing Mach 2 Convair B-58 Hustler and the Mach 3 North American XB-70. The sheer visceral thrill of the former was captured in *The Convair B-58 Hustler Supersonic Bomber – Champion of Champions*, a promotional film made in 1962. The laid-back narrator is USAF Reserve Brigadier General James Stewart, a decorated wartime B-24 Liberator combat pilot who later flew the B-47 and the B-52 – better known as the leading Hollywood actor who, in 1962, featured in both John Ford's *The Man Who Shot Liberty Valance* and Henry Hathaway's *How the West Was Won*. The air force film opens with a crew climbing out of a newly landed B-58. The pilot is, of course, James Stewart.

The B-58 was undoubtedly a star, its striking good looks at once magnificent and strangely unsettling. A little frightening, too, with its four engines projecting like lances from its sharp delta wing, and a sinister H-bomb pod bulging beneath its slim, wasp-waisted fuselage. The B-58 was a rare beauty by US standards, with a maximum deployment of ninety aircraft in 1964. Rare, too, in that in what seemed like the blink of an eye – protected by anti-glare glasses, of course – it was gone,

Short-lived, striking-looking, superfast Convair B-58 Hustler

retired within ten years. In terms of sheer speed and the promise of accurate bombing, the B-58's performance had not been in question. Powered by four afterburning General Electric J79 engines, it had a maximum speed of Mach 2 (1,319 mph) at 40,000 feet, and a 4,100-mile range helped by a lightweight construction making extensive use of honey-comb aluminium panels and representing just 13.8 per cent of the aircraft's maximum take-off weight.

The B-58 design team was led by Robert Widmer, with NACA (National Advisory Committee for Aeronautics) aero-dynamicist Robert T. Jones advising on the fuselage. Jones had pioneered research into swept and delta wings independently of German aviation engineers and scientists. The B-58 scythed through the air. When E. Stanton Brown, a Convair engineering administrative supervisor, was told how it would perform, he commented, 'Sounds like it'll really be a hustler.' The name stuck. The whole point of the B-58 was its speed.

The trade-off between speed and range haunted aircraft designers and air force commanders alike. The B-36 was slow but could fly a very long way and carry a heavy bomb load. Convair's first thoughts in terms of speeding up the delivery of nuclear bombs on enemy targets in the late 1940s had been the GEBO, a Mach 1.3 'parasite' carrying a singular nuclear bomb and ferried by the B-36. Quite how the GEBO would return home, no one really knew. The B-58 relied on sheer speed to avoid enemy aircraft, turning back after delivering its single H-bomb. It could certainly go.

On 26 May 1961, B-58A *Firefly*, assigned to the 43rd Bombardment Wing, Carswell Air Force Base, Texas, and commanded by Major William Payne, hustled from Washington DC to Le Bourget, Paris, in just under 3 hours and 40 minutes. He covered the New York to Paris stage of the flight – the first supersonic Atlantic crossing – in a little under 3 hours and 15 minutes, at an average speed of 1,089 mph. Payne slowed from Mach 2 only to refuel from a Boeing KC-135 tanker. At Le Bourget, the Hustler parked on the same spot Charles Lindbergh had when, in May 1927, he brought the *Spirit of St. Louis* to land after making the first solo non-stop flight across the Atlantic. James Stewart had played Lindbergh in Billy Wilder's 1957 film *The Spirit of St. Louis*.

With a fresh crew commanded by Major Elmer Murphy, *Firefly* went out of control a week after it landed at Le Bourget while performing a display at the Paris Air Show. All three crew members were killed. The B-58 could certainly bite back. It was difficult and demanding to fly. And, if the commander-pilot had his work cut out, so did fellow crew members shoehorned into claustrophobic cubby holes, one behind the other, and with virtually no view out from the aircraft. It was a late-flowering analogue supersonic aircraft. Crew members could pass notes to one another with the help of a string and pulley track running along the cabin wall; sextants were still used in navigation.

The B-58's test programme had involved thirty preproduction aircraft. Of the twenty-six B-58s destroyed in accidents, more than half were lost in tests. To give crews a fair chance of survival, the pressurized and air-conditioned B-58s were equipped with individual, all-enclosing, clam-shell ejection capsules designed to operate at up to 70,000 feet and at Mach 2. The capsules floated on water, serving as life rafts. Tests were made using live animals, including a two-year-old black bear named Yogi. Ejected at 35,000 feet at an air speed of 870 mph on 21 March 1962, Yogi survived, but was then killed and cut up (as were other military test animals) so medics could study the effects of the ejection and subsequent parachute drop on his internal organs. Were B-58 pilots meant to be built like bears?

The Hustler's key operational limitations were its heavy fuel consumption and complex and lengthy maintenance procedures. It required a great deal of maintenance; by general consent thirty-five hours on the ground for each one in the air. Concorde's chief British test pilot, Brian Trubshaw, flew ten hours in total in a B-58 from Edwards Air Force Base, California. Those ten hours, he recalled, 'took nearly one month as it was necessary to change one of the engines after each flight due to unforeseen circumstances'.

From 1965, the bewitching supersonic bomber was asked to fly low-level missions now that Soviet air defences could take out high-flying enemy aircraft, even those with supersonic performance. This was not ideal for the high-flying Hustler, despite *Champion of Champions* featuring a bravura clip of one of the aircraft on a supersonic flight made from Texas to California at 500 feet and below. In late 1965, US Secretary of Defense Robert McNamara announced the B-58's retirement by the end of January 1970. The B-52, of course, would fly on. And on.

Washed and waxed, on 16 October 1963, B-58 *Greased Lightning* commanded by Major Sidney J. Kubesch made the longest recorded supersonic flight, from Tokyo to RAF Greenham Common via Anchorage – 8,028 miles in 8 hours and 35 minutes, at an average speed of Mach 1.5 (938 mph). This kind of performance – a still-unbroken record in *Greased Lightning*'s case – and the way the aircraft looked, earned the Hustler its place in aviation history. When Lieutenant Colonel Kubesch died – a devout Catholic from rural Texas, he had

The sensational Mach 3 North American XB-70 Valkyrie bomber

picked cotton and worked in his family's grocery store to pay for his first flying lessons – the family asked, 'In lieu of flowers, please support the Grissom Air Museum [Peru, Indiana] with donations to build the "Hustler Hut" – an enclosure to enshrine Sid's B-58 supersonic jet for posterity. The Museum's Hustler was based at Bunker Hill-Grissom Air Force Base during some of the hottest days of the Cold War, and your donations will help preserve this amazing piece of military aviation history and honor the life of an esteemed member of the group of pilots who flew such aircraft.'

The North American XB-70 Valkyrie aimed to reconcile speed, duration and bomb load. With its six engines, Concorde look and Mach 3 performance, the Valkyrie was in a league of its own. For a brief moment it looked like the future. But when in May 1960 Gary Powers was shot down at 70,500 feet by that S-75 Soviet missile while flying his U-2 spy plane over Russia, the dream was dispelled. Even if an XB-70 had been able to fly at 80,000 feet, an S-75 would still have been able to bring it down. As it was, just two XB-70s were built, one of which was lost in a collision over California in 1966, by which time the project had been cancelled.

Even before the U-2 incident, the writing had been on the wall for the Valkyrie. The project had been approved in 1958, yet within a year General Thomas White, Chief of Staff of the USAF, told a meeting of the Joint Chiefs of Staff that the Soviets would 'be able to hit the B-70 with rockets'. Moreover, President Eisenhower told his chiefs of staff that 'we were talking about bows and arrows at a time of gunpowder when we spoke of bombers in the missile age'. And, as it would take perhaps eight or ten years to get the B-70 into production, missile technology would surely have moved on, very possibly in leaps and bounds. The Valkyrie was always a political shuttle-cock. In the end, the two aircraft built and first flown in 1964 (AV-1) and 1965 (AV-2) were used not as bombers, but to research Mach 3 flight.

AV-2 flew at Mach 3.05 on 6 June 1966. Two days later, while formation-flying with four other General Electric–powered military aircraft – the McDonnell Douglas F-4 Phantom, Northrop F-5, Northrop T-38 Talon and Lockheed F-104 Starfighter – for a company photoshoot, the Starfighter veered into the Valkyrie, causing it to spin and crash into the ground. AV-1 was retired in 1969. This superb-looking aircraft is on display at the National Museum of the USAF at Dayton. Some bow and arrow. Eisenhower, though, had been right.

The USAF moved on through the new era of ground-to-air and air-launched cruise missiles and Airborne Early Warning and Control Systems with stealthier heavy bombers – among them the mighty swing-wing supersonic Rockwell B-1B Lancer, offering the speed of the B-58 with the range and payload of the B-52, as well as the subsonic B-2 Spirit flying wing and the forthcoming B-21 Raider. And still, the B-52 flies on.

As does the Tupolev Tu-95. Like the B-52, the 'Bear' – as NATO knows this large, long-distance four-engine turboprop bomber first flown in 1952 – remains in front-line service, and will do so until the 2040s. Its virtues are much like those of the Stratofortress. Endurance. Reliability. Flexibility. In its long life it has performed numerous roles. Its combat debut, however, was not until November 2015, when a modernized version – Tu-95MS – carried out cruise missile raids on Syrian militant positions. In the West, we have known reconnaissance versions of the Tu-95 for as long as most of us can remember. Rarely has a month gone by over the past sixty years without references in the national media to Tu-95s flying to the north of Scotland and being intercepted by, successively, Lightnings, Tornados and Typhoons. Images of RAF fighters intercepting the Bears and their crews waving have changed little over the passing decades.

In an era of ICBMs and SLBMs, quite what Tu-95 crews want can seem hard to know. Testing NATO defence reaction times? Generally nosing around? Whatever they are up to on any given mission, it remains important for the F-35 Lightnings of the Royal Norwegian Air Force and the RAF's Typhoons to intercept the Russian bombers and escort them away from Scandinavian and British airspace. As Russian military crews refuse to communicate, the presence of their aircraft poses a danger to airliners and other civil aircraft. For RAF Lightning pilots from the outset of the '60s to the late '80s, it was also a matter of protecting Britain's V-Force bases from possible attack.

A product of the Tupolev design bureau, the Tu-95 was derived from the Tu-85, a prototype of a much-enlarged Tu-4 long-range piston-engine bomber – which, in turn, was an unlicensed and reverse-engineered B-29 Superfortress. The Americans had refused to supply the Soviets with B-29s, but Tupolev got hold of three that had made emergency landings in Soviet territory while on missions to Japan in 1944. From their perspective, the Americans were right to have been cautious. The Tu-4 flew for the first time in 1947, by which point the USSR was no longer the ally it had been between 1941 and 1945. Although it might not have been able to get back home afterwards, through lack of fuel or missile strike, the Tu-4 – which the Americans knew pretty much inside out – could reach targets in the United States.

Like George Schairer and Boeing, Andrei Tupolev benefited from German science and technology – the Tu-95 featured a 35-degree swept wing and Ferdinand Brandner's powerful NK-12 turboprop engines. Suitably powerful jet engines were not yet available. While Tupolev worked simultaneously on the

Tupolev Tu-95 bomber displaying its huge contra-rotating propellers

design of what proved to be the equally successful Tu-16 twin-engine jet bomber, the Tu-95 went ahead with turboprops. It might be seen as the ultimate development of the B-29, the world's first nuclear bomber.

In the Alice-through-the-looking-glass-darkly world of the Soviet Union, Tupolev had drawn up designs for the Tu-95 while still nominally a prisoner of the state. In 1937, he and his engineer colleagues were arrested on trumped-up charges of espionage and supporting Fascism. This was the time of Stalin's Great Purge, a reign of terror that witnessed the summary execution of some 750,000 people, while a further million, at least, were sent to forced labour camps. Sentenced in 1940 to ten years in prison, Tupolev was not formally rehabilitated until 1955, a year before Stalin's successor, Nikita Khrushchev, denounced the purges he had supported at the time. Tupolev was well aware of the dangerous uncertainty of Russian politics; in 1911, during the reign of Tsar Nicholas II, he had been arrested for supporting revolution. He was pleased to be made an honorary member of both the Royal Aeronautical Society of Great Britain in 1970, and the following year the American Institute of Aeronautics and Astronautics.

In its original role as a nuclear bomber, a Tu-95V, painted anti-flash white, had the dubious honour of dropping the most powerful nuclear device yet detonated. This was the 'Tsar Bomba' (meaning 'Emperor Bomb'), 1,500 times more powerful than Little Boy or Fat Man. The aim seemed clear enough: to show the world what the Soviet Union was capable of – destruction on an untold scale. The 26-ton bomb, carried Tallboy-style beneath the Tu-95's bomb bay, was flown 600 miles from the Olenya airbase, north of Murmansk, to Severny Island in the Novaya Zemlya archipelago. Home to few people, but to a wealth of walruses, whales and polar bears, these mountainous Arctic islands rarely witness temperatures above zero degrees.

At about 11.30 a.m. on 30 October 1961, the thermonuclear aerial bomb was released – its fall slowed by parachute – and detonated at 13,000 feet. Major Andrei Durnovtsev, the Tu-95 pilot, and Lieutenant Colonel Vladimir Martynenko, commanding the Tu-16 reconnaissance laboratory jet flying with the bomber, had barely enough time to escape the blast. Its mushroom cloud rose 42 miles into the atmosphere, approximately eight times higher than Mount Everest.

It is hard to know for sure, yet it seems that the size and destructive power of the Tsar Bomba have not been exceeded. In practical terms, such a huge weapon was difficult to deploy. It made more sense for both the Soviet Union and the United States to develop smaller bombs that could be carried by regular combat aircraft. It was also increasingly clear to all nuclear powers that the US stockpile of 20,000 megatons of nuclear bombs at the time of the dropping of the Tsar Bomba was vastly more than could be justified. If that stockpile had been ten times less, it would still have been more than enough to devastate life on Earth.

Tu-95 long-range reconnaissance missions have continued, with brief interruptions, ever since – many crossing Arctic airspace, proving time and again how this Soviet veteran might reach US targets from the north. The sheer duration of the Tu-95 in flight was shown to impressive effect in July 2010, when a pair of the bombers flew non-stop for forty-three hours, with aerial refuelling, across the Atlantic, Arctic and Pacific Oceans and the Sea of Japan. The German turboprops turned reliably and noisily, allowing the T-95s to cruise steadily at 440 mph.

Over its long life, the Tu-95 has been upgraded many times. The most important version is probably the Tu-142, for maritime patrol and anti-submarine warfare, which has been in service since 1972. With its ability, from 1984, to launch cruise missiles, the Tu-95 has retained its position as a strategic nuclear bomber. Otherwise, the Tu-95 has been in evidence wherever the Soviet Union or Russia has fought or snooped in recent decades: reconnaissance in the South Atlantic during the 1982 Falklands War; launching cruise missiles on militant positions in Syria in 2016; the opening assault, in February 2022, of Vladimir Putin's war against Ukraine. The Bear growls on through global skies.

As does the Tupolev Tu-16, in the guise of the Chinese-made Xi'an H-6, which remains in production as of 2025. This was the Soviet Union's first jet bomber, devised as early as 1948 and manufactured from 1952 to 1962. A graceful, swept-wing machine, it seems much smaller in photographs than it really is. About the same size as a Victor B.1, it is a large aircraft, flown by a crew of six or seven, bristling with defensive 23mm AM-23 cannons and powered by a pair of Mikulin AM-3 turbojets housed – like the Sapphires of the Handley Page Victor and the Avons of the de Havilland Comet airliner, contemporaries of the Tu-16 – in its wing roots. The aim had been for a bomber operating closer to the Soviet Union than the Tu-95. Aleksandr Mikulin's powerful AM-3 turbojets were too thirsty at the time for application in the long-range Tu-95.

Like the Tu-95 and the B-52, the Tu-16 – retired from the Russian Air Force in 1993 – owed its longevity to its adaptability. Like V-Force bombers, it was never asked to fight a nuclear war, and its Soviet combat history was limited to conventional bombing raids made during the tortuous, decade-long Afghan War (1979–89). Tu-16s carpet-bombed Mujahidin insurgent positions much as USAF B-52s had bombed the Vietcong in Vietnam.

Tupolev Tu-16, the first Soviet jet bomber, cruises past USS Hewitt

The Soviet equivalent of the B-58 Hustler, the supersonic Tu-22 – first flown in 1962 – was not a success. The inverse of the old maxim 'what looks right is right' was at play here. The Tu-22 looked wrong. It was an awkward-looking aircraft – very pointy, with a wing swept back 55 degrees and twin Dobrynin RD-7M2 afterburning turbojets set on top of the rear of the fuselage on either side of the stabilizer. It was hard for the single pilot to fly – taking off too slowly, landing too quickly, with poor visibility and subject to aileron reversal, a very dangerous condition indeed whereby the wing controls do the opposite of what the pilot tells them to do. Other disturbing quirks included the downward ejection seats. These could only be used when the 'Awl', as the Soviet pilots knew the

Tu-22, was above 1,350 feet – not much use during take-off when accidents can be waiting to happen. The oddest quirk, however, was the evaporator used to cool the cockpit air. The coolant was a mix of 40 per cent ethanol and 60 per cent distilled water. Vodka. *Na zdorovie!* The result – sozzled air crews.

The swing-wing supersonic Tu-22M which took to the air in 1969 and was placed in service with the Soviet Air Forces and Soviet Naval Aviation from 1972 was, despite its classification, a new aircraft: larger, faster, and with a bigger bomb-carrying capacity than the Tu-22. It was designed with the new Kh-22 missile, an anti-shipping weapon with or without a nuclear warhead in mind. The Tu-22M was chosen partly in place of the Sukhoi T-4, a Soviet response to the American Mach 3 XB-70 Valkyrie. While the T-4, only one of which was flown between 1972 and 1974, proved to be an expensive proposal, the Mach 2 Tu-22M appeared to be a cost-effective choice. This has not been the case in practice, however. The Tu-22M has been in combat in Afghanistan, Chechnya and Ukraine, its operating limits firmly within the Russian geographic sphere of influence. It has been an expensive aircraft to maintain.

Tupolev was back on form with the Tu-160, known to the Russians as the 'White Swan', which it does indeed resemble in flight with its anti-flash white colour scheme and when its great swing wings are outstretched. In service since 1987, and in production again from 2022, the Mach 2 Tu-160 is the world's largest, heaviest and fastest bomber. Its engines are the most powerful fitted to a combat aircraft. And, for once in a post-Second World War Russian bomber, the Tu-160 has no 23mm cannon in its tail, relying on sheer sustained speed to keep safe. The Kh-BD cruise missiles it has carried since 2023 – a dozen mounted on a rotary launcher – have a 6,500-kilometre range.

The Tu-160's chief designer, the Kazakh-born Valentin Bliznyuk, had worked for Tupolev since completing his aviation engineering degree. He also made a significant contribution to the development of the enduring Tu-95. Although the Tu-144 supersonic jet airliner was not a success, Bliznyuk, who led the programme with Aleksey Tupolev, incorporated ideas and lessons learned from the Mach 2 aircraft into the design of the Tu-160. In retirement, Bliznyuk continued to work and then to advise on upgrades of the Mach 2 bomber. In 2006, a Tu-160 was named in his honour.

In striking comparison to these big, heavy, complex and dramatic US and Soviet Cold War bombers, the Dassault Mirage IV was a featherweight. When France formed its own *Force de frappe* aside from NATO – its sole independent nuclear deterrent before the employment of ICBMs and nuclear submarines in 1971 – it was with this trim delta-wing jet that from most angles looked no bigger than a jet fighter and strangely akin to Britain's 1950s record-breaking Fairey Delta 2 delta-wing jet.

Well, perhaps not so strange. The Fairey Delta 2, tested at Toulouse as well as Farnborough, was well known to the Dassault team working on the Mirage III fighter. The Fairey's lead designer, Robert Lickley, had played key roles in the development of the RAF's Hawker Hurricane, Typhoon, Tempest and Sea Fury. With such a pedigree, the Fairey Delta caught the eye of the RAF, which wanted a production version as a front-line fighter. It was not to be. In 1957 Harold Macmillan's Conservative government cancelled the project. Dassault, meanwhile – influenced by the Fairey Delta 2 – produced its superb Mirage III, the first European jet to exceed Mach 2 in level flight. Blink and you might have thought you had seen the Delta 2 when a Mirage III shot by. Serving in the air forces of twenty countries, 1,422 Mirage IIIs were made and sold. It was a fine aircraft, a commercial and military success.

In comparison to the single-engine Mirage III, the twin-engine Mirage IV was a limited edition with just sixty-two production aircraft built. Twice the size and twice the weight of the Mirage III, the Mach 2.2 Mirage IV was just a third of the weight of the Vulcan B.1. Its purpose was the same as the British V-bomber: to fly to targets in the Soviet Union, release an H-bomb and, if possible, return to base. This might just have been possible given that Mirage IVs flew in pairs, one carrying an H-bomb, the other serving as a fuel tanker. The svelte bomber had excellent performance at both high and low levels.

Flown at low level (450 knots at 600 feet) from 1966 to keep below enemy radar and thus missile launches against them, the bare aluminium Mirage IVs were now painted in camouflage colours. They served with the French Air Force's *Force de frappe* from 1964 to 1971, and then as a strategic bomber until retirement in 1996. The reliable and much liked Mirage IV, a success from its maiden flight, flew with enthusiastic pilots at the controls in a reconnaissance role until 2005.

A French nuclear deterrent had been discussed since 1945, but it was only when General Charles de Gaulle was installed at the Élysée in January 1959 after the chaotic and financially challenged years of the Fourth Republic (1946–58) that the process moved forward *à toute vitesse*. French nuclear research was highly advanced and French scientists confident of making an atomic bomb independent of the British and Americans. An atmospheric atomic bomb – 'Gerboise Bleue' – was tested in February 1960 at Reggane in the Algerian Sahara. Three more were exploded in the atmosphere before – in response to protests – testing moved underground to In Ekker in the Hoggar Mountains, continuing there until 1966. The French liked to say these areas were deserted, yet they have been home for countless centuries to nomadic tribes, while camel caravans continue to pass through. Coincidentally or not, this was the time that the crocodiles, cheetahs and African wild dogs there – all native to the region – disappeared.

The Mirage IV, meanwhile – a joy for its pilots to fly – pointed the way to the employment of much smaller aircraft than the Soviet, American and British bombers. It was not long before fighters were able to carry and, if necessary, deliver nuclear weapons – as is possible with the RAF Typhoons based at former V-Force airbases today. Of course, they had nothing like the range of US and Soviet intercontinental bombers, but, with the advent of high-altitude surface-to-air missiles, for a while at least the days of these behemoths seemed limited.

To prove the effectiveness of the Mirage IV as a nuclear bomber, a live test took place in the Mururoa lagoon, French

Polynesia, in July 1966. One of the pair of Mirage IVs chosen for the mission (F-THAH) sailed to Hao on board the new amphibious landing ship *Ouragan*. The other (F-THBI) flew from Mont-de-Marsan air force base in south-west France to Hao via fuel stops in the Azores, Massachusetts, California and Hawaii. It was the first French military jet to cross the Atlantic non-stop. With its 50-kiloton bomb detonated at 3,000 feet above the lagoon, F-THAH flew back to France via the US and the Atlantic.

Were the Soviets impressed? Albert Grenier, General Electric GE90-115B technical program manager for the Emirates B777 fleet, Dubai, and a former French Air Force engineer, tells a funny story about a diplomatic incident involving the Mirage IV:

> During a state visit to the USSR, President Georges Pompidou was invited by First Secretary Leonid Brezhnev to visit the USSR Strategic Command. During the visit Brezhnev casually asked President Pompidou if he could depress a button. Having done so, Brezhnev told Pompidou: 'You just destroyed France!' President Pompidou is reported at the time not to have appreciated Brezhnev's sense of humour. Later, when First Secretary Brezhnev paid his return visit to France, it happened that the very day of the State Dinner, a Mirage IV returning from a 'Circus' [reconnaissance] mission over the Mediterranean caught a Soviet crew off guard, who were sunbathing and playing cards on the deck

of their surfaced submarine. A photo album with suitable comments was swiftly compiled and presented by President Pompidou to the First Secretary. Such was the Cold War...

The big difference between British V-Force bombers and their Soviet and American counterparts was that the former were never intended to have the range of the latter. With their more closely focused purpose, the V-bombers were not, like the B-52 and Tu-95, all-rounders, although the Victor made a fine aerial tanker. Hard-pressed financially and governed by politicians over the years with an ever-decreasing understanding of design, technology, manufacturing and defence, Britain has largely abandoned independent aircraft manufacturing. Meanwhile, with or without machine guns and cannons, Russian, American and Chinese heavy bombers continue to fly in service in the mid-2020s – echoes of the Cold War and enduring symbols of nuclear state power.

NINE

What Might Have Been

July 1954. Seven months before the Valiant entered service with the RAF, discussions had already begun within the military, industry and the Ministry of Supply as to what future nuclear-capable aircraft might replace the V-bombers. In the interim, V-Force might be reinforced profitably with a long-range supersonic reconnaissance aircraft that could map targets accurately without getting itself shot down over enemy territory. A tender for this highly advanced aircraft type was issued the following January, when late model F.24 Spitfires were still flying from RAF Kai Tak to protect Hong Kong. The brief called for an all-weather, day-and-night aircraft with a range of 5,000 nautical miles, capable of Mach 2.5 at 70,000 feet. In 1955 an aircraft with a higher performance specification than Concorde was, however, little more than a pipe dream.

While five companies responded – Handley Page, English Electric, Short Brothers, Vickers and Avro – the tender conference held on 13 September 1955 – attended by, among others, the Royal Aircraft Establishment's Morien Morgan, whose wartime work at Farnborough had greatly improved the high-speed performance of the Spitfire – expressed a preference for the Avro contender. Matters moved apace. On 11 November, Avro was awarded a £25 million contract to develop its proposal and to build a prototype. The Avro 730 was to fly by November 1959 and join V-bombers in service in 1964. Nothing quite like it had been seen or flown before.

Even before the tender for the supersonic aircraft type had been issued officially, there had been *sotto voce* calls for a bomber version, not least from Air Marshal Thomas Pike DFC & Bar, Deputy Chief of the Air Staff. What might Pike have made of Avro's design for its 730? I ask this not because Pike – trained as an aero-engineer with the RAF and a decorated former night-fighter pilot who flew the fast and powerful Bristol Beaufighter during the Second World War – would have furrowed his brow studying the drawings of what was a remarkably futuristic machine, but because as a newly commissioned fighter pilot in 1923, the first aircraft types he had flown, from Biggin Hill, were the Gloster Grebe and Armstrong Whitworth Siskin. Henry Folland and Major F. M. Green, the designers of these 150-mph biplanes, were in their teens when the Wright Brothers made their momentous first powered flight at Kill Devil Hills, Kitty Hawk, North Carolina, on 17 December 1903. The Avro 730 looked as if its future chief pilot ought to be the *Eagle*'s Dan Dare.

The pace of change from the Wright Brothers' *Flyer*, Major Green's Siskin, Leslie Frise's Beaufighter, Roy Chadwick and Stuart Davies' Vulcan to this space-age supersonic jet from Avro, whose Lancaster bomber had been a staple of Bomber

Command until 1953, had been as dizzying and as exhilarating as a spin in a Siskin. From the perspective of the mid-2020s, the Avro 730 still looks like an aircraft of the future, or a prop from *2001: A Space Odyssey* or *Star Wars*.

Rocket-like profile aside, what still gives the 730 a slightly alien air is its lack of a cockpit canopy. Its crew of two were to take off and land with the aid of a retractable periscope. Nothing, not even a streamlined glazed canopy, was allowed to interrupt the flow of air over this super-fast aircraft. To 1950s eyes it would have seemed strange, with its tail-forward design, its small main wings set far back along its needle-like fuselage and its engines attached to its wingtips.

On the drawing board in 1955, the futuristic Mach 2.5 Avro 730

Slim the 730 might be, yet the specification was for a big aircraft, formed from a high-tensile steel honeycomb structure designed to cope with intense heat. It would be much longer than a Victor or a Vulcan, with a take-off weight of 226,000 lb – considerably more than that of a Vulcan B.1. Much of this weight would have been the fuel needed to fly the 730 to the Soviet Union and back. The weight grew as the project edged forward.

Initial design drawings – the 730 was revised time and again as it progressed – show four engines housed in wingtip nacelles. This arrangement would have made it easier to service and change the engines than with the Vulcan, Victor and Valiant engines housed in the V-bombers' wing roots. The proposed engine was to have been the as-yet-unbuilt afterburning Armstrong Siddeley P.159, designed to produce a thrust of 20,750 lb. A pair of Armstrong Siddeley rockets were to have boosted take-offs.

Rival designs considered in September 1955 included the Handley Page HP.100 – with a slim delta wing, a view from the cockpit and a dozen Rolls-Royce RB.121 engines – and Vickers' more conventional R.156, designed for a maximum speed of only Mach 2.3 despite its sixteen RB.121 jets partially buried in the wing.

While Avro worked on shedding weight from the 730 and on figuring out how it would carry and deliver an atomic or nuclear bomb, in June 1956 discussions concerning *its* replacement took place. Cold War thinking was moving at a white-hot pace. In February 1957, work began on the first 730 test fuselage at Avro's Chadderton factory, a handsome late-1930s design now largely demolished. The following month, the government published its Defence White Paper. The 730 was among the aircraft cancelled.

Quite how useful the Avro 730 would have been as a bomber by the time it entered service was a question raised early on by some in the RAF. To bomb accurately, the 730 would have to slow from Mach 2, making it vulnerable to Soviet interceptors. Even then, its speed would not have been high enough to protect it from the latest ground-to-air missiles. The 730 was an exciting project at the outset, but events and fast-moving military technology caught up with it all too soon while it was still in the early development stage. There were those who lamented its cancellation, but a care – indeed a passion – for faster, more exciting futuristic aircraft was no match for the reality of dangerous missiles. Legend has it that the partially built fuselage of what would have been the first prototype was cut up and made into wastepaper bins for the Avro factory offices.

It might have made a fine spy plane, yet to do so, again it would have had to be faster than Avro could promise. Significantly, Lockheed's SR-71 Blackbird spy plane, in service with the USAF from 1966 to 1998, had a maximum speed of Mach 3.3 (or 3.5, as pilots claimed). Constructed from titanium, the Blackbird was a much lighter aircraft than the proposed 730, but titanium came at a premium cost. Thirty-two Blackbirds were built. Twelve of these were lost in accidents, although none was shot down.

In the future, meanwhile, entirely new British military aircraft projects would be given official approval, as we have seen, only if they were from one of the newly merged aircraft companies forged as a consequence of the 1957 Defence White Paper. One of these aircraft was TSR-2, a product of BAC (British Aircraft Corporation), the company formed in 1960 from the merger of English Electric, Vickers, Bristol and Hunting. An exceptional design, the TSR-2 was to fall foul of politics, but not before a prototype had been built and flown.

What was TSR-2? A bit of everything. A Mach 2 all-weather, day-and-night tactical and strategic bomber, capable of hugging the ground (at 200 feet) at speeds of Mach 1.1 to 1.3, or flying high at Mach 2. A replacement for the Canberra in long-range reconnaissance roles. A jack-of-all-aerial-trades. And, according to its test pilot, Wing Commander (retired) Roland Beaumont DSO & Bar, DFC & Bar, a joy to fly. It must have been exciting to witness Beaumont flying the prototype at 450 knots (517 mph) over the MOD's Boscombe Down runway at 100 feet.

As chief test pilot for English Electric, Beaumont had put both the Canberra and the Lightning, two of Britain's finest military jets, through their paces. A Battle of Britain fighter ace, in the final weeks of the Second World War he had been planning to escort RAF Tiger Force bombers – Avro Lancasters, Avro Lincolns and Consolidated Liberators – based at Okinawa on long-range missions to Japan with the new Hawker Tempest Mk II. Beaumont knew a good plane when he flew one.

Flying the Tempest I the previous year, he had destroyed thirty-two German V-1 flying bombs aimed at civilian targets in London. While the Tiger Force Tempest IIs were ready to go, USAAF B-29s put an end to the war with Japan when they dropped the atomic bombs on Hiroshima and Nagasaki. Beaumont himself had only recently walked out of the Stalag III-A prisoner-of-war camp at Luckenwalde when the German guards legged it in May 1945. He got home a fortnight after his 22-year-old wife, WAAF officer Shirley Beaumont (née Adams), died. The one blot on Beaumont's immaculate RAF copy book was a court martial in December 1941. Against regulations, he had flown a WAAF officer in a single-seat Hawker Hurricane to a dance at RAF Pembrey, Carmarthenshire. That was Shirley.

A complex aircraft produced by a design team 1,100-strong from what until very recently had been individual companies, the design of the prototype TSR-2 took some while to resolve. Its first flight, planned for 1963, was a year behind schedule, by which time it had its detractors, not least the Chief of the Defence Staff, Admiral of the Fleet Lord Mountbatten (a navy man, he championed the low-flying, subsonic Blackburn Buccaneer), Sir Solly Zuckerman, the government's chief scientific advisor, and the newly elected Labour prime minister Harold Wilson. There were those in right-wing political and military circles who believed Wilson was a Communist and a Soviet spy. Cancelling the latest aircraft – 138 TSR-2s were, at one stage, to have been built by 1973 – and undermining Britain's defences and nuclear deterrent would, obviously, be in his paymasters' interest. While this was nonsense, it is a colourful reminder of the febrile politics of the Cold War.

The argument for TSR-2 was that it would fill the gap between the V-bombers after Skybolt had been cancelled in December 1962 and the launch of the Polaris submarines in June 1968. If the V-bombers were not to be equipped with stand-off nuclear missiles and thus unable to attack Soviet targets, TSR-2 would manage the job. It would be able to perform short take-offs from makeshift airfields, fly with an autopilot under radar and very close to the ground to deliver a nuclear weapon, and, when necessary, fly high and more than twice as fast as V-bombers at a maximum speed of Mach 2.35. Its technical abilities were way in advance of existing military aircraft. Unlike the 730, it offered its crews excellent visibility and – a radical innovation – head-up displays, which were hugely useful in low-level high-speed flight. Its engines, requiring further development in 1964–65, were the mighty Bristol-Siddeley Olympus afterburning jets (employed in the Vulcan), which would become the heart of Concorde's hugely effective and reliable power system. RAF officers argued that TSR-2 could replace the V-bombers as well as the Canberra in its reconnaissance capacity. Just one aircraft type for all principal Bomber Command roles.

Sir George Edwards, executive director of BAC, distinguished aircraft engineer and in charge of Britain's development of Concorde, said, 'In my thirty years of designing aeroplanes I have learnt that by one means or other they can all be made to work. Every now and again the basic design conditions are met, or exceeded, right through the whole aeroplane. When this happens... then there is very little alteration from the prototype to the production aircraft. All the available evidence points to this being the case with TSR.2.' He had barely spoken, when on 1 April 1965 the Cabinet approved the cancellation of the project.

The government rejected TSR-2 on grounds of cost. 'The trouble with the TSR-2,' Denis Healey, Minister of Defence, said later, 'was that it tried to combine the most advanced state of every field. The aircraft firms and the RAF were trying to get the government on the hook and understated the cost. But TSR-2 cost far more than even their private estimates, and so I have no doubt about the decision to cancel.' The cost of the project had risen from a starting point of £330 million in 1960 to £750 million five years later.

Famously, at least in aviation circles, Sir Sydney Camm – whose successful designs for Hawker included the Hart, Fury, Hurricane, Sea Fury and Hunter, together with his contributions to the P.1127 and Kestrel FGA.1 jump jets – said, 'All modern aircraft have four dimensions: span, length, height and politics. TSR-2 simply got the first three right.'

The politics were certainly awry. Having cancelled TSR-2, the government backed a version of the General Dynamics F-111, a US swing-wing Mach jet, but rising costs and delays to the project led, soon enough, to this being cancelled, too. Finally, in 1979, the RAF took delivery of the first of its swing-wing Panavia Tornado jets. Smaller and lighter than the F-111, the Tornado was an international venture between Britain, Italy and Germany. It flew in action many times before its retirement from the RAF in 2019. It was not quite a TSR-2 replacement, yet it proved how far military aircraft design had moved on and away from the heavy V-Force bombers. Fast, nimble, multi-role and increasingly stealthy tactical strike air-craft were becoming the order of the day. That order can and may change, of course, as politics and the mindsets of political leaders are never certain.

Intriguingly, between 1967 until 1984, details of the Tornado were passed to the KGB by Manfred Rotsch, head of Messerschmitt-Bölkow-Blohm's planning department. Some things, like espionage, are certain. Rotsch, an aircraft design engineer, had been smuggled into West Germany by the KGB from the German Democratic Republic in 1954. He pursued his career as a spy for thirty years before being arrested weeks before his retirement. Sentenced to eight and a half years, the investigation revealed that he had written reports in secret ink on the back of regular letters he posted to a fictional 'Aunt Ulla' in East Berlin.

In Britain, all documents, secret or otherwise, relating to TSR-2 – along with tooling and assembly lines – were destroyed. Too far ahead of its time, the secrets of the Mach 2+ aircraft were not to be shared. XR221, the aircraft tested by Roland Beaumont, was dispatched to the MOD site at Shoeburyness, Essex, where it was used for target practice. Fortunately, two airframes have survived: one, XR220 at RAF Museum Midlands, the other, XR222, at the Imperial War

Museum at Duxford. Both aircraft are painted in anti-flash white, as was XR221 – a reminder of TSR-2's intended role as a future Cold War warrior.

Soaring costs brought the fine, all-purpose TSR-2 down to Earth

TEN

Post-Polaris

Polaris was not a case of game over for the V-bombers. While the Royal Navy had usurped their nuclear deterrent role and Blue Steel squadrons stood down between September 1968 and August 1969, Victors and Vulcans continued to play valuable and surprising roles with RAF Strike Command – formed in 1968 when Fighter and Bomber Commands were merged – over the next twenty-five years.

Based at Waddington, Scampton and Finningley, Vulcans remained nuclear-capable until 1982. From 1969, however, their NATO role was strictly tactical. If the Soviet Union was to have attempted a ground invasion of Western Europe, Vulcans armed with the WE.177, the RAF's last nuclear bomb (withdrawn in 1998) – with a blast yield of 450 kilotons, or thirty times more powerful than Little Boy dropped on Hiroshima – would fly low-level strikes to vaporize enemy military infrastructure. With their crescent wings showing signs of structural fatigue caused by years of enforced low flying, Victors would not have joined their delta-wing siblings in combat.

Surviving Victors did, however, find important new purposes. After the sudden withdrawal of the Valiant fleet in January 1965, including its two tanker squadrons, Victor B.1/B.1As were converted to take on the air-to-air refuelling ops. Conversion work was carried out on twenty-four B.2s, following the demise of Handley Page, at the Avro works, Woodford, and the first – designated K.2 – entered service in May 1974. The five-month 'Oil Crisis' had come to an end in March, along with Britain's Three-Day Week as coal miners and railway workers finally refuelled the nation's power stations after prolonged and bitter industrial action. In April, ABBA won the Eurovision song contest with 'Waterloo'. This was a very different era from Harold Macmillan's 'You've never had it so good' years, when gleaming white Victors first entered squadron service in April 1958, between work beginning on the M1 motorway and the Queen opening Gatwick Airport. The Crickets, with Buddy Holly on lead guitar and vocals, were riding high in the UK charts with 'Maybe Baby', recorded at the Tinker Air Force Base Officers' Club in Oklahoma.

Other Victor B.2s had been modified, post-Valiant, to fly long-range maritime photo reconnaissance and radar surveillance missions of up to eight hours with 543 Squadron, mostly over the Atlantic. Between them, five Victors – their bomb bays now loaded with cameras for both day- and night-time photography – could radar-survey the ocean in just seven hours. A part of their job, which came to an end in 1974, was mapping the activities of Soviet warships. The Victors were replaced by Vulcan B.2s of 27 Squadron. These flew until March 1982.

And then, on 2 April 1982, Argentina invaded the Falkland Islands, and the next day, South Georgia. Lying 1,200 miles south of Buenos Aires and 300 miles from the Patagonian coast, the Falklands had long been a self-governing British Overseas Territory defended in principle by Great Britain, 8,000 miles away. Since the 1820s, Buenos Aires had made sovereign claims on the islands it knew as the Malvinas. Its attempt to do so in October 1832, with the aim of establishing a penal colony, was short-lived. Instructed by the Foreign Secretary Lord Palmerston, the Royal Navy set sail to raise the Union Flag once again, which it did on 20 December without a shot being fired from either the decks of Commander John James Onslow's 16-gun sloop HMS *Clio* or the accompanying HMS *Tyne*, a 28-gun frigate.

One hundred and fifty years later, General Leopoldo Galtieri, president of Argentina – a brutal military dictatorship since 1976 – decided to try his luck. Argentina's economy was in poor shape; the junta was unpopular. A promising little war would be just the thing to get the crowds cheering. In this, at least, Galtieri succeeded. How they cheered. How would there be any stopping Argentina? For years, British governments had toyed with the idea of unloading the islands onto Buenos Aires, including the Conservative government of Margaret Thatcher elected in 1979. Its 1981 Defence White Paper recommended the withdrawal of the lone British presence in the region, HMS *Endurance*, an Antarctic patrol boat keeping a weather eye on the Falklands while intercepting Argentinian military radio signals. The fact that the British government was willing to decommission *Endurance* was interpreted in Buenos Aires as a sign that Westminster had little future interest in protecting the islands.

Washington, meanwhile, would presumably turn a blind eye. In December 1981, Galtieri had made a big impression while on a visit to DC. President Ronald Reagan saw him as a bulwark against Communist rebellion in Latin America, while the US national security advisor, Richard Allen, described him as a 'majestic general'. The Argentinian army's notoriously brutal Batallón de Inteligencia 601, reporting directly to Galtieri, had also won favour in Washington through its training of US-backed operatives in sadistic Contra operations against the new Marxist government of Nicaragua.

At home, between 22,000 and 30,000 Argentinians – students, artists, journalists, trade unionists, and pretty much anyone considered in any way opposed to the ruling junta – had been seized, tortured and murdered in the government's infamous Dirty War against its own people (1976–83). After torture, many were injected with Pentothal, stripped, packed aboard navy aircraft and dropped into the Río de la Plata or out over the Atlantic Ocean.

Among the most extreme of Argentina's torture enthusiasts was Admiral Jorge Anaya, a member of Galtieri's three-man ruling junta, a former CIA agent and naval attaché in London, and the chief plotter of the Falklands invasion. The actual invasion was commanded by fellow physical-abuse aficionado

Vice Admiral Juan José Lombardo. Rear Admiral Carlos Büsser – who took Port Stanley, forcing Governor Rex Hunt, a former Spitfire pilot with 5 Squadron in India, to surrender – was also keen on physical and human rights abuse. Addressing the Argentine admiral, Hunt, dressed in full plumed regalia, said, 'You have landed unlawfully on British territory, and I order you to remove yourself and your troops forthwith.'

Büsser and his soldiers responded by sniggering aggressively, yet Britain struck back, and surprisingly quickly, through Operation Corporate. On 5 April a Task Force of 127 ships comprising Royal Navy and requisitioned merchant vessels – among them the troop-laden cruise liners RMS *Queen Elizabeth II* (QE2) and SS *Canberra* – set sail for the South Atlantic. The British supply line was the longest in the history of warfare.

The RAF and Fleet Air Arm flew from Britain to Ascension Island, a halfway stopover for aircraft and Task Force ships alike on the long transatlantic haul to the Falklands. This isolated equatorial volcanic outcrop, claimed by the British in 1815, has been used as a staging post by the Royal Navy ever since. In 1942, the Americans had built an airfield here – Wideawake, named after the island's ever-restless and clamorous colony of sooty terns – a vital halfway house for USAAF aircraft and personnel on their way to join the North African campaign against Germany and Italy.

The first aircraft to land at Wideawake, in June 1942, was an unexpected Fleet Air Arm Fairey Swordfish biplane torpedo bomber on an air-sea rescue mission from HMS

Archer, a *Long Island*–class escort carrier built in the US. The Swordfish pilot, Lieutenant Eric Dixon-Child, who had helped to sink the German battleship *Bismarck* the previous May, was carrying a message to be dropped over the island for onward relaying by radio to the Admiralty in London. Spotting the nearly complete airfield, Dixon-Child decided to land. The Americans responded in their time-honoured 'shoot first, ask questions later' fashion. Machine-gun fire hit the Swordfish and the pilot's shoulder harness. Fortunately, someone on the ground identified the British plane. Dixon-Child landed, delivered his message and flew safely back to *Archer*. Ever since, the British and Americans have shared Wideawake Airfield amicably.

During April and May 1982, Wideawake, managed under contract by Pan Am, was one of the world's busiest airports, hosting up to 500 aircraft movements a day –that is, one every three minutes around the clock. Navy and RAF Harriers flew from England to the island, where April temperatures hover around 30°C, before being shipped on the aircraft carriers HMS *Hermes* and HMS *Invincible* to the Falkands, where April temperatures are typically just above 0°C. These were among the longest flights ever made by solo military pilots. Meanwhile, the sheer variety of aircraft landing at Wideawake during the conflict was exceptional – an opera of RAF Victors, Vulcans, Phantoms, Hercules, Nimrods, VC10s and helicopters, interspersed by the comings and goings of a chorus of USAAF Lockheed Galaxies, Starlifters and Boeing 707s.

General Galtieri misread the Americans. While there was marked opposition to British military action among Ronald Reagan's colleagues, in a personal message to the prime minister at 10 Downing Street, the president promised every possible help. In practice this meant a replacement US aircraft carrier should either the *Hermes* or *Invincible* be lost, as well as Sidewinder missiles, satellite intelligence and millions of gallons of fuel. While US support was to prove critical, sceptics in Washington were concerned with the fact that this was uncharted territory. How might the Soviet Union respond? Might armed conflict in the South Atlantic open a political and military Pandora's box? This, after all, was the first confrontation between Western powers since 1945.

It had certainly come as something of a surprise to RAF Harrier pilots. Wing Commander Peter Squire's entry in No. 1 (Fighter) Squadron's Corporate Diary for 2 April reads: 'The Squadron is... committed to play in a five-a-side football competition... at 1415hrs. Needless to say, however, the crew room conversation is dominated by news of the Argentinian invasion of the Falkland Islands. The GLO [Ground Liaison Officer], Major John Moseley, is asked to look out a map in order to confirm the exact whereabouts of the islands.'

Britain's rapid response to the Argentine invasion was made possible in no small measure by 55 and 57 Squadron Victor K.2 tankers flown south from RAF Marham. In a complex aerial relay, Victors enabled the Harriers to fly to Ascension Island while keeping one another in the air along the way. The first Victors arrived on Ascension Island on 18 April. Two days later, XL192, flown by Squadron Leader John Elliott, took off early in the morning on a 6,500-mile reconnaissance mission over the South Georgia region. The information gathered was to help with the decision of when an attempt to recapture icy, wind-buffeted South Georgia might best be made.

Elliott's crew of six flew for nearly fifteen hours that day – including ninety minutes over South Georgia – investigating 150,000 square South Atlantic miles, supported on the outward run by four fellow Victors and four on the return leg. It must have been slightly disquieting for the Victor's crew to be flying so very alone over that vast inhospitable ocean once the outward K.2s turned back. Undaunted, Elliott commented thoughtfully on the wondrous sight of the southern stars mapped out so very brilliantly above and around the crescent-wing jet.

The Victors had been equipped with up-to-the-minute MMR (multi-mission radar). They had also been fitted with cameras for photoreconnaissance, practising just before they left for Ascension Island at low level over the Scottish Highlands and islands. One idea, quickly discarded, had been for the Victors to make a low-level recce of the Falklands combat zone. In practice, this would have been suicidal.

The K.2's surveillance role was superseded later in the conflict by the de Havilland/BAC Nimrod. Based on the de Havilland Comet 4 airliner, the Nimrod was packed full of the latest surveillance equipment. It could also attack targets with bombs, depth charges and air-dropped torpedoes, and defend itself with Sidewinder missiles while offering its twelve-strong crew a more comfortable flight than the Victor. The 111 sur-veillance and intelligence missions flown by Nimrods during the undeclared war were, however, supported throughout by K.2 tankers.

Victors also refuelled Vulcans engaged in the stirring, if contentious, Operation Black Buck missions made between 30 April and 12 June with the aim of putting Port Stanley airfield and its radar defences out of action – and perhaps the fear of the Roman god of fire and certainly Strike Command into the imaginatively beribboned breasts of Argentine generals and the cheering citizens of Buenos Aires.

Unsurprisingly, the events of the Black Buck raids have been well documented. They were extraordinary. Each of the seven planned operations, given the go-ahead on 27 April, required a single Vulcan to negotiate its way, non-stop at night in poor weather, over 8,000 nautical miles of landless ocean, and to hit Port Stanley airfield or ancillary instal-lations there with either high-explosive 1,000-lb bombs or AGM-45A Shrike anti-aircraft radar missiles. The Vulcans would not be entirely alone. Each would be accompanied by a back-up Vulcan for the early stages of the mission, to ensure all was well with the leading aircraft before it broke off and returned to base, while in the Vulcans' wake flew a flock of eleven Victors, refuelling the delta-wing bombers as well as one another several times, over a turbulent Atlantic crackling with electric storms. Nimrods were to be on hand to direct the Vulcans to Victors on their return leg from Port Stanley.

*Swansong B.2 Vulcan with flight and ground crew and
full array of weapons*

None of this was anything like easy, not least because the five Vulcans finally selected had to be refitted with, among other mission-critical equipment, renovated refuelling probes – these had been removed from the B.2s some years earlier and were not, when uncovered, in the best condition – before they left England for Ascension Island. To ensure refuelling went to plan, each Vulcan carried a sixth crew member – a Victor air-to-air instructor.

The first Black Buck mission was the most successful. Commanded by Squadron Leader John Reeve and Flight Lieutenant Martin Withers, Vulcans XM598 and XM607 (their undersides newly painted a dark sea-grey) made the nine-hour flight from Waddington to Wideawake on 29 April, departing at 0900hrs and arriving at 1800hrs GMT. The following night, each loaded with twenty-one 1,000-lb bombs, they took off for Port Stanley, with Reeve leading. Unable to pressurize XM598's cabin, Reeve was forced to turn around, leaving Withers and his crew flying in the dark and radio silence to complete the mission.

Some hours later, the BBC World Service announced, 'Earlier this morning, a lone Vulcan bomber attacked the airfield at Port Stanley.' At that moment, XM607 was still in the air, heading back to Ascension Island on what, at sixteen hours and 8,000 nautical miles, was the longest bombing mission yet flown by any country's air force. It was certainly heavy on fuel, so much so that the Victor that had last refuelled XM607 (XL189, flown by Squadron Leader Bob Tuxford) was left with insufficient fuel to get home to Wideawake. Unable to break radio silence until Withers sent a coded signal to say the mission was complete, Tuxford could only bide his time before a K.2, flown by Wing Commander Colin Seymour, was able to meet him 1,000 miles south of Ascension Island. Withers, meanwhile, had been seriously short of fuel on his way back from Port Stanley and was an hour late when he found Squadron Leader Barry Neal's Victor waiting patiently for him.

In the event, Withers had hit the runway at Port Stanley sufficiently hard to deny landings and take-offs to Argentinian fast jets if not to transport planes. Tuxford had helped him there. Withers was awarded the DFC (Distinguished Flying Cross) and Tuxford the AFC (Air Force Cross). Squadron

Leader Neil McDougall was also awarded the DFC, in his case for piloting XM597 to a safe landing at Rio de Janeiro's Galeão International Airport, following a botched attempt at air-to-air refuelling on the return leg of Black Buck 6 – a successful strike on a Port Stanley radar installation on 3 June – broke the Vulcan's fuel probe.

Once McDougall had committed to an emergency landing at Rio, the crew jettisoned classified material in a holdall from 43,000 feet but were unsuccessful in their attempt to rid the plane of the last of its four Shrike missiles. While an armed RAF bomber spiralling down in an attempt to land, out of the blue, at an airport of a foreign country might have sparked a major incident, the Brazilians handled matters diplomatically. The recalcitrant Shrike was unloaded and impounded, and the crew were held for seven days in the officers' mess at Galeão Air Force Base. The conditions of their incarceration were rather enviable. The airmen were invited to a barbecue, played five-a-side football against their hosts, and were taken on an intoxicating tour of Rio's ebullient and seductive nightlife on the orders of Brazil's Chief of Air Staff, who toasted the Queen's official birthday before the Vulcan was refuelled and the crew waved off on 10 June. It was all a very long way from the Falklands, from Wideawake and from Waddington, too. The Brazilian government had refused demands by Buenos Aires for the airmen to be handed over as prisoners of war.

Perhaps the makeshift nature of Operation Black Buck might best be summed up by Barry Masefield, XH558's air electronics officer, quoted in Tony Blackman's *Vulcan Boys*:

'One of the simplest pieces of electronic warfare equipment we were given was a small tape recorder and a
tape in Spanish to be used should we be illuminated
by the Argentine radars. The tape stated that we were
an Argentine transport aircraft that had lost its radio
receiving capability and was lost but was trying to land
at Port Stanley airfield so please do not shoot at us as we
approach the airfield. Sounds like a good ploy! It might
well have worked, but when I played the tape to my
navigator, Jim Vinales, who is a Gibraltarian and fluent
in Spanish, he was alarmed to hear that the Spanish was
so grammatically correct that no-one actually spoke the
language that way. He thought that it could be a danger
rather than a help and so we decided not to use it.'
Squadron Leader John Reeve thought it 'sounded more
like Jeeves explaining something to Bertie Wooster'.

Bar two cancelled missions, the Rio incident, and the mar-
ginal damage the long-range bombing sorties caused, Black
Buck was a glorious, if somewhat quixotic, show that demonstrated the prowess of Vulcans, Victors and their crews. Some
dismissed it, then as now, as a PR stunt and a waste of precious
fuel. Did it really prompt the Argentinian air force to redeploy
its Mirage III fighter jets to the defence of Buenos Aires, in
case Vulcans attempted to bomb the city? How greatly did it
disturb Argentine forces occupying the Falklands? Had the
Audacious-class aircraft carrier HMS *Ark Royal* still been in
service in 1982 (it was decommissioned in 1979), its heavily

armed Buccaneer S.2 strike aircraft might have been able to take the fight much closer and possibly more effectively to the Falklands than the Vulcans.

In January 1972, Buccaneers of 809 Naval Air Squadron had, to some degree, proved the point, flying 1,300 miles from the deck of *Ark Royal* – itself rushed at full steam from the North Atlantic to near Bermuda – to buzz Guatemala City in a show of British military strength aimed at deterring Guatemala's murderous, US-backed military regime from invading and seizing neighbouring British Honduras. The jets flew for 5 hours and 50 minutes, covering 2,600 miles. Their presence over the Guatemalan capital proved effective. Colonel Carlos Arana Osorio, Guatemala's president – a soldier whose experience of combat extended as far as capturing, torturing and killing thousands of his fellow countrymen and wiping out entire Mayan villages – backed off.

Although Osorio had ordered his air force to the Honduran border, its clutch of veteran P-51D Mustang piston-engine fighters would surely have been no match for modern British jets. In fact, unbeknown to Osorio and his colleagues, the British were far away, and the Buccaneers, which were not dog fighters, at the limit of their range. While the RAF could have fronted Buccaneers in 1982, flying them from Ascension Island was out of the question. They would have required far too many air-to-air refuellings. The Vulcans were left to perform their knife-edge South Atlantic wizardry.

British Honduras, meanwhile, had gained its independence in 1981. Some 1,500 British troops were on duty there until

1994 to ensure the former British colony, now Belize, stayed independent. Guatemala's sabre-rattling took many years to quieten down. Between 1975 and 1993, GR.3 Harriers of RAF 1 Squadron – versatile aircraft and, as Sea Harriers proved in the Falklands, more than competent dog fighters – were stationed in Belize. The Guatemalan air force was not prepared to take them on.

There may never be a final word on the effectiveness of the Black Buck raids. The action was perhaps best summed up by Marshal of the Royal Air Force Sir Michael Beetham, Chief of the Air Staff and Acting Chief of Defence Staff in 1982, and Admiral Sir John 'Sandy' Woodward, Senior Task Force Commander during the Falklands War seminar run by the Centre for Contemporary History in June 2002. As Beetham said:

> We were looking to give all the support we could to the taskforce and Port Stanley airfield was key to Argentinean operations... it was primarily a military purpose to do what we could with the resources that we had. But it did have a secondary deterrent effect, in the sense that the Argentineans must have raised their eyebrows and the thought would go through their mind (which we certainly didn't try to stop them having) that if we could do that, we could bomb the mainland. We had looked at this, but discarded it because it would have been a major escalation. But the Argentineans wouldn't have known that and therefore their Mirages and their other forces were being

aware and taking defensive measures in case we bombed the mainland, which took a little bit of the pressure off the forces which were deploying against the Falklands.

To which Woodward responded:

I very much agree with what you had to say about it. My dark blue aviators [Navy] said, 'Oh, it's the Air Force just trying to get in on the act,' but I said, hang on a minute, there will be two things. If they do hit the runway, that can't be bad, they can disrupt it and we haven't got the weapons to do that with the Harriers, because you have to drop them from a reasonably high level to penetrate the ground. So it can't be bad if they do that, but also it will have exactly that effect of causing them to think they could come at us on the mainland. It is showing reach and therefore it is deterrent. And I suspect it made them hold back some of their Mirages, which could have acted as top cover for their A-4 raids [Douglas A-4 Skyhawk single-seat jet fighters sank the destroyer HMS *Coventry* and caused significant damage to six other Royal Navy ships]. So I signed up for it and told my aviators to shut up.

In terms of the bigger picture, both V-bombers performed well in this unexpected theatre of war, contributing to the Argentinian surrender on 14 June 1982. The upshot of this was General Galtieri's forced resignation three days later, the fall of the junta and the restoration of democracy. And a victory parade held in the City of London on 12 October, a day of glum, drizzly grey weather curiously reminiscent of the conditions the conflict was fought in. Mrs Thatcher and a large lunchtime crowd watched 1,250 soldiers, sailors and airmen who had fought in the Falklands march past the balcony she shared at Mansion House with the mayor of London, military top brass and the leader of the opposition, Michael Foot, a veteran of CND demonstrations when V-Force was newly fledged. Protestors from the Greenham Common Women's Peace Camp turned up to make a point of turning their backs on the parade.

Above patriots, prime minister, protestors, broadcasters, the merely curious, and the gaze of the mounted Duke of Wellington – his statue cast from the bronze of French cannons captured at Waterloo – flew V-formations of Sea King, Wasp, Lynx and Wessex helicopters, Lockheed Hercules, and three Victor K.2s – accompanied, like heraldic pages, by two Sea Harriers and two GR.3s and, after them, three imperious Vulcans. Clattering and thundering past, this ariel flotilla of South Atlantic warriors coursed touchingly above the indomitable dome of St Paul's.

Whatever one thought or thinks now of such pomp and pageantry, the Victor had truly distinguished itself in the South Atlantic. It deserved to be celebrated. Victors had flown hundreds of sorties during the Falklands War (published figures range from 530 to 600), only three of which were called off – and these through no failing of the aircraft themselves. Victors were to remain on duty, operating from Wideawake, refuelling the Hercules charged with maintaining an 'air bridge' between Ascension Island and the Falklands, until a new airbase on the islands, RAF Mount Pleasant, was completed in May 1985, ready to accept large jets.

While Victors had been in their element in the South Atlantic, flying high for the most part over long distances, they used up much of their remaining flying hours. From July 1986, just one Victor squadron – 55, based at RAF Marham – remained. Four years later, the Victor was back in action. Expect the unexpected. On 2 August 1990, Saddam Hussein, president of Iraq, ordered the invasion of the neighbouring emirate of Kuwait. He claimed that Kuwait was a part of Iraq, rather as Osorio thought of Honduras as part of Guatemala, Galtieri insisted that the 'Malvinas' were Argentinian, and Vladimir Putin believes Ukraine to be Russian.

Saddam's claim was spurious, although Kuwaitis had largely supported unification before the emirate began exporting oil in 1946, thus becoming, for several decades, immensely rich. Kuwait had supported Iraq during the war with Iran (1980–88), lending Saddam's government US$65 billion. Now it wanted the money back, annoying the short-fused Iraqi president, who began accusing Kuwait of stealing Iraqi oil through illegal cross-border side-drilling operations.

Britain had significant interests in Kuwaiti oil, too. By 1961, Kuwait supplied Britain with 40 per cent of its oil. When Iraq's president, General Abd al-Karim Qasim, threatened to invade Kuwait in 1961, Britain reacted by sending a Task Force to the Gulf. Operation Vantage was led by the aircraft carrier HMS

Victorious steaming from Hong Kong, and comprised destroy-
ers, frigates, landing ships, some 6,000 troops, reconnaissance
Canberras, a squadron of Hawker Hunter FGA.9 fighters and
Victorious's own company of Supermarine Scimitars and de
Havilland Sea Vixens. Qasim backed down. British troops
remained in Kuwait until 1971.

Saddam took a gamble on the international reaction to his
invasion. But he had good reason to. Washington and sections
of the US media had long praised him as 'Iraq's Strong Man'.
Donald Rumsfeld, President Reagan's special envoy to the
Middle East, had been sent to Baghdad in 1983 to pump the
dictator's hand and stroke his ego during the long, drawn-out
Iraq–Iran War, and both Britain and the US had supported the
Iraqi military at the time with arms, satellite intelligence, and
the selection of Iranian targets for missile attacks. Saddam,
however, misread both the Americans and the British.

Within five days of the Iraqi invasion, President George
H. W. Bush initiated Operation Desert Shield, deploying huge
air, land and sea forces to the region, supported by Britain.
Very quickly, 55 Squadron Victors were in the air refuelling
Tornados, Jaguars and Buccaneers, flying from their bases
in Britain and West Germany to Tabuk and Dhahran, Saudi
Arabia, as well as Bahrain International Airport, formerly
RAF Muharraq. In early January 1991, eight Victors led
by 55 Squadron's CO, Wing Commander David Williams,
were posted to Muharraq. Their primary duty was to refuel
Tornados south of the Iraqi border, 90 miles away, before the
Mach 2 jets shot off to their targets.

Operation Desert Storm was unleashed on 16 January, with the RAF's 135 aircraft – flying under the umbrella of Operation Granby – part of a 2,790-strong allied fleet. These included RAF Vickers VC10 and Lockheed TriStar tankers operating from Riyadh's King Khalid Airport. The Victors, painted in a desert livery of hemp and pale grey and some named after the wives and girlfriends of groundcrew – *Teasin' Tina*, *Maid Marian*, *Saucy Sal*, *Lucky Lou* and *Slinky Sue*, complete with appropriate artwork by Corporal Andy Price – flew 299 missions without a single failure, turnaround or loss during the 42-day operation that put an end to Saddam's intentions in Kuwait. As well as supporting the RAF Tornados, the K.2 Victors also refuelled aircraft from US carriers, along with Canadian, French and Saudi combat jets.

The Victors' mission in the region extended to 177 sorties from 3 September 1992 refuelling RAF Jaguars of 54 Squadron based in Turkey during Operation Warden. This was to protect Kurdish refugees in northern Iraq from attacks by Saddam. From December until September 1993, Victors were back at Muharraq, flying 202 sorties supporting Tornados and US strike aircraft and fighters in Operation Jural no-fly-zone patrols – keeping what remained of Saddam's air force on the ground – over southern Iraq. At home, Victors remained busy in exercises, including those that took them across the Atlantic, until 15 October 1993 when 55 Squadron was disbanded.

The squadron ensured the Victor bowed out with a bang. 55's Victors appeared at several air shows that year, took the press up for a farewell flight in September – complete with an air-to-air photo sortie – and made a three-ship V-formation flypast over Marham on 15 October. When on 30 November the very last Victor flight was made, from Marham to RAF Shawbury, Shropshire, Johnny Allam was on board XH672. He had been first to fly both the production Victor B.1, in 1956, and the B.2 three years later.

No Victor has flown since, although on 3 May 2009, XM715 *Teasin' Tina*, living up to her name, appeared to try her best. Caught on video, the preserved Victor, passed for making fast taxi runs at Bruntingthorpe Aerodrome, Leicestershire, took off briefly in the course of a Cold War Jets Day demonstration when the co-pilot, a young mechanic with no flying experience, failed to follow his captain's order to throttle back. Roaring down the runway, *Tina* climbed to about 100 feet before landing safely. The pilot, seventy-year-old retired Group Captain Bob Prothero, saved the day through sheer professional skill. He had flown Victors, including XM715, with the RAF between 1964 and 1980. To anyone watching, it was as if the Victor had a mind of its own, wanting to be up and away, reliving its glory days.

Many in the RAF beside 55 Squadron's air and ground crews were fond of the Victor. Of course, it was outdated by 1993 and individual aircraft, no matter how well maintained, were showing their age. But what if the RAF could retain a Victor and fly it at air shows? The suggestion was made that year and taken to the top by Air Chief Marshal Sir Brendan 'Benny' Jackson – a Victor veteran, former station commander at Marham, and Air Member for Supply and Organisation at the

Ministry of Defence. The idea was shot down by a partly sympathetic Air Chief Marshal Sir John Thomson, head of Strike Command. Technical reasons aside, Thomson said, 'the weight of public interest in "V" aircraft has always focused primarily on the Vulcan'. He added: 'I would be surprised if the Victor was regarded as other than a sort of placebo for its demise.' And that was the Victor brought back down to earth, with a line of service stretching back to its glory days as a highly visible and key component of Britain's nuclear deterrent.

In 2025, Britain's nuclear deterrent is still borne by the Royal Navy's four *Vanguard*–class submarines. Commissioned between 1993 and 1999, any one of these formidable machines – as long as and twice the weight of the navy's latest Type 45 destroyer – might be anywhere in the world's oceans at any one time. Each is armed with sixteen Mach 24 Trident II missiles. With a 4,000-mile range, each missile carries three individually targeted 100-kiloton warheads. The fleet is scheduled to be replaced in the 2030s by four *Dreadnought*-class subs, three of which are under construction. They will be the first Royal Navy submarines to provide separate living quarters for women crew members.

And the RAF? Today, it has no dedicated bombers, operating instead two types of multi-role combat aircraft: the stealthy, information-gleaning Lockheed-Martin F-35B Lightning II and the supremely agile Eurofighter Typhoon. Typhoon QRA squadrons operate from RAF Lossiemouth and RAF Coningsby, the latter the former 617 'Dambuster' squadron base of Lancaster and Vulcan fame. Like their predecessors, they still intercept Russian Tu-95s, reminders of the long Cold War.

A flight of Typhoons, constantly on the alert, defends the Falkland Islands, South Georgia and Ascension Island. With NATO, Typhoons patrol the Baltic and Black Seas on the lookout for Russian and other potential aggression. While few in number, these machines are formidably capable, each able to carry a battery of hi-tech and conventional weapons, from 27mm cannons to laser-guided bombs, infrared and ram-jet-powered radar-guided air-to-air missiles and Brimstone guided missiles for air-to-ground attacks.

Lockheed-Martin says the Lightning 'is more than a fighter jet, it's a powerful force multiplier with advanced sensors and communications suites operating close to the battlefield and from an elevated position significantly enhancing the capabilities of networked airborne, maritime, space, surface and ground-based platforms'. The Lightning is an intelligence-gathering and electronic warfare machine as well as an air-to-air and air-to-ground missile platform. It will be joined in years to come by the even stealthier and more technologically sophisticated Tempest. Flown manned or unmanned, the Tempest, designed by a team led by BAE Systems, will make extensive use of AI and the latest in materials and weapons technology. It will be a complex component in attack, defence, and intelligence gathering and sharing, capable of controlling a swarm of attack and reconnaissance drones.

The one other RAF combat aircraft is the Protector RG Mk 1, a turboprop-powered long-range drone. No pilot.

Forty-hour endurance. Indefatigable. Fitted with bombs and missiles, the Protector's primary mission is what the RAF calls ISTAR (Intelligence, Surveillance, Target Acquisition and Reconnaissance). To give some idea of its size, its wingspan is more than twice that of a Second World War Spitfire and it is more than twice as long as, and much heavier than, the Supermarine fighter.

While the USAAF and Russian Air Force operate numerous advanced aircraft types and maintain fleets of nuclear-armed and nuclear-powered submarines, both still fly Cold War bombers – the B-52 and Tu-95 – that were once rivals of the Valiant, Victor and Vulcan.

The Vulcan was grounded in September 1992. The last in service was B.2 XH558, retained by the RAF after its retirement in September 1984 as an aerial tanker for display flying. Between 1985 and 1992 it was a hugely popular attraction at air shows. While the Victor had its fans, and still does, the Vulcan was always the star of the V-Force show. The way it looked, the way it howled, its fighter-like characteristics, its service record. Neither the RAF nor air show crowds – nor even a wider public – wanted the Vulcan to go. Like the Spitfire, Lancaster and Concorde, it had flown itself into the consciousness and the heart of a nation. When XH558 was finally silenced there was a true sense of loss.

ELEVEN

Vulcan to the Sky

How many people, turning the pages of the July 1992 issue of *Flight International*, would have stopped at the advert on the following page, with its badly cut-out and pasted photo of a B.2 Vulcan, and thought *that's the one for me*? Assuming the postman was unlikely to deliver it to your front door or to a safe place if you happened to be out, you would have needed a pretty serious airfield to hand before thinking of sitting down and writing to the MOD to register your interest.

David Walton had just that. In 1983, the Waltons had bought Bruntingthorpe Aerodrome in Leicestershire. Built for RAF Bomber Command in 1942 for training Wellington crews and then testing Meteors for Frank Whittle's Power Jets, it was rebuilt as a USAF base for the B-47 Stratojets of 100th Bomb Wing. The Waltons hosted aviation adventures at Bruntingthorpe including air shows, and ran the Cold War Jets Collection. On 'Rolling Thunder' open days, several of the museum's aircraft could be seen taxiing at speed along the aerodrome's 9,843-foot runway. These included Lightnings, Jet Provosts, Blackburn Buccaneers, a Canberra, a Hawker Hunter and *Teasin' Tina*. The Vulcan would be in good company.

THE MINISTRY OF DEFENCE
is planning to dispose of the last flying
VULCAN B 2 AIRCRAFT
During the last quarter of 1992

Preservation Societies, Aeronautical Museums, Organisation, Companies and Individuals with an interest in preserving this unique aircraft are invited to register their interest to the address below no later than 31 July 1992.

Delivery, subject to meeting certain safety requirements, may be arranged.

Director, Disposal Sales
(Vulcan Disposal)
Room 1/146 Ministry of Defence
St. Christopher House
Southwark Street
LONDON SE1 0TD

Advert in Flight International, *July 1992*

It had been well looked after by ground crews of 55 Squadron and flown regularly on brief sorties and tight circuits from October 1992. Dispatched from RAF Waddington on 23 March 1993, XH558 made a three-and-a-half-hour tour of England and Wales before touching down at Bruntingthorpe. Lorries brought eight spare Olympus 202 engines and 17½ tons of Vulcan parts included in a sale from the RAF Maintenance Unit at Stafford. From the moment the 33-year-old Vulcan, bought for approximately £25,000, landed at Bruntingthorpe, there was a realistic hope it might fly again.

For its part, the RAF missed XH558. This, after all, had been the first Vulcan B.2 to enter RAF service, in 1960, and in 1984 the last to be retired. Tony Blackman had been the first to fly XH558 – which served as a bomber from 1960 to 1973, in a maritime reconnaissance role from then until 1982, and as a K2 tanker for the following two years. The only hostile encounter XH558 had experienced in its military career was at RAF Scampton in November 1975, when a seagull flew into, or was ingested by, the bomber's No. 3 engine. This broke up, blowing a large hole through the aircraft's starboard wing. The Vulcan was out of action for several years.

Retirement should have come earlier than it did. The last operational Vulcans, including XH558, had been with 50 Squadron, RAF Waddington, until it was disbanded at the end of March 1984. XH558 was to have been broken up at RAF Marham but was flown back to Waddington to serve from 1985 with the Vulcan Display Flight. Initially this comprised two aircraft, but from December 1986 and for a further six years, XH558 – reconfigured from a tanker back to a B.2 and maintained by RAF volunteers – flew alone, performing for large and enthusiastic crowds. From the perspective of the mid-2020s, it seems remarkable that the RAF was allowed to fly XH558 Vulcan as a form of ceremonial mascot for as long as it did. But then, the RAF's Battle of Britain memorial flight continues to enthral crowds wherever its Spitfires, Hurricanes and Lancaster heavy bomber go. The Vulcan was easily as popular as these famous Second World War aircraft. It was a calling card for the RAF, just as the force's aerial displays had been since the giddily aerobatic and carnival-like Hendon air shows of the 1920s and '30s. The Vulcan might even have escaped MOD's cost accountants' eyes and flown beyond 1993 if a major and costly service had not brought it down to land and caused it to be put up for sale.

There is something in the British psyche that makes us want to experience machines, from mild-mannered paddle steamers, veteran buses and double-deck trams to exhilarating racing cars, steam locomotives and aircraft – and not just in photographs and films, but in full working order. Some of us have been told time and again that restoring old machines, reviving abandoned railways and, maddest of all, building accurate working replicas or creating improved new-build versions of original designs simply cannot be done. If, however, there is an appetite, a collective will, and funding to do so of course, pretty much anything is possible. The success of the A1 Steam Locomotive Trust in building a brand-new London and North Eastern Railway–designed express passenger A1 Pacific at Doncaster, Yorkshire, between 1994 and 2008 proved what could be done if an ambitious engineering project won public backing. A significant part of the £3 million needed to build the engine – the first new mainline British steam locomotive since 1960 – came from thousands of individuals the length and breadth of the country who wanted to see and ride behind an A1, a class of locomotive that had become extinct in 1966. The A1 project was an inspiration for those seeking to get the Vulcan back into the sky.

In 2009, the completed A1 Pacific, 60163, was named *Tornado* – after the front-line RAF jets – by the Prince of Wales, a steam enthusiast, and the Duchess of Cornwall at York station. A *Tornado* flew over to mark the occasion, accompanied by a pair of Hawk jet trainers. The locomotive was adopted by the Royal Air Force Association, its nameplates bearing the crests of former Tornado bases RAF Marham and RAF Leeming. The Leeming nameplate was unveiled in 2016 by Group Captain Rich Davies, station commander and Tornado pilot. 'We are delighted to affiliate RAF Marham in our centenary year with the magnificent achievement that No. 60163 *Tornado* represents,' he said. 'Its sheer power and presence being reflective of that of the Tornado aircraft that operate from RAF Marham and have been the backbone of the RAF for the past thirty years.'

On several occasions *Tornado* has been the choice of locomotive for the Royal Train. It is the first British steam locomotive to have run at 100 mph in the twenty-first century. It featured in a race from King's Cross to Edinburgh on BBC TV's *Top Gear*, and in a comic chase sequence in *Paddington 2*. On 21 December 2009, when snow stopped electric train services in Kent, *Tornado* rescued commuters who would otherwise have been stuck, taking them home from Victoria station in proper coaches and real style and dropping them off on the way from London to Dover. The BBC broadcast the story. Mark Allatt, chairman of the A1 Trust, who was on the train, said, 'It was a nice way to finish for Christmas, though I think some of the rescued passengers didn't realise they'd even been travelling on a steam train until they got off.' A spokesman for Southeastern Trains congratulated Allatt on what it called his 'moment of glory'. 'I'm sure those passengers were saved from a lengthy wait, all credit to him.' A joy to experience in steam,

Tornado has formed an enduring bond with the royal family, the RAF, and the British public at large.

Since 1998, capacity crowds of 150,000 have flocked to the Goodwood Revival, a glorious annual event held in the grounds of Goodwood House, West Sussex. Here, spectators have been able to see racing cars in action that, collectively and for decades, they knew only as black-and-white photographs in old magazines or as cold, oil-free museum pieces. To see and hear a fabled 1950 Grand Prix BRM tearing around the Goodwood circuit, its 1.5-litre, 600-hp V16 howling like some mechanical banshee, is like living a dream. To watch white-boiler-suited German mechanics, flown to Sussex for the occasion, fettling mighty 1930s Mercedes-Benz and Auto Union 'Silver Arrows' that are then unleashed on the track is a gloriously surreal experience.

'As a child,' says the architect and pilot Norman Foster, 'I lived in a fantasy world inhabited by these cars and their legendary drivers – Bernd Rosemeyer in the rear-engine Auto Union and Rudolf Caracciola in the Mercedes-Benz, racing at Nürburgring, Tripoli and Monaco.' Foster commissioned a replica of Buckminster Fuller's futuristic Dymaxion cars – road-going spaceships that the American inventor and futurist had said would be very fast, if not quite so fleet as the contemporary Silver Arrows. Completed in 2010, Dymaxion No. 4 – the sort of car Buck Rogers rather than Rudolf Caracciola might have driven – was built by Crosthwaite & Gardiner, the Sussex-based racing car restorationists recommended to Foster by David Nelson, one of his long-term studio partners and co-designer of the supremely elegant, ultra-modern McLaren Technology Centre, producer of racing and 240-mph road cars.

Like these examples of high-end rail and road engineering designs, XH558 was more than just an example of a popular aircraft type. It was a talisman of the Cold War, of the Jet Age, and of a time when British aviation design was inventive and memorable – and British invention, engineering and manufacturing at least the equal of those of any other leading industrial nation. Having performed fast taxi runs at Bruntingthorpe for several years, the Vulcan was finally restored to full flying order and named *The Spirit of Great Britain*. The restoration was inevitably long, complex and expensive.

One might still ask, why just the Vulcan? Why not a Victor, too? And what about the Valiant? To a significant extent, the conservation and restoration of special and historic machines has often been a matter of luck. While it is sad to think of all the ships, trains, cars and aircraft we have lost because either no one thought of preserving them or they were simply destroyed, gleefully or not, in a rush for 'modernization' and gratuitous change, we are lucky to be able to experience some of the very best British machines – buildings, too – that, one way or another, have made it into the twenty-first century by the skin of their teeth. While there have been, and are, official lists of what ought to be kept, these have long been contentious.

One of the best judges of what to keep for the future continues to be sheer, unbridled enthusiasm – whether for a ship, railway locomotive, car or aircraft. In 1951 a group of enthusiasts, led by the engineer and author Tom Rolt, took over the Talyllyn narrow-gauge railway in North Wales. It had survived – just – in the ownership of Sir Haydn Jones, longstanding Liberal MP for Merioneth, who had promised to keep it going until his death even though the slate quarry that sustained it closed in 1946. Sir Haydn's widow, Barbara, handed the railway over to the care of Rolt and his fellow enthusiasts, who brought it back to the full life it has enjoyed ever since. Rolt set a precedent. The Talyllyn was the world's first railway to be preserved and run by volunteer enthusiasts. If enthusiasts could rebuild and run a railway, why not a four-engine, delta-wing Cold War bomber?

Luck, enthusiasts, contacts, anniversaries and public support are just some of the factors that determine what we choose to or are able to save for future generations. Media presence can certainly help. The Vulcan was resurrected in the public mind in 1982 when it flew those headline-stealing Operation Black Buck missions from Ascension Island to Port Stanley, while the RAF itself had kept XH558 in the public eye after its retirement from regular squadron service. The Valiant, meanwhile, scrapped from early 1965, is very much the forgotten member of V-Force. None have flown since then and just one survives intact: XD818, the Valiant that dropped Short Granite, Britain's first H-bomb, over Christmas Island in May 1957.

I went to see XD818, tucked inside of the hangars of the RAF Museum Midlands. My decision to go by train was not a clever one. The five-hour cross-country trip across the East

Midlands, through Birmingham and on up the Shropshire line by grim trains to a glum, exposed and unstaffed Cosford station was, at best, penitential. There was a half-mile walk from there in driving rain. But the sight – not just of the sole surviving Valiant, but of all three V-Force bombers housed there – was the reward for my pilgrimage.

The Valiant, I learned, had been converted to a tanker in 1961, repainted in camouflage in 1964 and grounded that December. Today, the aircraft is a white-painted shell, her Rolls-Royce Avon engines sold in 1973 to the Swiss Air Force for use in their Hawker Hunter fighters, retired in 1994. Beyond Cosford, cockpit sections and nose cones of four other Valiants remain, like the relics of saints, on view in scattered shrines for aviation devotees.

The Victor B.2 at Cosford – XH672 – retired in October 1993. It had been a bomber with the RAF from 1965 to 1978. Among the duties it performed was a survey in 1967 of SS *Torrey Canyon* after the Liberian-registered supertanker, on lease to BP, struck a rock between the Scilly Isles and mainland Cornwall and spilled 30 million gallons of crude oil into the sea. This was the world's biggest oil spill, a true environmental disaster. Harold Wilson's government ordered the RAF and Fleet Air Arm to set fire to the oil and sink the tanker. To the embarrassment of both forces, it took 161 1,000-lb bombs, 16 rockets, 3,000 gallons of napalm and 11,000 gallons of kerosene to complete the task. Of the bombs dropped by Buccaneers, Hunters and Sea Vixens, a quarter missed their stand-out target.

After the Victor bomber fleet was stood down in 1968, XH672 went on to take part, as a tanker, in Operation Black Buck and Operation Desert Storm before retirement. Victor XM715, sold to the Walton family, remains caged like some stuffed circus lion at Bruntingthorpe, having performed fast taxi runs there for several years and, like a captive lion yearning to be free, taking off if only for a few seconds. I never went to see these taxiing events. To watch an aircraft restrained in this way, at the very point of take-off, seems, if this is the right phrase, contrary to nature.

There is one other complete Victor which, like XM715, could yet fly. This is XL231, a veteran of the Falklands and Gulf War, owned by businessman and aircraft enthusiast Andre Tempest and kept in tip-top condition at the Yorkshire Air Museum, Elvington. It was the Vulcan, though, that ultimately won the hearts of air show audiences, even though the one and only time I witnessed the Victor and Vulcan flying together, it was hard to decide which made the greater impression. This was the Falklands victory parade flypast over the City of London on 12 October 1982, the V-bombers appearing fleetingly, if vocally, through the clouds, like ghosts of some strange and far-distant battle – which in a sense they were. They sent shivers up my spine.

A quarter of a century later, a Falklands memorial flypast over The Mall and Buckingham Palace on a sunny June day was made without Sea Harriers (single-engine jets had been banned from flying over London), Victors or Vulcans. While the Victors had long gone, it was hoped that XH558 would be ready to route over London, but it would be another year before it flew again. 'This is a great loss to the flypast,' said Vice Admiral Peter Wilkinson, Deputy Chief of Defence Staff and former commander of HMS *Vanguard*, the Trident-armed submarine, who was in charge of organizing the anniversary event. 'The Vulcans' Black Buck raids were a great logistical achievement and iconic to the conflict.' The Vulcan would have been the star of the show.

At Bruntingthorpe, meanwhile, the Waltons clearly wanted XH558 to reach for the sky, inviting key Vulcan personnel to join their new Vulcan Operating Company. David Thorpe, the Vulcan's last crew chief, signed up, as did Andrew Edmondson, expert in jet restoration and, later, co-author of the every-home-should-have-one *Haynes Avro Vulcan Owners' Workshop Manual* (2010). Edmondson was to become the project's full-time engineering director. Marshall Aerospace of Cambridge – an outfit with more than ninety years' experience in maintaining and overhauling military aircraft – was brought on board to carry out the design work necessary to convert XH558 from a military to a Civil Aviation Authority–approved civil aircraft.

The project took wing in April 2000 when Robert Pleming, a British aviation enthusiast, left his high-flying job as a special projects director of Cisco Systems, the US-based multinational digital communications corporation, to join the team full-time and set up the Vulcan to the Sky Trust. Pleming had been involved with the Vulcan Operating Company for some years, on behalf of which he had formed a Project Steering Team with aerospace managers and engineers and former members of the Vulcan Display Flight. The new Trust to which XH558 was transferred was to be chaired by Air Chief Marshal Sir Michael Knight, former head of RAF 1 Group Strike Command in charge of Victor and Vulcan squadrons and himself an enthusiastic pilot.

The biggest challenge was not so much the intricate restoration of the Vulcan, nor meeting all the many regulations, but finding the money the project would inevitably devour. Felicity Irwin, a former TV presenter and experienced fundraiser, joined Pleming and the team in November 2000. With an eye to National Lottery funding, Irwin began by involving local Leicester villages, asking anyone who felt able and willing to donate a pound. The response was immediate. The trust received 60,000 replies to Irwin's mailshot – 'all of them', she told *Dorset Life* in September 2012, 'with £1 coins taped to them. Our postman was very understanding.'

Irwin knew how to draw attention to the Vulcan cause. At the opening of the Royal International Air Tattoo at RAF Fairford, Gloucestershire, in 2002, she performed a fundraising Boeing Stearman biplane wing-walk. 'I was followed by a plane trailing a banner which said, "Support Vulcan to the Sky". It was a truly awesome experience, both frightening and totally exhilarating at the same time, standing above the propeller in the open air, at times just a few hundred feet above people's gardens.' And then there was a skydive 'beginning in freefall V formation... in support of "Vulcan to the Sky" as well as Starlight, the children's charity. It too was awesome and to jump with the Red Devils [the British Army parachute display team] was again a once in a lifetime treasured experience.'

Born in New Zealand, Felicity Irwin had what she calls 'very fond memories of the Vulcan flying out to open Wellington airport when I was a child, so when I heard that the last one was due to be scrapped, I knew I had to act'. One of the very first Vulcans flying in New Zealand on an extremely windy 25 October 1959 very nearly came to grief, as Irwin will recall. Three Vulcans of 617 (Dambusters) Squadron had flown halfway around the world on a goodwill and proving tour, leaving RAF Scampton, in fog, on 14 October and stopping on the way to New Zealand at Akrotiri (Cyprus), Karachi (Pakistan), Penang (Malaysia) and Darwin (Australia).

When XH498, flown by the highly experienced Squadron Leader Tony Smailes, came to land after a display tour of New Zealand, turbulence and wind shear caused the Vulcan to come down short of the runway. Its port landing gear clipped an embankment and was badly damaged, prompting the port wing to drop perilously close to the ground. If the wing had struck it, the Vulcan may well have spun into the crowd. Recorded on film, we can see how quickly Smailes managed to balance the Vulcan and lift it, full-throttle, back into the air. The danger was not over, though. The hit on the embankment had clearly caused further damage to the aircraft. With fuel escaping at speed, Smailes's CO suggested the crew abandon ship and bail out over the sea. But the crew chose to stay with their skipper who, flying on to RNZAF Ohakea, landed safely, maintaining a level attitude along the runway supported by just the nose and starboard landing gear. As the air speed fell, so did the port wing. The Vulcan skewed safely onto grass on the side of the runway. A repair team dispatched from England enabled XH498 to fly home on 4 January 1960.

Meanwhile, at Wellington that blustery day in 1959, the drama intensified when the RNZAF display team comprising four de Havilland Venom jets disappeared into sudden cloud blown by wayward wind over the airport as they were diving vertically from a loop in tight formation. The CO was unable to give the order 'Break, break', at which pilots would normally have fanned out from one another before climbing safely away. Zero visibility meant that the slightest impromptu movement could have caused the Venoms to collide. The drama was caught on film. The cloud scudded away with just enough time – mere seconds – for the Venoms to avoid the ground. For Felicity Irwin, her family and friends, it had certainly been a day to remember.

In 2002, the National Lottery Heritage Fund, which had yet to give money for an aircraft to fly, turned down the Vulcan to the Sky Trust's application. The trust, it insisted, had to prove the educational value of the V-bomber. It did. The Vulcan's role as a nuclear bomber was key to a fresh bid, not least because the Cold War had become part of the national curriculum for history in schools. A second application, made in 2004, was successful. The Vulcan to the Sky Trust could now go about restoring XH558.

The extensive work, recorded in detail, can be studied through the trust's website (https://vulcantothesky.org/). In brief, it involved five Marshall Aerospace technicians and twenty design engineers supported by up to ten trust engineers at any one time, along with logistics and admin staff. Some of the details make curiously unsettling reading. As the trust notes, 'A particularly unpleasant skin repair was needed in the bomb aimer's blister, where the aluminium was badly exfoliated and corroded. The blister was where any spilt liquids (and bodily fluids!) tended to gather, causing both corrosion and a nasty smell.' Quite why bomber crews flying for many hours at a time were meant to be immune from calls of nature is a question that has been asked many times and around the world since the 1940s, and never satisfactorily answered.

The total number of work hours involved in addressing a list of 3,000 repair tasks exceeded 100,000. It was clearly an expensive business, with top-up funding required along the way, from pounds from schoolchildren's pocket money to a £500,000 donation from Sir Jack Hayward, the British businessman and philanthropist. Signing up at the outbreak of war in 1939, Hayward had flown Dakotas for RAF Air Command South East Asia during the Second World War, in close support of General Slim's 'Forgotten' 14th Army.

Echoes of that war were unmistakable when on 31 August 2006, and after £6.5 million had been spent on it, XH558 emerged from its hangar in camouflage livery and to the sound and sight of the Battle of Britain Memorial Flight's Lancaster performing one of several flypasts for the occasion. A congratulatory message was received from the Prince of Wales: 'His Royal Highness has fond recollections of his flight in Vulcan XL392 at RAF Waddington and was thrilled to hear that XH558 is to be rolled out of its hangar.' That flight – Operation Eagle – took place in July 1971, during Prince Charles's training as an RAF jet pilot. For Robert Pleming, thinking of all those thousands who had contributed to this special day, the unveiling confirmed 'what we'd always believed, that this is a People's Aeroplane, and there are so many people out there who want it to fly'.

Barry Masefield was one of them. Commissioned in 1979, he served as an air electronics officer with 617 and 50 Vulcan Squadrons, taking part in Black Buck 2. With the Vulcans gone, he flew for ten years with the Victors of 55 Squadron, including ops in the First Gulf War. Having retrained as a chiropodist and podiatrist after leaving the RAF in 1994, Masefield, his feet now firmly on the ground, set up his practice in King's Lynn. But the lure of XH558 was simply too great. Giving more and more of his time to XH558 as the years rolled by, he gave up his business in 2008 to devote himself to the Vulcan.

On 18 October 2007, the civilian-registered Vulcan G-VLCN *The Spirit of Great Britain* took to the sky over Bruntingthorpe. Its pilot was Squadron Leader (retired) Dave Thomas, who, after joining the RAF in 1962 when he was seventeen, had served as a fighter pilot – latterly with Hawker Hunters in Aden – before switching to bombers. He led the RAF's Vulcan Display Flight and flew the Lancaster for the Battle of Britain Memorial Flight. Now, chief pilot for the Vulcan to the Sky Trust, he continued to teach new generations of air cadets to fly at RAF Cranwell.

Vulcan XH558, The Spirit of Great Britain

The Vulcan was set to fly air displays in front of large and hugely enthusiastic audiences the length and breadth of the country. While the Vulcan's popularity was never in question, the trust estimated it would need to find at least £1.6 million annually, and possibly as much as £2 million, to keep it flying. A campaign to raise £1 million that year was endorsed enthusiastically by, among others, Richard Branson, founder of Virgin Atlantic, and the thriller writer Frederick Forsyth. While the trust could rely on income for air displays, this would never be enough to pay the Vulcan's way. Restricted to Visual Flight Rules – effectively daytime and good weather – XH558 was unable to climb above the clouds to find the smooth flying conditions that would prolong its structural life. The way it was forced to fly was an expensive proposition.

To put that £2 million operating cost into perspective, that of the new-build A1 Pacific *Tornado*, first steamed in 2008, is – according to Mark Allatt – approximately £350,000 a year. For Allatt, who did so much to bring *Tornado* to life, winning her friends including the Prince of Wales, the RAF and thousands of donors and volunteer helpers, the sound of *Tornado* at full tilt is music and the Vulcan's howl is 'freedom'.

While the Vulcan was a fundamentally safe aircraft flown by expert display pilots, there was always something that might go wrong. In May 2012, for example, silica gel desiccant bags were ingested into No. 1 engine, causing it to fail shortly before XH558 was due to take off on a practice flight from Doncaster Airport. Debris from the engine was drawn into No. 2 engine, causing that to fail, too. Both Olympus engines had to be replaced from the trust's diminishing stock. The aim had been to fly the Vulcan for eight years, but the last two required major work to its wings. An aircraft is under great duress in flight, no matter how accomplished those who fly it are and how compelling it is to those who watch it fly. There was no end to fundraising during the eight years the Vulcan took to the skies above Britain. But who watching XH558 soar above or below them, as they did at Beachy Head, accompanied now by two Lancasters, now by the Red Arrows, could say it wasn't worth the expense?

The Vulcan's history could also work against it in terms of fundraising. Like her siblings, XH558 had been designed to cause death and destruction on a scale that continues to defy description. Garbed in white, V-Force bombers were dark angels of death. Was this, perhaps, why XH558 was turned out in camouflage in 2008 rather than anti-flash white? After all, the substantial grant made by the lottery fund was for the Vulcan's role in the Cold War, not for its later service as a conventional, camouflaged bomber.

Martin Withers made the point that the Vulcan's 'original function was to keep the peace and not really to drop bombs. This is the whole thing about the nuclear deterrent, which I strongly believe in. It was not there really to drop bombs, it was about developing something that was capable of doing it to make sure nobody did attack you.'

What, though, most people saw and heard was a stunning-looking and charismatic aircraft. They loved the Vulcan's shape and sound, and the sense that it somehow evoked a British spirit that might only otherwise be caught in, perhaps, the music of Elgar. And there was little Edward Elgar liked better than being mistaken for a military man. Sometimes, it is best not to ask too many questions, or make too many assertions, but simply to revel in the sorcery of soulful machines that have been shaped through superb engineering and, in the case of XH558, imbued with the voice of some primal god.

The Vulcan's last flying season was 2015, its finale 28 October that year. By this time more than 2 million people in Britain (Holland and Belgium, too) had turned out to see it fly. The stock of spare Olympus engines, however, had run out. BAE Systems and other essential engineering concerns could no longer guarantee either the spare parts or the expertise specific to the Vulcan, because engineers and fitters who knew the aircraft inside out had retired. Even if the relevant skills had been available, XH558 would now require a comprehensive reconditioning to meet CAA requirements. It had clocked more flying hours than any other B.1 or B.2 at 7,658, quite something given that the Vulcan was designed for a life of 3,900 hours.

The last flights were captained by Squadron Leader (retired) Martin Withers DFC – who, of course, had bombed Port Stanley with Vulcan XM607 during Operation Black Buck. Thirty years later, Withers had flown XH558 over the new Falklands Memorial unveiled at the National Memorial Arboretum at Alrewas, Staffordshire.

But shortly before the Vulcan's final outing, something shameful and sad happened at the Shoreham Air Show, West Sussex, that put an end to jets performing over rapt crowds. On the early afternoon of 22 August 2015, the pilot of a Hawker Hunter T7 pulling up too low and too slow into an inside loop – a tricky manoeuvre at the best of times – crashed into the A27 road, killing eleven people and injuring sixteen. The Vulcan was due to follow the Hunter half an hour later. Its flypast over Shoreham was made as a tribute to those who were killed. It seemed like an epitaph for the XH558, too.

'People seem to really adore this aeroplane,' Withers told the press shortly before XH558's wings were clipped. 'I can't really explain it... We've seen plenty of tears this season. I've been on the ground at one or two air shows and people are just sobbing – grown men are crying on one another's shoulders and all the rest of it. It's really adored by people who aren't normally particularly lovers of aircraft.'

'Post-Shoreham,' said the Vulcan to the Sky Trust's Andrew Edmondson, 'there are questions over the future of this astonishing era of British aviation when our engineers really did rule the skies. Only very high standards of care and operational integrity will keep these aircraft flying.' The Vulcan last flew on 28 October 2015. Since then, it has been allowed to taxi, but not take off. The same is the case with two other Vulcans, XL426 at London Southend Airport and XM655 at Wellesbourne Mountford Airfield in Warwickshire. Chained eagles all.

I liked the *Guardian* review (30 November 2015) by Sam Wollaston of Channel 4's *Guy Martin: The Last Flight of the Vulcan Bomber.*

When they fire up the Vulcan's jet engines, it howls like a nuclear wind… Guy reads from the memoir of another pilot, whose post-strike advice was: 'Keep flying east and hope to settle down with a nice warm Mongolian woman.' What about if missus No 1 made it to Skye, though? Fortunately, Kennedy and Khrushchev came to a late agreement, averting the crisis and global bigamy in an uncertain post-nuclear world. Oh, and I like the story about the Vulcan's soup warmer, too. It goes like this: once upon a time, there was a soup warmer. It was rubbish, took 90 minutes to warm the soup, the end. You would think, given that this aeroplane was capable of melting entire cities and populations at the press of a button, it would take a little less than an hour and a half to heat the soup. Very British.

Afterword

V-Force occupies a special place in British political and military history between the dropping of the atomic bombs on Japan and the introduction of the Royal Navy's Polaris submarines. Relieved of their strategic deterrent role, Vulcans carried on for some years as conventional tactical – although still nuclear-capable – bombers, and both the Victor and Vulcan served as high-altitude and long-range maritime reconnaissance aircraft and air-to-air tankers. While there had been a concern from early on that, if called into action, the RAF's V-bombers would be vulnerable from increasingly competent Soviet jet fighters and, more disturbingly, from fast-evolving enemy ground-to-air-missiles, the Polaris programme which put an end to V-Force was as much a political as a military solution to how a nuclear war might be contained. Britain had been wrong-footed by the cancellation of the US stand-off Skybolt missile that would have kept V-Force in action for longer than it was, although even then the writing was in the sky. In cancelling Skybolt and offering Polaris instead, Washington, while seeming to make a generous offer, bolstered its position – not that this was seriously questioned by then – as senior partner in the Western alliance and NATO. The feats of the Falklands War aside – in which, of course, Vulcans played a much-feted role – Britain was no longer a major independent military power.

By the same token, Britain's aviation industry, both military and commercial, lost its independence. All those special names – Avro, de Havilland, Fairey, Handley Page, Supermarine, Vickers among them – disappeared. Corporate mergers, prompted by or in line with government policies and project cancellations, squeezed the industry into tightly reined control. Major new aircraft, especially as Britain was drawn further into an economic and political union with Europe, were to be joint ventures like the Panavia Tornado or Eurofighter Typhoon or Airbus – and in one sense all the better, perhaps, for it.

It ought to be remembered that government support for British aviation was at best patchy between the two world wars. It took the full horror and daunting scale of the Second World War to galvanize the government's approach to aircraft investment and production. Even then, an aircraft as brilliantly effective as the de Havilland Mosquito – the 'Wooden Wonder' – only just made it into service. V-Force was born out of warfare at its most alarming. Perhaps it was right as time went on for democracies to band together industrially as well as politically. Even so, concerns remain. In January 2020, following the referendum held four years earlier, Britain withdrew from the European Union. Meanwhile, and as it has been since 1941, the country is both a junction box and a buffer zone of sorts between the United States and Europe, and there is value in this 'special relationship'.

Whatever Britain's precise role in the military defence of the West today, the threat of nuclear warfare itself remains with us. In *The Butter Battle Book* (1984) by Dr Seuss, the Yooks confront the Zooks over a long wall set between them. The Yooks spread their bread with the butter side up, the Zooks with the butter side down. This fundamental difference in the right way to butter bread provokes an increasingly dangerous confrontation between them. Ever-more threatening weapons are produced on both sides, until at the end of the book both Yooks and Zooks wave identical, glowing red 'Bitsy Big-Boy Boomeroos' at one another. These are clearly nuclear bombs. Who will be mad enough to drop theirs first? Whoever does will, we assume, destroy Yooks and Zooks together.

The notion of Mutual Assured Destruction is terrifying, and yet, it has long been argued that the threat of atomic warfare is enough to stop it happening. No one could possibly win. Everyone would lose. This book is written at a time when the president of Russia, Vladimir Putin, threatens to place nuclear weapons in space and as the United States wants to send new nuclear weapons to military bases in Suffolk. And as newspapers and other media ask if we are about to plunge into World War III.

Mad perhaps, yet it does seem wise for countries threatened by such insanity to maintain some form of realistic deterrence. Britain, France, Russia, China, India and the United States all possess this in the form of stealthy nuclear submarines. Other countries may yet follow their lead. There is always the fear that rogue states that place little value on human or any other life, whether for political or theological reasons, may develop such weaponry and use it. Given such fears, generals are unlikely to throw away their guns anytime soon.

All kinds and types of contemporary military aircraft are capable of carrying and deploying tactical (more so) and strategic (less so) nuclear weapons, from the latest stealth jets to veteran American B-52 and Russian Tu-95 bombers. All this is sad and alarming. And yet, how hard it is not to be thrilled by some of the machines themselves, and to be moved by the story of how British ingenuity and manufacturing know-how produced aircraft that rivalled the world's best. Many of us would like to see them flying again, if only to delight us. Is it ever possible to separate the terrifying and ultimately insane purpose of a V-Force bomber from its sheer aeronautical allure? The answer, I think, is a very highly qualified 'yes'.

Acknowledgements

The author would like to thank Angus Mackinnon, Joe Coles and Andrew Nahum, Keeper Emeritus, Science Museum, for encouragement, advice and opinions; Group Captain (Rtd) Ken Edmonds and, along with at least 2 million others, the Vulcan to the Sky Trust for getting Vulcan B.2 XH558 *The Spirit of Great Britain* into the air between 2007 and 2015. Seeing and hearing a Vulcan fly again was the spark for this book. He is also grateful to Steve Holland, William Rudling, Dan Sharp and Jozef Gatial for help with illustrations; James Nightingale for commissioning *V-Force*; editors Ed Faulkner and Harry O'Sullivan at Atlantic Books; Gemma Wain for copy-editing; and Jessica Bullock and Sarah Chalfant of The Wylie Agency.

This book sets the story of the V-Force bombers in a complex historical, political, military, commercial and technical arena stretching from the aerial attack on Guernica in 1937, through the Cold War and to concerns of recent times. The author would be grateful for additional pertinent information and, where necessary, corrections. These will be credited and included in future editions.

Bibliography

Blackman, Tony, *Vulcan Test Pilot: My Experiences in the Cockpit of a Cold War Icon*, Grub Street, 2009.

Blackman, Tony, and Anthony Wright, *V Force Boys*, Grub Street, 2017.

Bowman, Martin, and Dave Windle, *V Bombers: Vulcan, Valiant and Victor*, Casemate, 2009.

Buttler, Tony, *British Secret Projects 2: Jet Bombers since 1949*, Crécy, 2018.

Cheshire, Leonard, *The Face of Victory*, Hutchinson, 1961.

Cocroft, Wayne D., and Roger J. C. Thomas, *Cold War: Building for Nuclear Confrontation 1946–1989*, English Heritage, 2003.

Coles, Joe (ed.), *The Hush-Kit Book of Warplanes*, Unbound, 2022.

Dorman, Andrew, Michael D. Kandiah and Gillian Staerk (eds), *The Falklands War*, Centre for Contemporary British History, 2005.

Edmondson, Andrew, *Haynes Avro Vulcan Owners' Workshop Manual*, Haynes, 2010.

Engel, Jeffrey A., *Cold War at 30,000 Feet: The Anglo-American Fight for Air Supremacy*, Harvard University Press, 2007.

Gaddis, John Lewis, *The Cold War*, Penguin, 2007.

Glancey, Jonathan, *Concorde: The Rise and Fall of the Supersonic Airliner*, Atlantic, 2015.

Glancey, Jonathan, *Harrier: The Biography*, Atlantic, 2013.

Goodall, Philip, *My Target was Leningrad: V Force: Preserving Our Democracy*, Fonthill, 2015.

Hastings, Max, *Bomber Command*, Michael Joseph, 1979.

Jackson, Robert, *V-Force: Britain's Airborne Nuclear Deterrent*, Ian Allan, 2000.

Jones, Matthew, *The Official History of the Nuclear Deterrent, Volume I: From the V-Bomber Era to the Arrival of Polaris, 1945–64*, Routledge, 2017.

Jones, Matthew, *The Official History of the Nuclear Deterrent, Volume II: The Labour Government and the Polaris Programme, 1964–70*, Routledge, 2019.

Laming, Tim, *V-Bombers: Vulcan, Victor and Valiant, Britain's Nuclear Deterrent*, Patrick Stephens, 1997.

Lanchbery, Edward, *A. V. Roe: A Biography of Sir Alliott Verdon-Roe, O.B.E.*, Bodley Head, 1956.

Penrose, Harald, *Architect of Wings: A Biography of Roy Chadwick – Designer of the Lancaster Bomber*, Airlife, 1985.

Redding, Tony, *V-Bombers: Britain's Nuclear Frontline in the Cold War*, Grub Street, 2024.

Seuss, Dr, *The Butter Battle Book*, Random House, 1984.

Slessor, Sir John, *The Great Deterrent*, Cassell, 1957.

Swift, Jonathan, *Gulliver's Travels*, Benjamin Motte, 1726.

Walls, Jim, *Flying Forwards Facing Backwards: Captivating Tales of a Vulcan and Nimrod Air Electronics Officer*, Grub Street, 2022.

Westad, Odd Arne, *The Cold War: A World History*, Cambridge University Press, 2007.

Websites

Key Military – https://www.keymilitary.com.

Key Aero – https://www.key.aero/.

Vulcan to the Sky Trust – https://www.vulcantothesky.org.

Illustration Credits

Page 1: © *Trinity Mirror / Mirrorpix / Alamy Stock Photo (B4K6FT)*

Page 10: © *Chronicle / Alamy Stock Photo (2M97NGM)*

Page 13: *https://thetartanterror.blogspot.com/2006/02/roland-roly-john-falk-obe-afcbar-1915.html*

Page 22: © *ROBERT / Alamy Stock Vector (2T7F43)*

Page 29: *Wikimedia Commons / User: Ducksoup / Public Domain*

Page 65: *https://johnknifton.com/2015/11/30/the-avro-lincoln-at-raf-cosford/*

Page 68: © *Trinity Mirror / Mirrorpix / Alamy Stock Photo (B57TX3)*

Page 72: © *Smith Archive / Alamy Stock Photo (2Y6K629)*

Page 75: *Wikimedia Commons / User: Kaboldy / CC BY-SA 3.0*

Page 90: *Wikimedia Commons / User: Materialscientist / Public Domain*

Page 95: *https://vulcantothesky.org/articles/the-birth-of-the-avro-vulcan/*

Page 98: *Wikimedia Commons / User: Kaboldy / CC BY-SA 3.0*

Page 109: © *Air Force Museum of New Zealand / CC BY-NC 3.0 NZ*

Page 114: *Wikimedia Commons / User: Kaboldy / CC BY-SA 3.0*

Index

About the Author

Jonathan Glancey is well known as the former architecture and design correspondent of the *Guardian* and *Independent* newspapers. A frequent broadcaster, his books include *Operation Bowler: The Audacious Allied Bombing of Venice*, *The Journey Matters*, *Concorde*, *Harrier*, *Giants of Steam*, *Spitfire: The Biography*, *Nagaland: A Journey to India's Forgotten Frontier*, *Tornado: 21st Century Steam*, *The Story of Architecture* and *London: Bread and Circuses*.